INTENSELY FAMILY

Wisconsin Studies in American Autobiography

WILLIAM L. ANDREWS
General Editor

INTENSELY FAMILY

The Inheritance of Family Shame and the Autobiographies of Henry James

CAROL HOLLY

The University of Wisconsin Press

Publication of this book was assisted by a grant
from the Publications Program of the National Endowment for the Humanities,
an independent federal agency.

The University of Wisconsin Press
114 North Murray Street
Madison, Wisconsin 53715

3 Henrietta Street
London WC2E 8LU, England

2   4   6   8   10   9   7   5   3   1

Printed in the United States of America

Library of Congress Cataloging-in-Publication Data
Holly, Carol, 1947–
Intensely family: the inheritance of family shame and the
autobiographies of Henry James / Carol Holly.
248 p.   cm. — (Wisconsin studies in American autobiography)
Includes bibliographical references and index.
1. James, Henry, 1843–1916—Family.   2. Authors, American—20th
century—Family relationships.   3. Authors, American—19th century—
Family relationships.   4. Authors, American—Biography—History and
criticism.   5. Family—United States—Historiography.
6. Autobiography.   7. Shame.   I. Title.   II. Series.
PS123.H63   1995
813'.4—dc20
[B]   94-39661
ISBN 0-299-14720-7. — ISBN 0-299-14724-X (pbk.)

For My Family

Contents

Acknowledgments   ix

Introduction   3

1. The Heritage of Failure and Shame in the
    Life of Henry James, Sr.   13

2. The Heritage of Failure and Shame in the
    Life of Henry James, Jr.   42

3. Strategies of Self-Protection and Vocational
    Success in *A Small Boy and Others*   74

4. Biographical Consequences of the Autobiographical Act   105

5. Divided Messages in *Notes of a Son and Brother*   137

Epilogue   185

Abbreviations   199

Notes   202

Index   224

Titles in Wisconsin Studies in American Autobiography   239

Acknowledgments

I wish to thank the many institutions and individuals who have supported my work on this book. The National Endowment for the Humanities and the St. Olaf Faculty Development Committee made it possible for me to take a leave from teaching in 1991–1992 by granting me a Fellowship for College Teachers and a Release-Time Grant for Tenured Faculty. St. Olaf College has also supported my work through the generous provisions of summer research grants and travel funds. My chairs in the English Department—Lowell Johnson, Ron Lee, and John Day—have encouraged me in countless ways, as have my departmental colleagues. Deans Jon Moline and Kathie Fishbeck have been unflagging in support both financial and moral. My former students, Maren Wolfe and Amy Rand, provided me with much-needed editorial assistance in the frigid winter of 1993–1994. Our department secretary Sue Ann Oines deserves special thanks for her hard work and expertise.

Throughout the years I have profited enormously from my conversations and correspondence with colleagues in the field of James and autobiography studies: William Andrews, Martha Banta, Charles Caramello, Daniel Fogel, Paul John Eakin, Tamara Follini, Alfred Habegger, Richard Hocks, David McWhirter, Suzie Naiburg, Cheryl Torsney, and William Veeder. To many of these colleagues I am also indebted for the opportunity to publish and give papers on preliminary versions of my work. I am grateful to Martha Banta and John Eakin for reading my manuscript with the close, critical attention no scholar can do without. Elizabeth Seaman has proved invaluable as a copy-editor for the University of Wisconsin Press, and my editors at the Press, Mary Elizabeth Braun and Raphael Kadushin, deserve thanks for being patient and exacting, even when I was not.

I am grateful to the Johns Hopkins University Press for granting me permission to incorporate into my Epilogue much of the material I published in the 1987 volume of *The Henry James Review* (" 'Absolutely Acclaimed': The Cure for Depression in James's Final Phase"). Thanks are due, too, to those knowledgeable staff members at the Houghton and Beinecke Libraries who for many years have faithfully provided help in person, over the phone, and by fax machine. Letters from Henry James to J. B. Pinker, and a letter from Charles Scribner to J. B. Pinker are quoted from by permission of the Yale Collection of American Literature, Beinecke Rare Book and Manuscript Library, Yale University. Additional material from the James Family papers is published by permission of the Houghton Library. The late Alexander James was always prompt and generous in granting me permission to quote from James Family papers.

My final thanks go to people closer to home who have upheld me in ways that are hard to describe. Karen Cherewatuk and Rich DuRocher, Ray and Charlotte DeVries, Olivia Frey, Linda Morrall, Elaine Nesbit, Ellen and Steve Polansky, Pamela Schwandt, and Mary Titus—through good times and bad, these friends and colleagues have kept me going. My parents, Cynthia and Roy Holly, have never failed to believe in me, and Alvin and Matthew Handelman have never failed to love.

INTENSELY FAMILY

Introduction

Henry James once claimed that when he began his autobiography in November 1911 he had intended to write a "Family Book" or memoir of William James based on a collection of his brother's early letters.[1] Most of us know what became of that intention. By centering the narrative in his own reminiscing consciousness and letting his memory flow, and flow and flow, James reconstructed the past through the imagined vision of his boyhood self. And the memoir of William or book about the family became "the history of the growth of one's imagination" James had envisioned in his preface to *The Portrait of a Lady* several years before.[2] Thus James determined in the summer of 1912 that in order to make use of his personal history, yet pursue his plan for the family memoir, two books would be needed instead of one—the avowedly autobiographical volume *A Small Boy and Others* (1913) and the sequel containing his *Notes of a Son and Brother* (1914). But in his attempt to clarify his thinking about the volumes, James mistakenly led William's family to believe that he was giving up the Family Book altogether. In September 1912 he wrote his nephew, Harry James, this expression of reassurance and regret: "I could shed bitter tears over my having so clumsily or so superficially expressed myself as to lead you to suppose that I am not becoming, at every step of my process, more intensely 'Family' even than at the step before."[3]

Intensely Family—James coined this phrase within a specific context and with a particular purpose in mind. Speaking metonymically, he wanted to inform Harry that, far from abandoning his book about the family, he was instead "being each day more & more immersed in what I see as constituting the only possible & workable form of it!"[4] He wanted to assure Harry that, far from pursuing his personal interests, he meant to serve the family with an intense sort of loyalty and devotion. By representing himself as "family" in this particular situation, James coined a phrase that describes what I see as a central feature of his entire

3

autobiographical project—the numerous ways in which it was shaped by his relationship with his family. As R. D. Laing explains, the *"family as a system* is internalized" in individuals as "an introjected set of relations"—and, I would add, a pattern of emotional behaviors—which in turn are "mapped back onto the family and elsewhere."[5] My purpose in this book is to identify those features of James's internalized family that were "mapped back" onto both his autobiographical project and the biographical experience to which it is intimately related.

Family, of course, is one of the central subjects of *A Small Boy and Others* and *Notes of a Son and Brother*. In *Notes*, James made good on his intention to write a book about William, about his "memories of our Father and Mother and the rest of us,"[6] and he quoted lengthy passages from family correspondence as the basis for his portraits of Henry James, Sr., William, and his cousin, Minny Temple. His Civil War chapters likewise contain brief memorials of his younger brothers Garth Wilkinson and Robertson James. When he focuses on himself in both volumes, moreover, James recreates his boyhood self against the backdrop of a family so close-knit that he describes its members as "fused and united and interlocked" (4). Thus James's personal history of his imagination cannot be understood apart from his relationships with individual members of his family. Nor can they be viewed apart from his sense of his family as a whole.

But the family dimension of his autobiographical act goes well beyond James's deliberate recreation of family in the past. As the September 1912 letter suggests, James often discussed the Family Book with William's eldest son, Harry James, and his widow, Alice Gibbens James. Indeed, he discussed it so often that the numerous letters he wrote to these relatives between 1911 and 1914, between the period in which he began *A Small Boy and Others* and the publication of *Notes of a Son and Brother*, comprise the most extensive and sustained commentary on a project written by James during his entire career. Sometimes these letters contained information about his thinking about or progress on the volumes; sometimes they enlisted the family's aid in obtaining packets of letters, in negotiating with his American publisher, or in providing the support he needed to keep writing during periods of illness and depression. But other times they were intended to straighten out misunderstandings about his plans for the books, and to the extent that they were painful for James, these misunderstandings launched so many explanations and apologies that the letters began to echo the often obscure and self-justifying language of the autobiographies themselves. At one point, James's communications with his family so strained his nerves that he appears to have fallen ill as a result.

The autobiographical act which embraces family as one of its subjects can thus be seen as having affected not only James's relationship with his surviving family but also his emotional and physical well-being. In turn, these contemporary events seem intimately related to such important themes in the autobiographies as the connections among illness, creativity, and family relations. There exists a mutually reflecting and clarifying relationship between James's autobiographies and his letters about them, between the autobiographical account of his life in the past and his epistolary account of his life in the present. To interpret this relationship, as I intend to do, will be to wed the textual analysis of James's autobiographical act with an examination of its immediate biographical context as revealed in family correspondence. A brief review of criticism on autobiography in general and James's autobiographies in particular, as well as a look at biographical studies of James's late years, will clarify the significance of this critical approach.

Until the 1950s autobiography was largely read as a historical document which provided a clear and uncomplicated view of the autobiographer's past. In response first to New Critical and then to post-structuralist theories of literature, autobiography has since been seen less as a transparent reflection of the autobiographer's past, and therefore as a reliable source for historians and biographers, and more as a fictional construction reflecting the artistic concerns of the autobiographer in the present. Accordingly, critics have begun to pay an increasing amount of attention to James's autobiographies as literary texts employing themes and techniques appearing in the fiction, and several efforts have recently been made to define the role of these texts in James's overall career. One recent critic argues that not only do the prefaces and the autobiographies form a "diptych, together claiming to furnish a complete history of the development of James's imagination," but there is "a fundamental continuity" as well "between James's fiction, which already contains an autobiography *in potentia*, and the explicitly autobiographical works that capped his career in the twentieth century."[7]

In his essay in *New Literary History*, Paul John Eakin further extended our understanding of the autobiographies by challenging the tendency to read autobiography either as a source of biographical fact from the past or as a narrative that fictionalizes such facts in the present. According to Eakin, an examination of James's "obscure hurt" passage in *Notes of a Son and Brother* suggests that autobiography "is not merely a source of biographical facts, it is such a fact itself." Not merely a fictionalization of biographical events, autobiography is a major "biographical event" in the present life of the autobiographer. But in an earlier study on the autobiographies as therapy, Eakin had interpreted this biographical event largely on the basis of what James's story of the past reveals of the autobiographer's immediate circumstances and preoccupations. Thus he argues that "to stress, as I have, the need to accord to the autobiographical act the status of biographical event is to suggest the importance of a *contextual* understanding of autobiography's recreation of biographical fact."[8]

What Eakin proposes is a reading of the autobiographical act that is grounded in the life of the autobiographer during the time in which he was writing his life story—or, to be more precise, in an interpretation of that life available in such biographical sources as diaries, letters, and other documents. By relying extensively on James's lengthy and largely unpublished correspondence in his final years, a correspondence that is richly personal and informative, I offer in this study the contextual reading of the autobiographies that Eakin describes. Because family issues are the common denominator of both text and context, my emphasis on family allows me to offer a tightly focused reading of the relationship between autobiography and experience in James's late career—or, to put it more exactly, between James's public account of his experience in the past and private version of his experience in the present. As such my book provides a detailed biographical study of a crucial period in James's late life, a more detailed and realistic study, in fact, than we have been given in Leon Edel's partial and idealized account of the elderly James.

To understand what I mean, consider first the final chapters of *Henry James: The Master*. Here Edel gives short shrift to the prolonged emotional and physical difficulties experienced by James in the years following his nervous breakdown in 1910, and then highlights what he calls the "new-found serenities of his old age" in the months following the publication of *Notes of a Son and Brother*.[9] In a subsequent essay, "The Portrait of the Artist as an Old Man," Edel articulates a theory about male artists and old age that helps explain his presentation of James's late years both in this essay and in *The Master*. The "portrait of the artist as an old man," he claims, "is that of the finished oak, standing strong and sometimes beautiful in nature, with a developed and nour-ished past. Most questions have been answered. The storms and stresses are over. The pain of growth, the anguish of aging, have been surmounted; the radiance and the suffering have ended in triumph and fulfillment, even if sometimes in penury and want."[10]

Heavily invested in an idealization of both James and old age, Edel not only slights the fact that, as family correspondence reveals, the years 1911 to 1914 were often extremely painful and anxiety-ridden for James, and that much of James's discomfort was directly related to his work on the autobiographies. He also eclipses the fact that, in spite of the healing that occurred by 1914, James never saw himself as having moved completely beyond the "storms and stresses" of the depression and illness that had beset him in previous years. He also ignores the fact that James's emotional well-being in 1914 was the result not only of his ability to gain strength from his suffering but also of the critical acclaim he received for *Notes of a Son and Brother.*

Readers who wish to go behind the biography and look at the evidence of the letters will encounter a similarly partial and idealized version of the Master. When he first published *The Letters of Henry James* (1920), Percy Lubbock included a selection of letters written by James during the years he was working on the autobiographies. But Lubbock also excised large portions of these letters, sometimes without indicating that he had done so, and as a result the volume emphasizes James's triumph over his difficulties rather than the difficulties themselves. As in the case of Edel, Lubbock was motivated by the desire to present an image of the Master in full possession of his soul and supreme command of his art. In "the presence of his work," says Lubbock, "he never knew the least failure of assurance; he threw his full weight on the belief that supported him and it was never shaken." Again he says, "His life as a creator of art, alone with his work, was one of unclouded happiness. It might be hampered and hindered by external accidents, but none of them could touch the real core of his security, which was his faith in his vocation and his knowledge of his genius."[11]

Edel's four volume edition of James's letters goes further than Lubbock's in presenting the letters relevant to James's work on the autobiographies and his complex emotional response to the family's involvement in the project. But these letters, too, represent only a selection of the dozens of letters James wrote to his family (and his agent) about both the autobiographies and the state of his health in his final years. And the letters selected for publication are often incomplete. A certain focus and economy has been gained by Edel's editorial decisions, but lost is our sense of the magnitude of this correspondence and, with it, of James's often thoroughgoing preoccupation with his work on the autobiographies, his painful anxieties over his family's response to the work, his abilities to elicit from the family the responses he desired, and his ongoing struggle with ill health. My point is that any analysis of James's autobiographical act as biographical event depends upon a fuller understanding of James's late years, particularly the years when the autobiographies were being written, and thus upon a familiarity with the entire family correspondence, housed at the Houghton library, not just with the letters published by Lubbock and Edel.[12]

But there is more to James's autobiographical act as biographical event than the interrelationship between life and life writing, between letters and autobiographies, in the last years of his life. Henry James did not come to this "intensely 'family' " experience without having first been raised in the family he recreates in *A Small Boy* and *Notes*. Some critics have observed, for example, that in organizing his autobiographies and recreating the past James is still driven by the feelings of inferiority to and rivalry with William that Leon Edel identified in his biography of the writer. James is likewise beset with feelings of ambivalence, even anxiety, about his father and younger brothers,[13] and he continually struggles with the conflict between his effort to insist on the autonomy of his perceptions of the past and his desire to feel one with the family and remain intensely loyal to its name. It is often a variation on these dynamics, in fact, that is enacted in his letters to Alice and Harry between 1911 and 1914. The following chapters therefore identify those features of James's internalized family of origin that were mapped back onto James's autobiographical act as biographical event. As such, my book offers a description of what Clifford Geertz calls the "piled-up structures of inference and implication," of patterns and relations, that informed the inter-relationship between life and life-writing in the last years of James's life.[14]

Clearly a project that attempts a doubly contextual or "thick description" of James's autobiographical act using family issues as its focus must look elsewhere for a psychological model than to the individualistic psychologies initiated by Freud and his followers.[15] It must look elsewhere than to the traditional psychoanalytical emphasis on the individual as an "autonomous psychological entity" and "the family only as a collection of relatively autonomous people, each motivated by his or her own particular psychological mechanisms and conflicts."[16] I have found this model in the concept of the "undifferentiated family ego mass" (or enmeshed group identity) that family therapists believe to prevail in families in which there are no clear boundaries among members and individuation becomes hard to achieve.[17] The assumption in such families is that negative affect will be repressed, shameful secrets suppressed, conflict avoided, and intense loyalty and dependency fostered for the sake of family harmony and order.

The cost of such codes of family conduct is exceedingly high. Beginning with research on schizophrenics in the 1960s, family therapists have shown that individuals who come from a highly enmeshed family system often have a multi-generational history of psychosomatic illnesses, chemical or process addictions, eating disorders, or other addictive or dysfunctional behaviors. More recently they have discovered in such families a complex of behaviors organized around and growing out of perpetuated shame. As recent theorists describe it, shame is the "invisible dragon" in families with "a self-sustaining, multi-generational system of interaction with a cast of characters who are (or were in their lifetime) loyal to a set of rules and injunctions demanding control, perfectionism, blame and denial. The pattern inhibits or defeats the development of authentic intimate relationships, promotes secrets and vague personal boundaries, unconsciously instills shame in the family members, as well as chaos in their lives, and binds them to perpetuate shame in themselves and their kin."[18] This multi-generational system of interaction creates, in other words, a shame-based "emotional field" which permeates, even imprisons, the emotional life of family members.[19]

Family therapists thus believe, says Howard Feinstein, that reconnecting not only the individual client but her family as a whole "with its revivified past" and its multi-generational systems "is the essence of the therapeutic procedure." Feinstein also argues that, while historical reconstruction of the family is central to family therapy, "family therapy theory" is useful to the historian "studying lives in the remote past." Moreover, he identifies a number of concepts taken from his work in family therapy—the family secret, the multi-generational hypothesis, and so on—that he found particularly useful in his "three-generation, biographical study of the family of William James." Feinstein justifies his use of these concepts on the basis of the James family's highly developed level of self-consciousness: "All of the family were talented correspondents, and their letters and journals have attracted many biographers. Keen observers of themselves and even keener of each other, they invite psychological study."[20] But my reading in the Victorian family in general and in the James family in particular suggests that we can take Feinstein's rationale for this approach yet another step further. For the patterns of psychological dependencies, intense family relations, and shame-based identities that family therapists now see as characteristic of dysfunctional families in the twentieth century had their roots in the changes in child-rearing techniques, assumptions about marriage, approaches to emotional conflict, and other middle-class family patterns that developed in England and America throughout the nineteenth century.[21] And the keen lens that the James family members trained on one another, and on their dynamics as a family, were but an outgrowth of a both culturally and privately sanctioned system that fostered a high level of psychological dependence and emotional enmeshment. As James said of his family in *A Small Boy and Others*, "We were, to my sense, the blest group of us . . . *so fused and united and interlocked*" (4; my emphasis). The point is not only that the self-conscious James family invites psychological study, but that it invites psychological study tailored to its complex and multi-generational pattern of enmeshed, shame-based emotions and behaviors.

Central to my approach to Henry James's role in the family, and therefore to the impact of family on his autobiographical act as text and context, is the portrait that has emerged in several family biographies, Feinstein's *Becoming William James* in particular, of the patterns of emotional enmeshment and psychosomatic illness encouraged in their children by the emotional climate created by Henry James, Sr., and his style of narcissistic parenting.[22] Looking particularly at the conflicts between Henry, Sr., and William, Feinstein believes this pattern of dependency and illness to be an outgrowth not only of Henry, Sr.'s, unresolved emotional conflicts with *his* father, William James of Albany, but also of his perpetuated shame and consciousness of his own lack of vocational respectability and success. Kept in place by the secrecy surrounding his disinheritance, and fostered by his dependency on his wife's caretaking abilities, Henry, Sr.'s, sense of deep, inward defectiveness—his sense of perpetuated shame—became an emotional burden that his children would struggle to shoulder in their own lives as well. Feinstein shows that while William was able to work his way out of the depression and illness that resulted from this vocational conflict and go on to become a successful psychologist and philosopher, Wilky and Bob took on the dark side of their father's emotional profile and, as a result of illness, alcoholism, financial mismanagement, and other problems, became increasingly dysfunctional in their lives as adults.

My goal in this study is, in part, to extend Feinstein's study by identifying more fully Henry, Jr.'s, position in the paternal legacy of vocational conflict and internalized shame. Thus I consider in Chapter 1 both the origin of shame, what Feinstein calls "negative identity," in the life of Henry James, Sr., and the perpetuation of shame in the family created by Henry, Sr., and his wife Mary. Chapter 2 goes on to consider the effects of this shame-based family psychology on the life of Henry, Jr., first by examining the source of his ambition in his fears of failure and then by looking at the psychological costs of professional failure later in his career. My central concern in the later portions of this chapter is James's severe emotional collapse in 1910.

Chapter 3 turns to *A Small Boy and Others*, the autobiographical narrative written by James between November 1911 and June 1912. Here I emphasize his struggle to define his boyhood self in relation not only to his eldest brother, but also and primarily to his devoted but incoherent and incompetent father. I contend that the inherited shame-based identity that was operative in James's collapse in 1910 emerges in

A Small Boy in the form of his conflicted autobiographical strategies for expressing his appreciation of his father yet defending himself from his progenitor's shame.

Chapter 4 moves from the autobiographical text that was largely completed in the summer of 1912 to an examination of James's correspondence with Alice and Harry James about the changes taking place in his plans for the Family Book. The main focus of the chapter is the complicated process of justification by which, in his letters to Harry, James redefined the nature and scope of the Family Book so as to privilege his autobiographical material, yet maintain the appearance of remaining loyal to the family, of becoming, as he put it, "more intensely 'Family' even than at the step before." Because the most distressing episode in this correspondence was followed by a severe and prolonged attack of shingles in September 1912, the chapter moves on to consider the politics of illness in the James family and the role of illness in James's efforts to maintain a positive sense of self-identity. My discussion in earlier chapters of a variety of interrelated issues—the James family system, the perpetuation of shame about the father, and the apologetic rhetoric of the autobiographical act—serve in part as a foundation for my analysis throughout Chapter 4 of James's complicated and often painful relationship with nephew Harry.

Illness or disability is also the subject of Chapter 5, not only the illness that James described at various points throughout the autobiographies but also, and primarily, his account of his "obscure hurt" in *Notes of a Son and Brother*. My theory is that because disability constituted an appropriate response to unacknowledged or unresolved conflict in the family, and to the unacknowledged shame that underlies this conflict, Henry uses his "hurt" both to express and to work through the emotional pain caused by the confusion in his family and thereby to resolve his vocational uncertainties. Once again his father plays a central role in the narrative, and his mother a brief but highly significant role as well.

Chapter 5 also considers the commemorative dimension or tribute to family in *Notes of a Son and Brother*. Here I address such interrelated issues as his rationale for including certain members of his family and excluding others (particularly his mother and sister) and his self-consciously protective attitude towards his presentation of family (and family friends). Accordingly, I expand here my discussion of an issue that will have been touched on in previous chapters—the James family tradition of suppressing painful knowledge and idealizing the family by means of what psychologists call the "family myth."

The Epilogue follows the history of the autobiographical act through the publication and British reception of *Notes of a Son and Brother*. It not only examines the nature of James's emotional and physical well-being in the spring of 1914, when *Notes* appeared, but it also posits a relationship between the optimism of some of James's letters during that period and the enthusiastic reception he received from the British press. I also examine James's efforts once again to justify to his nephew Harry his decisions about the Family Book, in this case the editorial decisions he made in his presentation of family documents to the public. As such, this chapter necessitates a consideration of the impact of the autobiographies on James's well-being throughout the years of composition and an examination of the ways in which the autobiographical act, as many claim, was therapeutic for James.

The Epilogue brings us to the end of my consideration of a particularly intense and fascinating period in James's life and to the end of a book that has scrutinized this period with the kind of detail necessary for an understanding of the autobiographical act as biographical event in the late life of Henry James. To be sure, James's experiment in autobiography was not an isolated act of autobiographical prose. The autobiographies are not the only writings that express James's emotional state in the final years of his life or the only writings that reflect the shame-based psychology he inherited from his family. But the pains and the pleasures, the contradictions and the inconsistencies, of James's autobiographies have long fascinated me, as have the blatant expressions of humiliation and shame both in James's autobiographical act and his writings about it. Tightly focused on the autobiographical text and its psychological context, *Intensely Family* is, for me, the inevitable result of this long-standing fascination.

1

The Heritage of Failure and Shame in the Life of Henry James, Sr.

I shall endeavor to screen him from infamy and as far as possible from reproach,
... I shall endeavor the best, to ward off the shame and reproach he is Creating
to his brothers and Sisters.

—William James (1829)

Henry James, Sr., grew up in a family dominated by a father who, by virtue of enterprise and hard work, rose from his status as an Irish immigrant to become in the early nineteenth century one of the wealthiest, most influential citizens of Albany, New York. Yet, as his grandson claimed in *A Small Boy and Others*, the lives of William James's children comprised "a chronicle of early deaths, arrested careers, broken promises, orphaned children" (10). Robert James, the son who in 1818 "succeeded his father 'in the superintendence of his commercial concerns,' " died in 1821 of undetermined causes. Ellen James King, William's eldest daughter, died in 1823 at the age of twenty-three, and each of his three other daughters, Jeannette, Catharine Margaret, and Ellen King James, died in their twenties or early thirties. Robert's twin brother William, who suffered intermittently from despondency and ill health, abandoned his career as a Presbyterian minister at age thirty-eight to live off his inheritance. Another son, John James, may have committed suicide in 1856 after incurring insurmountable gambling debts in Chicago. Finally, Augustus, the son who followed Robert into the family business, died in 1866 three months after declaring bankruptcy. Summarizing Mary James's account of the tragedy, Howard Feinstein claims that "Augustus' downfall had begun during the panic of 1857, but ... he had been too proud to acknowledge the loss. He tried to cover up and lived beyond his means until tragedy struck and left him pale and thin and weeping like a child, longing for death and threatening suicide."[1]

In this chapter, I discuss the arrested career and failed aspirations of the most well-known of these children, Henry James, Sr., in terms of a paralyzing sense of shame or inner defectiveness passed on to him by his father, William of Albany, and aggravated by the traumatic accident he experienced in his thirteenth year. This examination will provide the foundation for my discussion, later in the chapter, of the parenting styles of Henry, Sr., and his wife Mary, who, in spite of their obvious love for and devotion to their children, were responsible for establishing a shame-based emotional atmosphere in their home and perpetuating the feelings of shame or emotional woundedness in their children.

I

It is difficult to conceive of the wound'd
spirit of a man in my situation.
—William James (1829)

There is little doubt that William of Albany would have believed that his fourth son Henry repeated the pattern of "arrested careers" and "broken promises" established by his other sons, by William, by J. J., and even by Augustus. Not only was Henry addicted to alcohol by the time he entered Union College in 1828, but he had also begun to incur numerous debts for food, cigars, and clothing without his father's consent. He likewise refused to pursue the legal career chosen for him by his father and promoted by his father's associates at Union. In 1829, the conflict between father and son became sufficiently intense that Henry ran away to Boston and obtained work as a proofreader for *The Christian Examiner*. Pleased with himself, he wrote to a friend that his ambition to work and study was "awakened" by his situation in Boston.[2] But a letter to Henry from Archibald McIntyre, a family friend, reveals that his behavior at Union had jeopardized the faith of family and friends in his prospects for happiness and success:

I have heard and your friends generally have heard enough of your conduct to cause us much pain and solicitude for your safety and future usefulness. I consider you on the very verge of ruin, and am well satisfied that if you do not without delay stop short in the career of folly that you have for a time indulged in, (if you have not already stopped) and pursue with sincerity a different path, you are lost to the world, to your parents and to yourself. . . . Some consider you already lost, irretrievably lost. I am not, however, one of those. I cannot believe that a young man of good parts, with wealth to support him in well doing (but with none without performing his duty) with numerous and anxious friends, can

Failure and Shame in the Life of Henry James, Sr.

be such an idiot as to throw away all these advantages, and become a loathing to himself and his best friends.

Archibald concluded these remarks by claiming that, if Henry did not repent of his past and behave in conformity with his father's wishes, he would "lose all respectability, all support, independence, every thing valuable in life. You will be shunned by the good—you will be miserable."[3]

A letter written by William James a few weeks later reveals how closely McIntyre's admonitions to the rebellious son reflect the sentiments of the indignant father. Writing to McIntyre with the intent of "heaving a sorrowful load of [sic] my mind," James claims that his son Henry "[h]as so debased himself as to leave his parents [sic] house in the character of a swindler &c &c," that the details of the case are indicative "of his progress in arts of low vileness—and unblushing falsehood," and that his behavior will "lodge him in a prison of some kind directly." What is more, James writes, "[h]is mind and concett . . . [are] given to such low pursuits" that there appears to be "no hope of him" in the future.[4]

What is striking about these remarks is not only the heightened sense of wrongdoing with which McIntyre and James regard the rebelliousness of the student and son, but also the state of degradation and shame which they so readily impute to his character. Noteworthy too is the ease with which they predict for him a future of evil and ruin. Read in historical context, their language reveals both the concerns of men intent on controlling the future of a son who would be useful to William's financial empire and the expectations of men who had culturally-sanctioned reasons to expect unqualified filial submission. Insistence on controlling a son's future was, in fact, typical of the authority that early nineteenth-century parents expected to wield over their children. "A no less important feature of early 19-century society," argues Joseph Kett, "was the emphasis on the subordination of young people. Subordination had many antecedents. It was part of a tradition that decreed that sons and daughters were inferior members of the family hierarchy [and it] . . . led fathers to sound like commanding officers when they addressed even mature sons." An example of the expression of such authority appears in McIntyre's November 12, 1829, communication of William James's plans for his son Henry's future. William was, he writes, "inflexibly fixed on your studying the law, or at all events on studying one of the learned professions."[5]

In their letters, William James and McIntyre's promise of respectability and success to the errant Henry, and its obverse, their forecast of failure and shame, likewise reflect the strict values of right and wrong that were the stock-in-trade of William James's staunchly Presbyterian household. As Henry James, Sr., wrote of the behavior codes dictated by the family's "Orthodox Protestant faith," "we were taught" that on Sundays we were "not to play, not to dance nor to sing, not to read story-books, not to con over our school-lessons for Monday even; not to whistle, not to ride the pony, nor to take a walk in the country, nor a swim in the river; nor, in short, to do anything which nature specially craved." The general "pursuit of pleasure," in fact, was sufficiently frowned upon that Henry, Sr., claims to have been "plunged" by his boyhood tendencies towards self-indulgence into continual "perturbations and disturbances of conscience."[6]

The rhetorical strategies and shaming techniques that appear in the McIntyre and James letters, and that were undoubtedly used in the James household to excite "disturbances of conscience," were also characteristic of larger societal efforts to exert control over wayward young people and return them to the fold not only of moral but also of vocational respectability. The publications of the American Tract Society continually feature young protagonists who, having taken one step in the direction of prodigality and vice, rapidly begin the descent into moral and financial ruin. Self-help books promoting business success similarly draw parallels between the drama of economic and spiritual salvation: He who works hard at his calling is saved; he who slips into habits of prodigality, indolence, and sloth is lost.[7]

The advice literature also warned of the dangers of encouraging loose morals and laziness by bequeathing one's wealth to one's children.[8] That William James clearly subscribed to this philosophy can be seen by the stipulations he made in his will, shortly before dying in 1832. Leaving Henry and his elder brother William with only a small annuity, James insisted that his fortune was to be distributed only to those who did not lead a "grossly immoral, idle or dishonorable life." He thus hoped, as he said, "to discourage prodigality and vice, and to furnish an incentive to economy and usefulness." He may also have sought to protect his family, one of the leading families in Albany, from the dishonor of being related to an idle or immoral man. As he wrote to McIntyre (probably in 1829), "if you see him [Henry], tell him, that when he finds how base he has acted,—and when deceiv'd and despised by himself and all others;—to come to me and I shall endeavor to screen him from infamy and as far as possible from reproach,—and in the interim; I shall endeavor the best, to ward off the shame and reproach he is Creating to his brothers and Sisters."[9]

This letter speaks worlds about the permeable emotional boundaries of the patriarchal family of William James; the "shame and reproach" of the son automatically accrues to the siblings, and the father who stands somehow above the shame believes that he possesses the power to protect them all from their dishonorable condition. What is especially interesting in this regard is the possibility that, in admonishing his son, William James may have been acting out a family pattern in which, years earlier, he too played the role of the disobedient child. "There is a story extant," says Katharine Hastings, "that the father of William James wished him to enter the ministry, and that he came to America to escape from an uncongenial career."[10] The fact that William James then tried to control the career choices of his sons (McIntyre writes that he was "inflexibly fixed on your [Henry's] studying the law, or . . . one of the learned professions") suggests that his own inter-generational conflict had been left unresolved and, being unresolved, was now visited on the son in the form first of admonitions and then of disinheritance. When William James wrote, probably in 1829, that "[i]t is difficult to conceive of the wound'd spirit of a man in my situation," that of having a recalcitrant child, he may well have been reliving feelings experienced by *his* father forty years before.[11]

The animus of William James's indictment of Henry can be explained in the context of both the cultural expectations for dealing with an errant child and the intra-familial patterns of vocational conflict. But the possibility exists that multiple deaths in the family likewise contributed to James's powerful need to control his son. As the family record shows, William experienced the deaths of his first two wives within three years of one another. His first wife died in 1797, less than a year after they were married and eight days after giving birth to twin sons. William James married his second wife in December 1798 only to lose her in October 1800. According to Katharine Weissbourd, the record of James's business ventures during this period suggests that, "in contrast to his private life," James "worked very hard . . . to achieve a public identity of control and mastery." In May 1795 he "opened a store with a partner. In December 1797 he opened a second store for receiving country produce. In November 1798 he announced the building of a tobacco factory. A fourth store was opened jointly with a second partner in 1800."[12]

Might this record suggest, says Weissbourd, that "William absorbed himself in a successful public career" throughout the late 1790s "without facing the pain of his domestic life"?[13] To put it another way, might the absorption in work that led to James's impressive business success have been a more available alternative for the expression of pain and loss than the open expression of feeling? Certainly the prescribed method of dealing with death in early nineteenth-century America would have encouraged James in the direction not of therapeutic release but of Christian acceptance and resignation. As John James (William's nephew) wrote to his mother in Ireland following the death of his father, "I have been much consoled . . . [by] the fortitude with which you bare up this heavy blow. This my Dr. Mother your own good sense must teach you will be necessary. It is not in our power to oppose the will of the Almighty."[14]

What concerns me in this attempt to reconstruct the emotional life of the James family is the relationship between what grief theorists call "disordered" mourning and the sense of Christian fortitude that would have encouraged William James to compensate for his loss through his work. According to mourning theorists, grief becomes disordered when, among other things, "environmental conditions do not support the expression of disruptive emotions of mourning" or when an individual, proud of his independence and self-control, and determined to remain busy and efficient, attempts to carry on as though nothing had happened. When mourning becomes disrupted or remains unresolved it "can lie dormant and revive periodically throughout one's life."[15]

Unresolved grief also makes additional loss more difficult to deal with. The genealogical record shows that following the deaths of his first two wives William James went on to experience a series of new losses—the death of an infant son Henry in 1809, the death of his youngest brother John in 1813, the death in 1821 of the son (Robert) who went into the family business, the deaths of his daughter Ellen and his elder brother Robert in 1823, and then in 1824 the near loss of his fourth son Henry from an accident in a fire.[16] Indeed, if Henry's autobiographical account of his father can be believed, the accident and the amputation of his leg that followed jolted his father out of his characteristic detachment from his children and initiated a period of almost excessive sensitivity to and concern for the well-being of his injured son. "[R]e-sponding to other losses in his life," Weissbourd suggests, Henry's father "made a brief and uncharacteristic special effort to foster his son's survival."[17]

It appears, then, that the unresolved pain of previous losses resulted for William James in an almost unbearable anxiety not only over Henry's suffering but over his own potential loss as well. Temporarily becoming what John Bowlby calls a "compulsive caregiver," the father expressed through his anxiety for his injured son "all the sadness and neediness" that he was "unable or unwilling to recognize in himself."[18] It is thus likely that Henry's rebelliousness several years later reactivated his father's unresolved and accumulated pain. When William of Albany wrote to Archibald that "[i]t is difficult to conceive of the wound'd spirit of a man in my situation," he may well have been attesting to a wound that goes deeper than the 1829 intergenerational conflict alone, a wound, in other words, that is excessively painful for the very reason that other losses had not been resolved, a wound that is excessively painful because of his inability to control the possibility of additional loss.

Grief theorists also argue that unresolved grief often results in "unconscious reproach against the lost person combined with conscious and often unremitting self reproach." Thus the powerful, unsparing condemnation of his son both during the period of rebellion and in his will may represent the father's attempt to visit upon Henry some of the self-reproach and shame that went unrecognized and unresolved in his own life. As contemporary psychologists contend, inherited family shame often arises in families in which "parents feel they were to blame (or being punished)" for "bankruptcies, suicides, childhood deaths and accidents," and the "rules of shame-based systems" in turn "produce several generations of repressed affect."[19] The discourse of self-loathing that is so prevalent in the letters to and about Henry, by this account, would have emerged from similar feelings within the father's self, feelings he defends against by passing them onto his children. That Henry was named after another child who died in infancy adds to our sense that he became the object of many of his father's unresolved feelings of anger, grief, and loss.

This is not to say that other children in the family would not have fallen victim to their father's shame-based emotional system. Undoubtedly the discourse of shame that emerges in the letters of James to McIntyre reflects language that, in some form or another, would have been expressed not only during periods of crisis but throughout the daily life of the family. William James's powerful sense of family loyalty and honor, and the permeable emotional boundaries that accompanied this sense, would have taught all of his children that, because shame would be shared by the family, individuals must take the responsibility of screening one another from "infamy." And his orthodox Protestant sense of perfectionism and control would have taught his children that very thin indeed was the line between bad behavior and good, failure and success, shame and respectability. Having internalized this shame-based system, at least two of William's other sons, John and Augustus, were unable to withstand the emotional pressure of having broken its rules, John by incurring large gambling debts, and Augustus by having to declare bankruptcy.

But to say that other children in the family were likewise victims of the James family system does not negate the fact that William sought strenuously to control his second son first by shaming him and then by disinheriting him, even as he claimed that the wounds were his. The expectation of filial submission; the family history of inter-generational conflict; the hard-line Protestant approach to disobedience, deviance, and failure; the sequence of deaths in the family; the religious emphasis on self-denial; and, finally, Henry, Sr.'s, unfortunate accident and amputation—taken together, each of these factors helps explain the force of William of Albany's disapproval of Henry when the son failed to comply with his father's rules and expectations. But what about the emotional life that Henry, Sr., would have brought to the conflict with his father?

Any attempt to theorize about Henry James, Sr.'s, emotional life during the years of conflict with his father must, above all, take into account the traumatic accident that occurred when Henry was thirteen. As biographers have explained, the boy's leg was badly burned when, along with some classmates, he attempted to extinguish a fire in a barn. Infection set in, "some sharp surgery was required," and, not once but twice, portions of the boy's leg were amputated. Two to three years were then spent recuperating in bed before, as Edel claims, the "dismembered young man . . . one day found himself at the end of his adolescence, erect again, facing the world on a solitary foot."[20]

Biographers who have written on the subject of the accident emphasize at least one concern central to our understanding of James—the incident's capacity to exacerbate the boy's Calvinistic sense of God's powerful "supernatural being." For years, says Edel, James lay in bed, "face to face with the spectral eye, the God of punishment." Or, as Feinstein puts it, "[t]hree years of confinement would have provided ample opportunity for a theologically talented young man to speculate on the meaning of his misfortune. Was it punishment? If so, what was his transgression?"[21] James's fictional autobiography suggests that he had already suffered agonies of "self-abasement" over the sins he committed as a child, among them his having become "addicted to alcohol" during boyhood revels with friends. The possibility exists, then, that the trauma of the accident, in itself remarkably severe, would have been made more severe by his boyhood terrors of God's wrath, by the wrath, that is, of a stern and exacting heavenly Father. As James says in a passage associating these terrors with the sensation of burning: "I doubt whether any lad had ever just so thorough and pervading a belief in God's existence as an outside and contrarious force to humanity, as I had. The conviction of his supernatural being and attributes was burnt into me as with a red-hot iron, and I am sure no childish sinews were ever more strained than mine were in wrestling with the subtle terror of his name."[22]

Biographers have also hinted at the "emotional problems" that would have resulted from the loss of a leg at the age in which James would otherwise have been marching sturdily into manhood: an attitude of helplessness, confusion, or loss of self-respect.[23] Recent research on the victims of catastrophe highlight the extent to which such problems could have been created in James by the trauma of the accident and the amputations that followed. One psychologist contends, for example, that much of the trauma that results from catastrophe derives from the shattering of "basic assumptions that victims have held about the operation of the world"—assumptions about personal invulnerability, about the world as meaningful and comprehensible, about self-worth and personal decency. Indeed, the experience of being victimized leads to a serious revision of one's self concept. "People generally operate under the assumption that they are worthy, decent people; that is, they maintain a relatively high level of self-esteem." Victims, however, "see themselves as weak, helpless, needy, frightened, and out of control." Their sense of helplessness can serve as catalyst for a loss of self-esteem, and can even lead them "to experience a sense of deviance. After all, they have been singled out for misfortune and this establishes them as different from other people. The self-perception of deviance no doubt serves to reinforce negative images of oneself as unworthy or weak," especially, we might add, if the victim brings to the accident an already highly developed Calvinist sense of sin.[24]

Consider, then, the emotional burdens that both father and son brought to the intergenerational conflict of 1829—the father the unresolved and accumulated pain of a series of losses, including the pain of his son's trauma of several years before; the son not only a powerful sense of vulnerability created in him by both the accident and the religious interpretation of its significance but also a loss of self-respect associated with his maimed condition, his own wounds, as it were, both physical and emotional. For all of his reputed spirit and pluck, for all his courage and bravado, Henry would have been acutely vulnerable both to the language of condemnation heaped upon him by his father in 1829, and then to the official act of disinheritance made public in 1832 with his father's death. Feinstein suggests that James's "first encounter with unreasoning authority," the accident, "left him without a leg," and the "second round," the battle with his father, "left him without self-respect."[25]

But to understand fully the force of the identity James carried into adulthood, we must think of each of these encounters not as isolated and discrete but as cumulative and convergent; the trauma of the accident made the pain of the 1829 conflict more intense, and the pain of the two together made the public shaming of the disinheritance more painful still.

Of course, the death of the father in 1832 was another loss, one undoubtedly fraught with inner conflict for the son. And it was followed in the subsequent decade with yet more acts of rebellion—the breaking of the father's will, the undermining of the estate inherited by his brother Augustus, and, following the inheritance that left him "leisured for life," the abandonment (after two years at Princeton Theological Seminary) of the attempt to pursue one of the respectable vocations earmarked by his father. As Feinstein has shown, Henry paid a heavy emotional price for this repudiation of his father's expectations and values. In breaking his father's will he took on the guilt of defying his father and undermining Augustus, his father's favored heir. Additionally, by failing to pursue a respectable vocation, Henry unconsciously assumed the identity that his father and friends imposed on him during his years of rebellion—the shameful identity characterized by such labels as "idle" and "dishonorable." To make matters worse, he failed to succeed at the role he tried to define for himself in the early 1840s as writer and lecturer on religious subjects. As he wrote to Emerson in 1841, "I came home tonight from my lecture a little disposed to think from the smart reduction of my audience that I had about as well not prepared my lectures, especially that I get no tidings of having interested one of the sort (the religious) for whom they were wholly designed."[26]

Henry, Sr.'s, solution for vocational uncertainty in the early 1840s was the same as his remedy for spiritual confusion in the late 1830s—travel.[27] In 1843 he packed up his rapidly growing family and set sail for England. His motives, as he explained them to Emerson, were somewhat indistinct: "My affairs, in various regards, seem to indicate this as the advisable course. How long I shall stay, and whether I shall gain what I go for specially, or something instead which I have not thought of, and all questions of that class—I am of course in the dark about." In England in 1844, he then experienced an emotional and spiritual crisis that attests to the uncertainty and confusion that thus far had characterized so much of his adult life. As James tells it, the breakdown came when he was enjoying the comfort and "exhilaration incident to a good digestion" after dinner. Then "suddenly—in a lightning-flash as it were—'fear came upon me, and trembling, which made all my bones to shake.' To all appearance it was a perfectly insane and abject terror, without ostensible cause, and only to be accounted for, to my perplexed imagination, by some damnèd shape squatting invisible to me within the precincts of the room and raying out from his fetid personality influences fatal to life. The thing had not lasted ten seconds before I felt myself a wreck; that is, reduced from a state of firm, vigorous, joyful manhood to one of almost helpless infancy."[28]

James eventually came to believe that he had experienced a vastation, "one of the stages of the regenerative process" described by Emanuel Swedenborg.[29] Recounting the incident many years later, he thus shaped it according to the patterns of spiritual conversion he had encountered in

Swedenborg and, as John Owen King argues, in Bunyan, Edwards, and Mill.[30] Like these other writers of conversion narratives, James was particularly interested in using the incident to illustrate his belief that an individual's "proprium" or "selfhood" was illusory or dangerous, and he makes a point of highlighting the contrast between the personal comfort that preceded his experience of terror and the emotional chaos that followed. When he returns to the incident later in his text, he likewise emphasizes the experience of self-abasement so vivid in his core account: "When I sat down to dinner on that memorable chilly afternoon in Windsor, I held it [faith in selfhood] serene and unweakened by the faintest breath of doubt; before I rose from the table, it had inwardly shrivelled to a cinder. One moment I devoutly thanked God for the inappreciable boon of selfhood; the next, that inappreciable boon seemed to me the one thing damnable on earth, seemed a literal nest of hell within my own entrails." Elsewhere he speaks of the "conviction of inward defilement" that "took possession of me" during this experience.[31]

What is striking about this account is the resemblance between James's description of his vastation and the family's Calvinistic rhetoric of abasement and ruin. For however much James reshaped his account in the light of his reading and subsequent experience, the passage nonetheless attests to the force of the shame-bound identity quickened by his Presbyterian up-bringing, reinforced by his accident, and then conferred on him by his father. Gershen Kaufmann explains that shame in this sense is not a behavioral infraction but a sense of oneself as deeply defective—the Calvinists would call it original sin—and James's sense of his infant-like state, his "conviction of inward defilement," describes this defectiveness in particularly vivid terms. So too does the suddenness and intensity of the experience reflect the pattern that develops in shame-bound individuals whereby, having learned to internalize and perpetuate shame within the self, they reach the point of contending "with excessive shame, excessive beyond current capacity to cope or due to some failure of the supporting interpersonal environment."[32] The result is a depressive episode which reflects the sort of downfall that James's father and friends predicted for him on a worldly and, to a certain extent, on an psychological level. In a flash, James went from feelings of outer comfort and inner selfhood to a sense of abjectness, helplessness and deformity. As McIntyre and his father warned, he went from a situation of safety and advantages to one of self-loathing and ruin. The suggestion is that self-loathing and defilement lie just beneath the surface, ready to take one unawares, ready to reduce one from a state of manhood to infancy. The son in the shape of the "outraged view of the father" comes to life.[33]

Henry James, Sr., wrote about his vastation as if it were an isolated, self-contained crisis in his life, disconnected from the self recounting the experience. But, according to King, James's depression continued for two years after his horrifying vision.[34] What is more, the James family literature provides abundant evidence not only of the haunting presence of self-doubt and depression throughout James's life but also of the energy he expended attempting to ease the pain of these feelings, often through behavior that was confusing to his children. Family correspondence attests, for example, to the numerous occasions on which Henry, Sr., both referred to the "devil" of weakness, anxiety, depression, or sexual temptation with which he struggled throughout his life, and counseled his male children to banish the demons in their own souls by repressing their feelings, reflecting on the good side, and behaving in a manly fashion. Letters likewise attest to the mood swings, the "ups and downs as usual," that he appears to have experienced throughout his life and that, as Feinstein believes, led James to thoughts of suicide.[35] They broadcast James's dependence on his wife's strength and stability to ease the troubles in his soul. They hint at his tendency in the 1840s and 1850s to look for a solution to his problems by uprooting his family, traveling to Europe, and then, once there, keeping continually on the move. They likewise tell the story of the father's chronic problem with homesickness, and his inability to leave home for long without the presence of his family.

John Owen King claims that Henry, Sr., was the victim of an obsessional neurotic disorder resulting from his Protestant upbringing, a disorder characterized by "paralyzing doubts," "seemingly silly forebodings and apprehensions," "methods of self-castigation," and "feelings of loathing and self-hate." The psychology of shame would also argue that Henry, Sr., was the victim of a condition in which shame or self-loathing had become sufficiently prolonged as to be experienced as a cycle which gives rise to "oscillations of mood" or "recurring bouts with depressive episodes" and compulsive behaviors to control anxieties.[36]

The evidence of self-doubt that appears in the literature of the family takes on added importance when set against the personal preoccupations that appear again and again in James's writings for the public. The self-image of the prodigal, of the reckless, rebellious son, had been "impressed on him by William James and sealed by his testamentary rejection," says Feinstein; "Henry would carry it as a mark of shame for the rest of his life." But, Feinstein continues, Henry tried "to lighten that burden by fashioning an ideology to justify a rejected prodigal." Not only did he use his interpretation of Swedenborgian thought to privilege the absence of ambition and accomplishment in his philosophy, but he described as the only divine truth the experience of humiliation, failure, and defeat.[37] "I am not sure indeed," his son Henry wrote years later, "that the kind of personal history most appealing to my father would not have been some kind that should fairly proceed by mistakes" (*Notes of a Son and Brother* 301).

Further driving his compensatory need for the ideology of the prodigal were the dreams of professional success James entertained in the 1840s and 1850s. Writing to Emerson in 1842, he claimed that he might go about learning science and bringing "myself first into men's respect, that thus I may the better speak to them." Writing to his brother-in-law, Edmund Tweedy in 1852, James suggested that he might settle in Europe and write a "book—and a book moreover—O! you Mammonite!—that will sell." He went on to claim that "I shall eventually live abroad in all probability on the income of my writings. How much more honorable this than upon one derived from the merciless warfare of Cedar and Wall Sts?" He was encouraged to dream this dream by the fact that his most recent book, *Lectures and Miscellanies* (1852), was selling well. "It has recently had two very appreciative notices in the London *Leader*," he informs Tweedy, "and I doubt not by the first of January a new edition will be needed. Don't you feel, then, somewhat ashamed of your wicked insinuations?"[38]

Clearly the ideology of the prodigal was designed to defend against the disappointment of these dreams of worldly success (a success that would differ from his father's) and the teasings or "wicked insinuations" from his relatives. It was underscored in his work by the pervasive but not unrelated belief we have already seen articulated in his discourse of vastation, his belief in the essential corruption of the self. Over and again in his writings, James excoriates the private personality, "that cadaverous and lying thing"; over and again he calls for the "inward death to self in all its forms," for the expulsion of that "dead, corrupt, and stinking thing." "My father," wrote William, "seems in his early years to have had an unusually lively and protracted visitation of this malady . . . [s]elf-conceit and self-reproach . . . and his philosophy indeed is but the statement of his cure."[39]

James's preoccupation with the dangers of the self have led some biographers to assert that "the whole of his writing, an imitation rather than a repetitive copy of past spiritual struggles, becomes an autobiography."[40] But here resides one of the central contradictions of James's work. While the entirety of James's philosophical writings becomes an autobiography enacting the struggles of a lifetime—an autobiography in spirit, that is, rather than form—the self-avowed autobiographical writings of Henry, Sr., attempt to distance James from both the struggles and the worldly failures to which they are related.

Take, for example, the account of his vastation that appeared first in *Society, The Redeemed Form of Man* (1879) and then again in William's edition of his father's *Literary Remains*. As Alfred Habegger observes, his description of terror in terms of a "damnèd shape squatting" in the room—in terms, that is, of something "wholly *other*"—suggests the extent to which James was alienated from his feelings, first perhaps when he experienced his crisis and then when he recreated the crisis in writing. And the retrospective stance James takes on the experience, recasting it as his moment of conversion in the past, allows him to treat the feelings he does acknowledge as other and distant, part of the past as well. As King says of both Henry, Sr.'s, and William James's depiction of emotional crisis, the intense focus on the state of degradation or collapse "distract[s] the reader from the lengths of their suffering, from the periodic and extended depressions both men experienced following their convictions of fear."[41] So too does his description of the situation he enjoyed prior to the breakdown, not only physical comfort but also professional success, distract the reader (and James as well perhaps) from the lack of professional focus and success responsible for the breakdown.

We see the same kind of distance towards and ambivalence about his personal experience in the fictional autobiography James began for a volume entitled *The Immortal Life*. In this volume, James divides himself into two autobiographical narrators, the narrator who introduces the autobiographer, Stephen Dewhurst, and Dewhurst himself, each of whom he endows with qualities identifiable as his own. But he also endows them with other qualities foreign to his own experience, such as a worldy identity validated by professional status and, in Dewhurst's case, by his service to the country. As the narrator of the preface explains, Dewhurst not only "got a situation of trust in the Treasury Department at Washington, which his ability and probity qualified him to fill with advantage to the country," but, after the death of his wife and son, he also devoted himself "with forced activity to the increased labors thrown upon him in common with all the Government servants by our unexampled war."[42]

Perhaps James uses Dewhurst to compensate for the failings in his own life not only by having this fictional autobiographer pursue a socially acceptable profession and become a success, but also by endowing him with professional abilities and social commitments absent in his own experience—financial abilities suitable for a "position of trust" in the government's Treasury Department and, perhaps even more suggestive, strenuous "activity" on behalf of the government during the Civil War.

In the autobiography, James also endows Dewhurst with a sense of emotional certainty or, as Feinstein puts it, a "spiritually undivided self," and then highlights his wholeness by omitting from Dewhurst's record his own conflict with his father, William of Albany.[43] Indeed, through his portrait of Dewhurst's childhood, James portrays his father as an "easy" and, at the time of his accident, extremely solicitous and caring parent, and because he fails to continue the narrative beyond his childhood years, he is absolved of the responsibility of negotiating his subsequent painful history with his father and the difficult question of vocational choice. Given the gap between the preface and the autobiography, the impression conveyed is that vocations are acquired without histories, and conflicts with real fathers, rather than divine ones, are avoided. Indeed, by limiting his autobiographical writings to the unfinished autobiography of Stephen Dewhurst and the story of his vastation in *Substance and Shadow* and *The Redeemed Form of Man*, and by describing in these writings only his boyhood and the conversion experience of his early thirties, James creates a chronological gap in his personal history that, like the twenty year gap in *The Education of Henry Adams*, bespeaks the presence of a painful emotional fact. It should thus come as no surprise that, as Feinstein believes, the history of James's conflict with his father and the fact of his disinheritance was never mentioned to his family and friends but instead kept as a carefully guarded secret against exposure and shame.[44]

Alfred Habegger's meticulous research into the life of Henry, Sr., reveals that, in addition to keeping quiet about his conflict with his father, Henry, Sr., was similarly uncommunicative about his accident and amputations. In chapter 5 of his biography, Habegger discusses the "techniques of self-control by which," as a suffering teenager, Henry "sought to deflect his attention from the horror that mired him." Although his "letters are full of references to his frequent illnesses and indispositions, and he seems to have demanded a great deal of care from the woman he married," Henry, Sr., rarely talked "about his lifelong disability." He also failed to fulfill his promise to a friend at Princeton Theology Seminary to write a "*clinique*" disclosing "in orderly form those sinister personal or sentimental grievances of mine which first sensibly impaired my natural pride of life." When he wrote about his accident in his fictional autobiography, he described the accident as a "gun-shot wound in my arm" and emphasized not his own but his father's suffering.[45] Contained within and underscoring his silence about the rupture with his father, then, is the more painful, more shameful secret of his personal physical suffering and defectiveness.

Henry, Sr.'s, children would keep alive in their memoirs, autobiographies, and diaries the autobiographical impulse manifested in their father's personally expressive theology and his personally evasive fictional autobiography. They would re-enact in their writings about themselves and the family the distinctly ambivalent attitude towards secrecy and self-revelation that was founded, in part, on their father's preoccupation with his wounds, both emotional and physical. They, too, would describe their emotional terrors and psychological sufferings; they, too, would talk about their fears of personal disintegration and emptiness, about the illnesses or wounds that embodied those fears. Also like their father, the children would become expert in simultaneously distancing themselves from, disguising, or obscuring the truth about personal trauma in their lives or the life of the family. I turn next to a consideration of how the children became heirs to the family shame and thus to the pattern of concealing self-revelation established by their father.

II

"[A] certain wounded feeling which
had taken possession of me."
—Henry James, Jr. (1885)

Central to an understanding of the relationship between the psychology of Henry James, Sr., and that of his family is the belief among family psychologists that secrets are responsible for maintaining an individual's pervasive sense of shame or inner defectiveness. Yet secrets, and the system of denial on which they are based, also enable the shame of such individuals to become an invisible yet powerful presence in the life of their families. In their roles as spouses and parents, shame-based individuals not only demand that families live by the rules of the "control, perfectionism, blame and denial" so necessary to their psychic survival, but, by operating from these rules, such individuals unconsciously instill shame in the other members of the family.[46] Through the affective climate they create, in other words, parents who are raised in shame-based families will create a system by which shame is both perpetuated within themselves and passed on to the emotional life of their kin.

The threatening presence or damnèd shape of Henry James, Sr.'s, shame, by this account, would have been both communicated and perpetuated by the family system created by him, his wife Mary, and Mary's sister Kate. It would have been communicated, in particular, by the family's complicity in keeping secrets about Henry, Sr. Alfred Habegger has discovered that someone in the family suppressed evidence of Henry, Sr.'s, activities in the late 1830s, including the fact that he took not one but two trips to Europe and began to affiliate himself with radical theological groups. There is likewise evidence to suggest that the family destroyed letters concerning Henry James, Sr.'s, embarrassing exposure in *Woodhull & Claflin's* in 1874. (For more on this incident, see the discussion later in this chapter.) When Henry, Sr., died in 1882, the officious Aunt Kate took it upon herself to burn a good number of letters tucked away in a drawer of Henry, Sr.'s, dresser. "[S]he said they were family papers," Katharine Loring reports, "& she thought it better that 'the children' should not seem them."[47] In brief, secrecy about Henry, Sr., prevailed in the family and the unspoken message must have been twofold; something was wrong with or shameful about father, yet no one was allowed to name the malaise.

The threatening presence of Henry, Sr.'s, shame would also have been communicated by his habit of narcissistic parenting, a parenting style in which children learn to accommodate themselves to the emotional needs of the parent and, through this unconscious process, discover the parent's sense of anxiety and deprivation. Narcissistic parenting also requires that the psychic energy the parent invests in denial of his or her own emotional problems not be available for adequate mirroring of the children's emerging identities and for responding to the children's emotional needs.[48] Howard Feinstein believes, for example, that the James children quickly learned to avoid direct questions about or allusions to their father's sore point, the fact of his disinheritance. They learned to avoid direct reference to the origins or the presence of their father's shame. Yet they were continually asked to share in their father's episodes of emotional distress and to accompany him on the chaotic pattern of travel partly designed to alleviate this distress. A passage from Alice James's diary supplies an apt illustration. Calling her father a "delicious infant," Alice recalls instances during their travels in the 1850s when Henry, Sr., would return "at the end of 36 hours, having left to be gone a fortnight, with Mother beside him holding his hand and we five children pressing close around him 'as if he had just been saved from drowning,' and he pouring out, as he alone could, the agonies of desolation thro' which he had come."[49] Not only does this passage comment on the family's responsibility for comforting Henry, Sr., it also demonstrates what we will have the occasion to observe throughout this study—the tendency of James family members to reflect upon and to dramatize their dynamics as a family.

Evidence shows that specific relationships between Henry, Sr., and his children were also organized around the emotional needs of the parent. William once remarked to Bob, for example, that if "you have felt any lack of it [sympathy] in Father, it does not much surprise me, for his religious optimism has I think a tendency to make him think too lightly of anyone's temporal troubles, even to neglecting to look closely into them at all." When Henry, Sr., wrote to advise Bob on such troubles, he substituted Bob's concerns for his own need to have virtuous and untroubled children: "It would kill me if one of my boys, especially you, turned out [to be] an unkind husband, or a base man. Take a look at the goodness of God every day, and see how great our hope is, if you only keep from evil."[50] On another occasion, Mary James remarked to Henry, Jr., that "father" enjoys Alice's companionship more now than ever "because it is not marred by the old anxiety about her." And a passage from Henry, Jr.'s, autobiography, a passage we will consider in a different context in chapter 5, suggests that when Henry expressed anxiety about his father's lack of professional identity, Henry, Sr., responded with what Miriam Elsen calls "his own zestful amusement at his small son's dilemma rather than an empathic understanding of the child's need."[51] Behind these comments we see a father who, even as he addresses it, deflects attention from his children's distress, directs their actions to comfort himself, or substitutes their concerns for his own desire to articulate his philosophy or indulge in verbal display. We thus see a father who communicates to his children that their needs or troubles are somehow trivial, unacceptable or wrong.

The part that Mary James played in this family dynamic seems only to have strengthened it. Even more than her children, Mary James was expected to provide comfort for her husband and keep watch over his lapses and prodigalities. Henry, Sr.'s, letters suggest, in fact, that Mary James was available for comfort whenever he felt overwhelmed by anxiety and temptation. Yet her capacity to empathize with her husband's troubles appears not to have extended to her children. Not only was she impatient with William's frequent expressions of weakness and anxiety in the 1860s and 1870s, but she explicitly endorsed the patient, non-complaining posture of her second son Henry. Moreover, she seems to have been more comfortable caring for her children when their troubles took the form of physical illness rather than emotional distress.

These patterns, says James Anderson, hint at the "overwhelming anxiety" smoldering "just under the surface of her outer defensive structure." They hint at her tendency to protect herself from anxiety by distancing herself from her children's negative feelings, yet reassuring herself of her caregiving capacities by tending to their physical ills. And they point to the children's attempts to accommodate her needs by repressing their feelings and falling ill, a pattern that would have been reinforced by the narcissistic parenting of their father.[52] There is even a hint in *Notes of a Son and Brother* that Mary James further undermined the children's emotional security by endorsing their habit of teasing father about his "ideas." Remembering "free jokes and other light familiarities" directed at Henry, Sr., Henry, Jr., goes on to say that the "happiest household pleasantry invested our legend of our mother's fond habit of address, 'Your father's *ideas*, you know—!' which was always the signal for our embracing her with the last responsive finality (and, for the pleasure of it, in his presence). Nothing indeed so much as his presence encouraged the licence" (*Autobiography* 333).[53] In banter that seemed all "for the pleasure of it," everyone in the family was able to ridicule the absurdity of "father's ideas" and indirectly acknowledge the sore point or shame concerning his vocational ineffectuality. They did this by aligning themselves with their mother.

Perhaps Mary's participation in, even control over, this humorous ritual signaled the unconscious shame she felt about her marriage to an emotionally dependent and professionally ineffectual man. Perhaps it was her way of exercising control or expressing resentment in a marriage which, like so many nineteenth-century marriages, demanded that she sacrifice her identity for her husband. Alfred Habegger writes:

Leon Edel believes that the James father was dominated by his rigid and commonplace wife, to the degree that Henry, Jr., became virtually obsessed in his fiction with the figure of the viciously overmastering woman (Edel, *Henry James: A Life* 11–16). . . . But the preponderance of evidence indicates that he enjoyed a commanding relationship over his wife. She gave up her Christian orthodoxy in marrying him, accepted and defended his ideas, read less and less on her own, and remained silent in those family arguments where her husband's voice boomed loudest.[54]

What is more, Mary James was married to a man who publicly endorsed the view that, although she is "inferior" to man in "passion," "intellect," and "physical strength," woman nonetheless represents "nature's revelation to man of his own God-given and indefeasible self." She "represents to the imagination of man, a diviner self than his own; a more private, a more sacred and intimate self than that wherewith nature endows him." In addition, James claims that as a "form of *personal affection*," woman exists "simply to love and bless man" and thereby to provide for him what he lacks in himself. "This precisely then is what man finds in woman, the satisfaction of his own want, the supply of his own lack."[55] Henry James, Sr., may have enjoyed a commanding relationship over his wife, but that relationship was designed to fill the emptiness or ease the distress of his own shame-bound self. What, we wonder, were the psychological costs to Mary James and the emotional effect on the family of expectations which, as a woman of her time, she wholeheartedly endorsed?

What too were the costs of Mary James assuming the responsibility of maintaining to the world outside the home the image of the family as both proper and harmonious, or of enforcing this image through her children? Writing to Alice of the social obligations that William was expected to fulfill during his travels abroad in 1867, Mary claims, "I told him that I felt a great burden removed from my mind in hearing" that he had paid the expected social calls, "and indeed the social conscience of the whole family would be especially relieved when he had got through." Conversely, Mary felt the "social conscience" or image of the family had been tarnished when one of William's friends assumed that her son's departure for Germany was motivated by difficulties within the family. "Your friend Pratt made his appearance last evening," she reports to William: "The only reason he had heard given [for William's departure], was 'family reasons' which had evidently placed the whole thing in so equivocal an attitude to his mind that he had not dared even to speculate upon the subject—some dreadful family rupture had driven you to place the ocean between you and your offending family—this seemed the most natural solution to the mystery."[56]

In this letter, Mary James's snide and wounded tone expresses her indignation at the possibility of a "rupture" within the James family, or at the possibility that people might imagine such a rupture had occurred. Thus she indirectly echoes her husband's belief that "domestic discord" is the most "frightful of all discords" and reveals her sense of responsibility not only for maintaining harmony but for reminding her children of their responsibility as well. More self-assured, self-righteous, and socially conscious is a passage from an 1873 letter to Henry, Jr.: "Tell Will that old Mrs. Norton said to Alice the other day with quite a sympathetic but serious look, 'I hope your brothers are getting on harmoniously in Italy?'. . . . You may imagine Alice's consternation and the warmth of her assurances that her brothers never quarreled and that no mere differences of taste, even if they had any, which she disclaimed, could possibly produce a want of harmony between them."[57]

Taken together, these comments reveal Mary's insistence that "a want of harmony" is impossible within her family and that the image of harmony should be reflected both outside the family as well as within. As part of her role as wife and mother, she had assumed the responsibility of maintaining the family identity while divesting herself of her own.[58] But, as the letters suggest, this process creates for her a "burden" that could be relieved by passing it onto her children. For in each of the letters, Mary James not only reports the gossip about the family but reminds the children of their role in protecting the family from the implications of gossip. (In her letter from 1873, she even describes to one child the alacrity with which another child defended her brothers and upheld the family image.) One cannot help but wonder, of course, at the relationship between the need to defend the family against the imputation of conflict and the conflict that, as so many biographers have shown, was smoldering under the surface of the family's harmonious facade.

Like their father, the family learned the lesson of keeping secrets only too well. Indeed, it was in part the invisible presence of the father's secrets in the emotional life of the family that required Mary James to invest so much energy in maintaining the image of harmony and order. It was the invisible presence of family secrets that, in part, caused the family to become so emotionally enmeshed.

We have seen that, for all the rhetoric of care and concern for the children, the James family was in large part organized around the task of meeting the emotional needs of the parents, and the parent with the greatest needs was their father, Henry, Sr. It was the father's impulsiveness that determined the inconsistent nature of their travels, and his theories of education that led to the children's endless succession of tutors and school-masters. It was the father's rich but overpowering discourse that dominated the intellectual atmosphere of the household and shaped the children's attitudes towards self and society.[59] It was the father's emotional needs that drew on Mary James's seemingly endless capacity for comfort and reassurance, an ability she had cultivated early on in her own family, and it was the father's dependence that may have hindered Mary's ability to mother her children as consistently and attentively as she mothered her husband. (Mary, of course, must have found this arrangement conducive to her own emotional needs.) Henry, Sr.'s, inability to face the pain of his own life rendered him unable to face the pain of his children's lives; it directed him to substitute personal anxiety and religious platitudes for the attentive paternal presence the children required.

Yet it was the father's unacknowledged anxieties about personal and vocational failure that shaped his excessive involvement in the emotional difficulties, the illnesses, and the career choices of his children. Miriam Elsen explains that the "James children did not suffer the trauma of abrupt withdrawal or emotional inaccessibility: their trauma arose from their father's being so everlastingly *there* and of using their feelings and experiences to discharge his own." Using his children narcissistically to accommodate his feelings is a kind of inaccessibility, as I have explained. But it is an inaccessibility necessitated both by Henry, Sr.'s, tacit insistence that the family take on the responsibility for his feelings and compensate for his choices in life. Whereas Alice was raised to fill the role of her father's "darling daughter," William was raised to fill the role of the compensatory son. The "basic clue to understanding [William] James's search for a vocation," says Cushing Strout, "is provided by Erikson's remark in *Young Man Luther* that" a parent may plunge a "child into 'a fatal struggle for his own identity' " by electing that child as the "one 'who must *justify the parent.*' "[60] Driven by his own deep-seated

33

sense of failure, Henry, Sr., selected William as the son through whom he could be brought the better into men's respect, first through the vocation of artist, and then through a scientific career.

The struggle to accept the vocation selected for him by Henry, Sr., and to assume thereby a false, ineffectual sense of identity, resulted for William in a prolonged period of physical and emotional suffering. Throughout the 1860s and 1870s, William experienced a range of psychosomatic ailments—eye troubles, back troubles, problems with digestion, and so on—and at one point his intermittent struggles with depression became sufficiently severe that, like his sister Alice, he contemplated suicide. The frightening vision of a mental patient in *The Varieties of Religious Experience* is through to be veiled confession of the terror he experienced when, during this particularly trying period, William feared he was going insane: "it was as if something hitherto solid within my breast gave way entirely, and I became a mass of quivering fear."[61]

The similarities between this account and his father's vastation experience reveal that in attempting to justify Henry, Sr., through his choice of vocation, William also assumed the burden of his father's shame. As Feinstein puts it, the breakdown was "more his father's than his own." Perhaps that is why William's sense of helplessness during this period was so pronounced. "Nothing that I possess can defend me against" the fate of insanity, he declared, "if the hour for it should strike." Here William may be expressing the belief held by many nineteenth-century Americans that insanity, organically determined, was the sign of hereditary taint. But William may also be unconsciously acknowledging the legacy of his multi-generational emotional inheritance, that he was fated to experience emotionally what his father had left unresolved. He directly compared his debilitated state with his father's, in fact, when in recounting his own "panic fear" in the *Varieties*, William included a footnote to "another case of fear equally sudden," Henry, Sr.'s, account of his breakdown in *Society, the Redeemed Form of Man*.[62]

William took on the legacy of his father's failure in other ways as well. In editing his father's literary remains in 1883, he tried to rescue his father's reputation as a religious thinker. Privately William claimed that he had undertaken the project to atone for the fact that during his lifetime father "found *me* pretty unresponsive" to his ideas.[63] But his introduction to the *Literary Remains* reveals that he likewise hoped to make Henry, Sr.'s, ideas more appealing to the public. "It has seemed to me," he says, "not only a filial but a philosophic duty, in giving these posthumous pages to the world, to prefix to them some such account of their author's ideas as might awaken, in readers hitherto strangers to his writings, the desire to become acquainted with them." Though he attests to his inability to speak for his father—"I must screen my own inadequacy under the language of the original"—William goes on to provide an interpretation of Henry, Sr.'s, thinking that is more forthright and unequivocal than anything attempted by Henry, Sr., himself. And he creates a context for "father's *ideas*" that puts them in the most attractive light possible.[64]

William begins with this pithy summary of his father's thought and *modus operandi*:

Probably few authors have so devoted their entire lives to the monotonous elaboration of one single bundle of truths. Whenever the eye falls upon one of Mr. James's pages,—whether it be a letter to a newspaper or to a friend, whether it be his earliest or his latest book,—we seem to find him saying again and again the same thing; telling us what the true relation is between mankind and its Creator. What he had to say on this point was the burden of his whole life, and its only burden. When he had said it once, he was disgusted with the insufficiency of the formulation (he always hated the sight of his old books), and set himself to work to say it again. (9–10)

In these remarks, the phrase "monotonous elaboration" suggests that William is not unwilling to be critical of his father's writings. Yet before he goes on to elucidate his father's "bundle of truths," William pauses to put the blame for his father's situation not on the insufficiency of his father's "formulation[s]," but on the skeptical age in which he was forced to attempt them: "I have often tried to imagine what sort of a figure my father might have made, had he been born in a genuinely theological age, with the best minds about him fermenting with the mystery of the Divinity, and the air full of definitions and theories and counter-theories, and strenuous reasonings and contentions, about God's relations to mankind." "Floated on such a congenial tide," William imagines, and "furthered by sympathetic comrades," Henry, Sr., would have enjoyed a sense of intellectual stimulation and professional success impossible to achieve in this theologically "lifeless and unintellectual" age. If he had been "opposed no longer by blank silence but by passionate and definite resistance," Henry, Sr., "would infallibly have developed his resources in many ways which, as it was, he never tried; and he would have played a prominent, perhaps a momentous and critical, part in the struggles of his time, for he was a religious prophet and genius, if ever prophet and genius there were" (12).

Because Henry, Sr.'s, system of thought depends upon an "intensely positive, radical, and fresh conception" of our relationship with God, William also claims that the reader can appreciate his father's writings only by accepting "without criticism" his father's faith (12–13). He even concludes this section of his introduction with a plea that the reader "listen to my stammering exposition in a very uncritical mood of mind. Do not *squeeze* the terms or the logic too hard!" For "the core and centre of the thing" in his father "was always instinct and attitude, something realized at a stroke, and felt like a fire in the breast" (15–16). Apparently William wants to create in his readers, if not the spirit of a genuinely religious age, then a fresh state of openness to Henry, Sr.'s, ideas. The hope is that with the help of his "stammering exposition" readers will come to appreciate the prophetic genius so patent to the devoted son.

Likewise crucial to this effort of filial justification is William's approach to his father's autobiographical writings. William notes on the first page of his introduction that Henry, Sr., had often "been urged by members of his family to express his religious philosophy under the form of a personal evolution of opinion." But "egotistic analysis was less to his taste than enunciation of objective results, so that, although he sat down to his autobiographic task a good many times, it was at long intervals" (7). What he finally produced was the *Autobiographic Sketch of the Late Stephen Dewhurst* discussed earlier in this chapter. William claims that the "Stephen Dewhurst, whose confessions it is supposed to be, is an entirely fictitious personage" (7). But he is careful to correct the impression that the "fictitious" Dewhurst bears no relation to Henry, Sr. Not only does he provide footnotes that make the "items of personal and geographic fact . . . true of Mr. James rather than of his imaginary mouthpiece," but he makes a point of alerting us to his act of having "rectified" the facts (7–8).

By highlighting the referential status of the autobiographical sketch, then giving it a prominent place in *The Literary Remains*, William accomplishes a goal central to his aim of redeeming his father's reputation as a religious "genius." He follows his introduction to Henry, Sr.'s, writings with an account that, by concretely illustrating the evolution of Henry, Sr.'s, thought, makes the paternal "genius" more accessible and immediate to readers who might otherwise be confused by his father's "monotonous bundle of truths." But, as we have seen, the autobiography of Stephen Dewhurst is the story of Henry, Sr.'s, divided self. His use of the two narrators allows Henry, Sr., not only to present himself as more successful than he was but also to gloss over painful details of his personal history. His use of a fictional persona allows him to distance himself from the past even more. When William acknowledges the referential status of the narrative through his footnotes, he defeats his father's attempt to disclaim his autobiographical identity. But by publishing his father's fictional autobiography, he also contributes to his father's efforts to hide the truth about his past. He becomes complicit in his father's efforts to keep secret the fact of his shameful or failed self.

Unwittingly, William has performed this compensatory function not only for himself, not only for his father, but for the entire family as well. Like his grandfather fifty years before, he has attempted to ward off the shame that might accrue to a dishonorable or ineffectual man and, through that man, to his family. We have already seen how instrumental William was in alleviating the social conscience of the family, and how fully his mother pressured him and the other children to maintain for the family an acceptable facade. We have seen how instrumental William was in absorbing his father's shame and compensating through his vocational and emotional struggles for his father's sense of defectiveness and failure. Now, through the publication of the *Literary Remains*, the first book of his career, William has made yet another effort to rescue his father's reputation and thereby the ability of the family to remain loyal to their sense of his "genius." Henry James, Jr., says as much when he thanks William for his efforts: "I can enjoy greatly the spirit, the feeling and the manner of the whole thing . . . and feel really that poor Father, struggling so alone all his life, and so destitute of every worldly or literary ambition, was yet a great writer. At any rate your task is beautifully and honourably done. . . . And we [Henry and Alice] talked of poor Father's fading away into silence and darkness, the waves of the world closing over this System which he tried to offer it, and of how we were touched by this act of yours which will (I am sure) do so much to rescue him from oblivion."[65]

It is the public response to *The Literary Remains of the Late Henry James* that moves us in this chapter from William's ability to compensate for his father's shame to Henry, Jr.'s. Henry and Alice had spoken to each other about their hopes for the volume early in 1885 and, as we have seen, Henry promptly summarized their conversation in a letter to William. Far from rescuing him "from oblivion," however, the review of the *Literary Remains* that appeared in *The Nation* several weeks later afforded at least one critic an opportunity to ridicule Henry, Sr.'s, theological system. To "disgorge his bile," William immediately wrote Godkin, the editor of the *Nation*: "Does n't the impartiality which I suppose is striven for in the 'Nation,' sometimes overshoot the mark and 'fall on t'other side'? Poor Harry's books seem always given out to critics with antipathy to his literary temperament; and now for this only and last review of my father—a writer exclusively religious—a personage seems to have been selected for whom the religious life is complete *terra incognita.*" Godkin apologized, and William responded by clarifying the spirit in which he had launched his attack: "My *emotion* was less that of filial injury than of irritation at what seemed to me editorial stupidity in giving out the book to the wrong *sort* of person altogether—a Theist of some sort being the only proper reviewer."[66]

While this exchange was underway, Henry also wrote Godkin about the review, and Henry too received an apology. "Your delightful letter, in answer to my last," he explains to Godkin, "gives me more pleasure than I can say. I was morally sure that you had known nothing about the Review in the *Nation*, and that it had found its way in by accident." What distinguishes Henry's response from William's, however, is the second son's willingness to acknowledge the feeling of "filial injury" that William disavows. Godkin's letter, Henry admits,

soothes extremely, a certain wounded feeling which had taken possession of me. . . . I have a tenderness for my poor Father's memory which is in direct proportion to the smallness of the recognition his work was destined to obtain here below and which . . . fill[s] me with a kind of pious melancholy in presence of the fact that so ardent an activity of thought, such a living, original, expressive spirit may have passed into darkness and silence forever, the waves of time closing straight over it, without one or two signs being made on its behalf, to say, however little it might command general assent, how remarkable and rare it had been.[67]

The letters of both William and Henry demonstrate the brothers' loyalty to the family code of protecting their father's reputation. But Henry's letter attests more clearly to the transfer of emotions that occurred in the enmeshed family system of Henry and Mary James. Not only does Henry, Jr., reveal a poignant sense of empathy for the "poor Father" whose memory will be lost to oblivion but, through his "wounded" feelings, he identifies with the shame of his father's failings in the past. Helen Lynd tells us that "[e]xperiences of shame appear to embody the root meaning of the word—to uncover, to expose, to wound. They are experiences of exposure, exposure of peculiarly sensitive, intimate, vulnerable aspects of the self." Henry, Jr.'s, feelings are "wounded" by the attack on Henry, Sr., because he treats his father's exposure as his own. What is more, his attention to wounded feelings on behalf of the father recalls the language of William of Albany who, in expressing anger over Henry, Sr.'s, errant behavior, likewise attested to a feeling of woundedness: "It is difficult to conceive of the wound'd spirit of a man in my situation." As they passed down through the family, the painful feelings associated with Henry, Sr.'s, vulnerability and failings have thus become the complex inheritance of his sons.[68] The difference between William and Henry inheres in the fact that Henry actively feels the wounds and admits to the feelings while William keeps them at bay. At this, however, he is only partially successful. Though William claims his "*emotion* was less of filial injury than of irritation," he is so irritated by the negative review that he finds it necessary to "disgorge his bile."

Family history reveals that Henry, Jr.'s, sensitivity to his father's shame surfaced well before the publication of the *Literary Remains*. Alfred Habegger has shown, for example, that Henry, Jr.'s, "dislike of newspaper vulgarity" hardened "into a lasting hatred" after his father's embarrassing exposure in an 1874 issue of *Woodhull & Claflin's*. The episode began when, in order to express his opinion on free love, Henry, Sr., wrote a letter suggesting that his wife no longer appealed to him sexually. Through a complicated series of events, the letter found its way into the magazine of Henry, Sr.'s, former journalistic "enemy," Stephen Pearl Andrews. "On April 18, 1874," reports Habegger, "the whole world could read in the most outrageous paper of the day Henry James Sr.'s own confession that his wife had not afforded him full sexual satisfaction. Henry Sr.'s radical ghosts were out of the closet with a vengeance, and this time Henry Jr. was old enough to have to deal with them."

The family dealt with these ghosts, it appears, by destroying any family correspondence that alluded to his father's exposure. Henry, Jr., dealt with the ghosts by expressing in his fiction his hatred of "investigative candor" and " 'the complete effacement of privacy' " in modern life. "In this way," Habegger concludes, "the father's deep apostasy—his willed refusal to know himself and to let himself be known—was visited on his son."[69]

Henry, Jr., responded to the humiliating exposure in *Woodhull & Claflin's* with a gesture he had learned not only from his father but from his entire family as well—defensiveness about his father's "dark side," as Habegger calls it, and a tendency to assign blame.[70] Henry, Jr.'s, fear of public embarrassment and habit of defensiveness likewise extended to William when, shortly after their father's death, William's behavior began to resemble Henry, Sr.'s.

Having gone abroad for his sabbatical in September 1882, William determined after a few months to abandon his plans and return home. He "was unhappy in London," writes Gay Wilson Allen, "because he detested the city, and even found Henry's cherished flat uncomfortable." But Henry could not stand the thought that William would leave London for dull Cambridge—he himself was in Cambridge to settle their father's estate—and he wrote a number of heated letters attempting to keep William from coming home. "For you to return before the summer seems a melancholy confession of failure (as regards your projects of absence)," he wrote in January 1883, "and sort of proclamation of want of continuity of purpose"; to have to settle for makeshift housing in Cambridge upon his return, "would give a dreary and tragic completeness to such a collapse, and have the air of your having committed yourselves [William and Alice] to inconstant and accidental (not to say shiftless) ways." William recognizes that what Henry seems "so much to dread" is "the opinion of outsiders and their exclamations of 'failure.' " In his typically patronizing manner, William finds his brother's attitude sympathetic, but "comical." "Your allusions to my return continue by their solemn tone to amuse me extremely."[71]

The irony of this exchange becomes apparent when we read in William's correspondence to his wife his own expression of the fear of failure: "If I can only get to feeling decently & doing a little work beside letter writing, it will undoubtedly be by far the best thing; for I shall have the consciousness of having sat it through & of not coming home under a sense of defeat. I ought to be ashamed to keep up such a whining,—you had better not read it to any one else."[72] What William can express to his wife he apparently cannot express to his brother; Henry's open acknowledgment of the "confession of failure" seems, in fact, to harden William's resolve to mask his own anxieties and regard Henry's as "comical." William wishes to distance himself from Henry, from Henry's open expressions of powerlessness and fear; Henry thus enables William to assume a mask of indifference to the social pressures and the possibility of shame that both of them feel.

What neither of the brothers seems to recognize, however, is that Henry's anxiety about William's failure to make a success of his sabbatical is informed and exacerbated by an anxiety about his father that surfaces more clearly when, as an old man, he tries to write about his father's travels in *A Small Boy and Others*. (I discuss this episode at greater length in chapter 3). As William's son, Harry, explains, his uncle Henry retained "a very lively consciousness of his father's vacillations and impulses—as if the possibility of going home or going to Europe, going from one place to another, were always in the air and often realized to the disturbance of his, Uncle H's equanimity. He is also evidently self-conscious about the fanciful and inconsequent explanations and reasons which his father used to give to people, who expressed surprise or made inquiries."[73] Habegger argues that James's self-consciousness about his father's travels "had a long history," a history that goes back at least as far as Henry's quarrel with William's sabbatical. "Back in 1882," notes Habegger, "W. D. Howells had told the same story in his sketch of James's life and works: 'In his twelfth year [actually his thirteenth] his family went abroad, and after some stay in England made a long sojourn in France and Switzerland. They returned to America in 1860, placing themselves at Newport' ('Henry James, Jr.,' 25). It was undoubtedly James himself who fed this misinformation to Howells and thus made his youthful years appear more stable and regular."[74]

In these instances, Henry, Jr., seems anxious about the impression of uncertainty and the imputation of failure in the actions of a male member of the family, and in both he is extremely sensitive to, even "self-conscious" about, the opinion of outsiders. Karen Horney suggests that inhibitions resulting from "sensitivity to humiliation often appear in the form of a need to avoid anything which might possibly seem humiliating to others."[75] To fear humiliation for others, particularly a member of one's family, is to fear humiliation for oneself. When he assumed the responsibility articulated by William of Albany of warding off the "shame and reproach" associated with William and his father, Henry, Jr., was thus engaged in the activity of protecting the family. He had assumed the responsibility so soundly communicated by his mother that the image of the family was to be preserved at all costs. But he was also working to protect himself, to guard himself against the discomfort or "disturbance" he felt through his association with another's "appearance of failure." In the next chapter, we see not only that the "negative identity" that was William's inheritance from his father was Henry, Jr.'s, as well, but also that, to a certain extent, this inheritance shaped Henry's approach to his entire career.

2

The Heritage of
Failure and Shame in the Life
of Henry James, Jr.

[I]f once I can get rid of this ancient sorrow I shall be many parts of a well man.
—Henry James (1873)

The chapter "Consciousness of Self" in William James's *Principles of Psychology* neatly summarizes the source of identity or "self-feeling" for the men in the James family. A man's *"provocative* of self-feeling," William claims, "is one's actual success or failure, and the good or bad actual position one holds in the world." The man with the "broadly extended empirical Ego, with powers that have uniformly brought him success," is not likely to experience "the morbid diffidences and doubts about himself which he had when he was a boy." But the man "who has made one blunder after another, and still lies in middle life among the failures at the foot of the hill, is liable to grow all sicklied o'er with self-distrust, and to shrink from trials with which his powers can really cope."[1] The equation of self-worth with worldly success clearly reflects the fact that, as Burton Bledstein puts it, many nineteenth-century Americans began to identify themselves according to their "individual advancement in a career and by the degree of passion for the material symbols of success rather than by social rank, region, and community obligation."[2] But it likewise reflects the experience of a man whose father failed to succeed in this new standard of professional success. With the autobiographical thrust typical of so many of his father's writings, James's discussion of social identity tells the story of the son who not only dared to take on the values of accomplishment and success but, in doing so, attempted to "disassociate himself both from the uncertain boy he had been and from the negative vocational possibility modeled by his father and his younger brothers."[3] What is more, James reveals that a fear of shame determines the level of achievement to which he must aspire if the act of disassociation is to be complete: "I, who for the time have staked my all on being a psychologist, am mortified if others know much more psychology than I. . . . So we have the paradox of a man shamed to death because he is only the second pugilist or the second oarsman [or the second psychologist] in the world."[4]

William's analysis of identity or self-feeling in *Principles,* and the relationship between self-feeling and shame, speaks directly to the experience of his younger brother Henry as well. Time and again, Henry James's personal writings from the late 1860s to the early 1880s suggest that he built his impressive literary career out of a determined effort to disassociate himself from his own shame or negative identity, manifested initially in a history of psychosomatic complaints. Likewise they equate the debilitating features of this repudiated identity with the negative vocational models of other male members of his family, his father in particular but also his younger brother Wilky. While the point of the previous chapter was to trace the origin of this shame-based psychology in the experience of Henry, Sr., and to consider the effect of his negative self-feeling on his wife and children, the purpose of this chapter is, first, to identify the process by which Henry, Jr., attempted to distance himself from his own negative identity and then, on the basis of this discussion, to trace James's continuing struggles with shame through key periods in his career. In the end, I argue that the failure of James's massive act of disassociation and denial in 1909 and 1910 resulted in a nervous collapse resembling his father's vastation and the collapses and panic fears of other members of his family. Whatever the other reasons he went on to write *A Small Boy and Others* (this volume of autobiography is the subject of chapter 3), James attempted both to understand and to rectify this painful period in his life by attempting to repeat in his autobiographical act the process of disassociation that was not always successful in life.

I

I shall have been a failure unless
I do something *great.*
—Henry James (1882)

Manfred Mackenzie claims that as "one reads the mass of James's writing, one's overwhelming impression is that the central psychological experience delineated is shame . . . of sudden exposure, above all of a vulnerable or inferior self to the self; of almost grotesque blights or invalidism or woundedness consequent upon exposure of secrecy, and, on the other hand, of the extraordinary energy released in an effort to conceal and heal these effects of exposure; of secrecy."[5] Likewise the central psychological experience of James's younger self in the autobiographies is self-negation or shame and, to the extent that these narratives reflect what Eakin calls "the psychic truth of James's retrospective account," they reveal that, saturated with feelings of inferiority, James spent much of his boyhood learning to cope with painful moments of exposure, or avoiding the possibility of such moments, through his self-protective posture as a detached, gaping boy.[6] Edel contends that Henry's stance of self-protective inferiority was due in part to William's aggressive treatment of his younger brother. Not only was William known to have "pounced" on Henry for the "blunder[s]" he made as a boy but he continued "to the very end of his life to be a sharp and not always friendly critic of Henry's work."[7] We saw in chapter 1 that William was often critical of Henry's concerns and condescending towards what he called Henry's "powerless-feeling" personality.[8] But we can more fully understand Henry's fear of shame, his self-protective inferiority, if we consider William's reasons for being so critical of Henry and so invested in his personality.

Present in William's life, first of all, was the pressure Henry, Sr., put on his eldest son to compensate for his own failures through his choice of career and the publication of his posthumous writings. Present, too, was the benevolently abusive talk and the harsh judgments for which Henry, Sr., was known among his friends and the members of his extended family. His talk was not just a maʈer of carrying "freely into public his domestic habit of saying whatever would cause a shock and hence excite some sort of spirited reaction."[9] It was also a matter of condemning in others any manifestation of his or her selfhood. Habegger's research on Minny Temple reveals that through his "talk" Henry, Sr., tried to push Minny "to question her assertive individuality and self-trust." "[I] knew all the time . . . , " she wrote to a friend, "that he . . . disliked me for what he called my *pride & conceit.*" William himself claimed that Henry, Sr.'s, habit of criticism was so pervasive, and his respect for others' individuality so slight, that he once wrote to Alice, "if you or I or Mama were to die to-night, he would send off a contribution to the Daily Advertiser tomorrow tearing us to pieces."[10]

William turned his criticism on Henry because his own sense of individuality had been undermined by his benevolently demanding and verbally aggressive father and, in doing so, he became one of the sources of Henry's exacerbated sense of shame. William was not the only source, to be sure. Henry, Jr.'s, relationship with his father would have taught him to empathize with and feel shame for his father's ineffectuality and failure, as I suggested in Chapter 1. So too would Henry, Jr., have absorbed the talk about the evils of selfhood even as he sympathized with and admired his cousin for rejecting it.[11] Moreover, Henry may have been criticized by his parents for being too literary as a young man, and he once groaned "with shame" to his niece Peggy when he recalled that "No one took any interest whatever in *his* development," when he was a boy, "except to neglect or snub it where it might have helped."[12]

A letter that Henry, Sr., wrote to the editor of *Scribner's* reveals, in fact, that the father not only misinterpreted Henry's talents but also projected on his son his own sense of professional powerlessness: "Polonius-like, the elder Henry . . . went on to say that he was delighted that *Scribner's* so highly esteemed his son's work, added that Henry had 'no power to push himself into notice, but must await the spontaneous recognition of the world around him,' and promised that he would do his best to persuade his son to write the novel Holland requested. He also mentioned that it was his opinion that his son's gifts did not lie in the realm of fiction, 'his critical faculty' [being] . . . 'the dominant feature of his intellectual organization.' "[13]

Thus, like William, Henry suffered from his father's misreading and neglect of his interests and talents and, as the letter to Peggy suggests, this neglect was itself a source of self-negation or shame. But, as Kaufman claims, "the interpersonal transfer of shame usually follows the lines of the familiar pecking order, or dominance hierarchy which emerges in social groups . . . [w]hether it is in the *family*, the *peer group*, *peer setting*, or the *work setting*."[14] In the James family, William may have acted as an emotional shield for Henry by becoming the primary focus of his father's vocational issues and, as we will see, of his mother's disapproval. But through his aggressive criticism of Henry, William not only communicated the difficulty he had in establishing a "psychologically separate self," he also passed on to Henry the shame he had inherited from his father and internalized in his own development.[15] In other words, William helped construct Henry's sense of inferiority in order to bolster his own ego and, in doing so, he aggravated the shame that was developed in Henry through parental self-absorption and neglect.

The transfer of shame between the brothers was further aggravated by the fact that, given the injunction against conflict and assertiveness in the family, Henry was unable to defend himself against William's attacks. Research on Mary James suggests that the father's diatribes against egotism and self-assertion were reinforced by the mother's injunctions, both direct and indirect, against self-expression and assertiveness, particularly if that expression was colored by feelings of anger, unhappiness, or complaint. About Wilky she once wrote: "He began to walk when the baby was two weeks old, took at once into his own hand the redress of his grievances which he seems to think are manifold, and has become emphatically the *ruling* spirit in the nursery. Poor little soul! my pity I believe would be more strongly excited for him were he less able or ready to take his own part, but as his strength of arm or of will seldom fails him, he is too often left to fight his own battles."[16]

The inability to empathize with a child's overt grievance was likewise expressed in a comment about William that, in a letter to Henry, she made many years later: "This necessity he is under here to measure his strength every day, keeps his mind constantly fixed upon himself which is the worst possible thing for him." He is "still very morbid, and much more given than he used to be to talking about himself. . . . If, dear Harry, you could only have imparted to him a few grains of your blessed hopefulness, he would have been well long ago." A letter to William demonstrates not only how appreciative she was of what William called Henry's "angelic patience" but also how critical she was of William for "talking about himself." "*Of course*," she writes to William, "his 'angelic patience' shows forth, as you say but happily that side of his character is always in relief, and does not need great occasions (as it does with some of us) to bring it to view."[17]

James Anderson's psychological study of the relationship between William and his mother illuminates a number of po. s essential to my analysis of the transfer of shame in the family. For one thing, the "fragile self-structure" in William that we have traced to his relationship with his father is clearly reinforced both by Mary's lack of empathy for William's psychological difficulties and by William's unconscious recognition that his mother was emotionally unavailable.[18] We recall from chapter 1 that William was also under pressure from his mother to satisfy the "social conscience" of the family, and he was occasionally the reason that the family was being talked about in the Cambridge community in the first place. Moreover, his mother was constantly comparing him unfavorably with the "angelic" Henry. The psychological pressure that William was under in the family, then, was acute, and evidence of firm emotional support from both of his parents was lacking. Small wonder, then, that William was in the habit of pouncing on his younger and more vulnerable brother, on that "powerless-feeling" Henry.

The evidence of Mary James's parenting practices likewise illuminates the inner world of Henry and his helpless feelings. Anderson believes that, unbeknownst to his mother, "Henry was not actually hopeful [or patient] but had learned to put on an optimistic [or angelic] facade for his mother." He was one of those children who learned to develop an "as-if personality" or "false self" in order to accommodate parental needs and win approval. The problem is that children raised by unempathic parents are "plagued by anxiety or deep feelings of guilt and shame." Additionally, the injunction against anger in the family and the approval of "angelic patience" would have allowed "shame to proliferate" in Henry by rendering him "shamefully weak or by denying" himself the opportunity to defend himself "against attacks on self-esteem."[19] The psychological burden here for Henry is double; criticized by William, he is unable to respond with an overt expression of anger, and by adopting the defensive posture of an angel in the family he is likewise criticized by William for his "angelic patience" or "powerless-feeling" personality. Through his passivity, he also aligns himself with a feminine identity which, however useful as a survival strategy, was an additional source of shame.[20] Both the shame at being belittled by William and the anger that cannot be expressed would have been internalized, and, through internalization, James would have acquired the response typical of shame-based individuals—"to hold on to shame, to draw it out over time."[21]

A comment James made to T. S. Perry in 1913 is very instructive in this regard. "Fancy deliberately *stirring up* such an exhibition," he says of the organizer of Howells' seventy-fifth birthday party, fancy "pulling with a wanton hand the string to let loose the flood of shame otherwise for the time confined." In this passage, shame is a given amount of emotion that, like the water in a tank or reservoir, can be released by the mere pull of a string or a touch of a "wanton hand" by some person or some occasion that exposes you. Shame is a permanent part of the self that is "confined" only when exposure is avoided.[22] I believe that James characterized shame as a carefully contained "flood" because as a boy he had become a repository for much of the self-negating feelings experienced within the family. Indeed, the frightening dream he experienced in his youth, a dream in which he is threatened by a "monster" lurking behind a door, demonstrates James's unconscious awareness of the power of such feelings within himself. Writes Lady Ottoline Morrell:

Henry James told me of two dreams that he had in his youth, and which had obviously made a lasting impression on him. He awoke trembling in a great state of nerves. He had become aware that a terrible beast had entered into the house where he was. He realized that the room in which he was had four doors. He rushed to the first, the second and the third, turning the key; when he arrived at the fourth he was aware that there was something awful behind it, and he began to hold the door to with all his strength. But as he was doing this, he felt a sudden *volte-face* within himself, and he called out, "What a vile, cowardly creature you are to be afraid." He dashed open the door and determined to pursue the monster; as he opened it he found he was on the threshold of a long beautiful gallery, flooded with sunlight. He rushed out, waving his arms, and at the far end of the gallery he saw a monster rushing away, and as he fled after it he woke.[23]

In his analysis of a later version of this dream, that of the Galerie d'Apollon in *A Small Boy and Others*, Edel claims that the monster in the dream is William and the act of routing the monster equivalent to Henry's act of vanquishing William in the world of his fiction.[24] Given its likeness to the frightening fetid shapes of Henry, Sr.'s, and William's nervous breakdowns, however, I would identify the monster as the emotions in Henry that were transferred to him from the family and that William was instrumental in transferring—the threat of illness and invalidism, the fears of impotence and ineffectuality, and the obscure sense of individual and family shame. Indeed, his position as second son and thus his vulnerability in relation to William may be the reason that, more so than William, Henry is keenly aware of and sensitive to the "monster" in the family, and to shameful situations both for himself and for others in which the monster emerges. It may also be the reason that his attempt to rout the monster, to disassociate himself from family emotions and patterns, is so clearly expressed in his early writings about his evolving manhood and aspirations for his career.

The language that the young Henry James uses to describe his struggles to succeed at his vocation and to move into manhood is often the language not of the emotions but of the body, of a series of vague bodily complaints that kept him constantly attuned to his state of health and the hope of recovery. During his first solo trip abroad in 1869 and 1870, a trip central to his literary apprenticeship, his letters about his travels are punctuated with updates on what he calls his "moving intestinal drama." At one point he claims that "my digestive organs are the bane of my existence," at another point that "my back . . . is so chronically affected by my constipated state." Somewhat later he says he has "derived invaluable relief" from the cure of an Italian doctor, but is unsure he can regard this "as an improvement."[25]

As Feinstein said of William, it would be possible to describe Henry's invalidism "as a unique experience inextricably tied to his personal uncertainties. But he was not alone in his neurasthenic struggles. A twentieth-century reader of the James letters is startled to discover how many of their friends, not to mention family members, devoted themselves to, in Alice James's phrase, the 'life-long occupation of improving.' " Like many nineteenth-century illnesses, James's can be seen in the context of the anxieties about leisure experienced by affluent Americans. Though travel for the sake of amusement was suspect, travel for the sake of health was justified. During the late 1860s and the early 1870s, sickness became a means by which the James children, Henry and William in particular, competed for the family resources that would enable them to travel for personal and, sometimes vaguely, for professional edification—and to postpone their full entry into the world of work.[26]

We must acknowledge that James's reports on his "intestinal drama" attest to his adeptness at manipulating his parents to ensure the continuation of his travels. But sickness was also a way to express anxiety and shame in a family in which the overt expression of such feelings was unacceptable and the value of self-suppression was supreme. Central to James's gastrointestinal drama, in fact, are his frequent equations of illness with characteristics of a self-negated, failed identity—weakness, inaction, suffering. Conversely, his "struggle" with what he once called his "enemy"—a term similar to the "monster" of his youthful dream—is constantly equated with his efforts to become his "better self" and achieve a life of work and respectability. He describes himself as "slowly crawling from weakness and inaction and suffering into strength and health and hope." He claims that "if once I can get rid of this ancient sorrow I shall be many parts of a well man. . . . I shall march straight ahead, I think, to health and work." Using a metaphor appropriate for a man whose father had only one leg, James likewise equates learning to function in the world with "lifting me fairly onto my legs."[27] Illness may have served to justify the travel necessary to gather impressions for the writing, but as the manifestation of "weakness and inaction," helplessness and incompetence, illness was also the condition that both expressed and confirmed his feelings of inferiority and shame. As James wrote to Grace Norton in 1883, "Try not to be ill—that is all; for in that there is a [failure]."[28]

Related to and clarifying James's dilemma is the fact that his language of invalidism merges with language descriptive of anxieties created by his role in the family—about his use of family funds, in particular, and the impression his use of such funds is making on his parents. "To have you think that I am extravagant with these truly sacred funds sickens me to the heart," he writes in May 1869: "I attach not only so much value to the money you have given but so much respect and gratitude to the temper in which you gave it and I can't bear to have you fancy I may make light of your generosity. I incline I think to take my responsibilities to my little fortune too hard rather than too easy and there have been moments when I have feared that my satisfaction here was going to be very seriously diminished by a habit of constant self-torturing as to expense."[29]

A number of significant issues emerge in this letter. Among these is James's need to justify himself to his parents, to remind them of his gratitude, and to assure them that his "habit of constant self-torturing" would not be exceeded by his personal satisfaction. But I am chiefly concerned here with James's use of the word "sickened" to describe his feelings about his communication with the family. "Symptoms in a family member," explain Roman and Blackburn, are usually "masks for unacknowledged . . . pain," not only in the individual but in the entire family, and when James says he is "sickened" by his misunderstanding with his parents and then moves to justify himself, he neatly points to the connection between his "intestinal drama" and the family's unacknowledged pain regarding the relationship between self-worth, vocational usefulness, and, in this case, the expenditure of family funds.[30] We have already seen that Henry, Sr., focused his vocational issues on William and that, as a result, William himself not only had trouble achieving autonomy in the family but also suffered for years from depression and neurasthenic illness. So, too, did Henry, Jr., express through his body the struggle to separate from his family, particularly from its preoccupation with self-negation and failure. As Feinstein writes, "In young adulthood, which Erikson has labeled a time of identity formation, following one's will becomes a paramount issue once more. In a family context that has made separation difficult"—indeed that has fused the identities of fathers and sons—individuation "may have to be fought out symbolically, once again through control of one's own stool."[31] Looking back on this period in his life, James himself blamed his difficult abdominal conditions on a behavior associated with the need to establish control and express emotional distress, a practice, he writes, of "real *under-feeding*—into which I tend rather easily to fall—as the result of an old hatred of the whole act & business of eating, the source for me, in the past, of so much misery—black to look back upon."[32]

James's symptoms—his costiveness, his digestive difficulties, his problems with eating—expressed the extent to which he was enmeshed in the psychology of his family and communicating its collective, unacknowledged pain. But they likewise expressed his struggle to free himself from the entanglements of the family's emotional system and from his father's legacy of ineffectuality and failure. A letter to his parents written in 1869 reveals that even as he demonstrates his dependence on his parents' opinion of him and renders that opinion in monetary terms, James wishes to define himself in opposition to the paternal pattern:

The more fool you, you'll say, to have spent so much and have got so little [from his trip]. But really I have got a great deal. Wait till I get home and you behold the glittering treasures of my conversation—my fund of anecdote—my brilliant descriptive powers. . . . To say nothing of my making your universal fortunes by the great impetus with which I shall have been launched into literature. Consider therefore what you know me to have done and what you believe me to have gained and try to think that my return will not be altogether that of the prodigal.[33]

James begins this passage by justifying himself to his parents in terms of "treasures of conversation," something at which his father excelled. But he quickly moves beyond the social value of his travels to the promise of the "fortunes" he will make for them by "the great impetus with which I shall have been launched into literature." By then using the word "prodigal" to define what he is not, or what he almost is not, James further suggests that he hopes to justify himself by not taking on the role of his father. (The prodigal son, after all, was the image by which that shame-haunted man frequently defined himself.) The investment his grandfather made in his father, the investment that did not pay off, will in the career aspirations of the second son thus see a return in the next generation. As he said in a later letter to his parents, "I will be a *credit to you* yet."[34] Not only will he be a source of honor to the family but, in doing so, he will have warded off or compensated for his father's shame. And he will have done so in the terms established by their entrepreneur grandfather—"universal fortunes." Unfortunately, achieving distance from his father's prodigal identity by making the family's "fortunes" or being a "credit" to them in the future is but another way of remaining enmeshed in the family's shame.

James's desire not to appear as the fool or prodigal and thus both to distance himself from and justify himself to the family—indeed to justify the family itself—is further clarified by the histories of other members of the family. When Henry left for Liverpool in 1869, for example, William and Alice had been suffering from a variety of illnesses for several years. Their cousin Robert Temple had, as William put it, "thrown away in the past" every chance he had "of making something of himself" and now, William was certain, would abuse "whatever future chance might be furnished him . . . just as carelessly & cold bloodedly" as he had squandered opportunities in the past.[35] His brother Wilky's Florida plantation had begun to fail by 1868, and the ever-erratic Bob had left a job with the railroad only to return to it after he found the Florida experiment intolerable as well. Only a few years before, Uncle Augustus had gone bankrupt and, as we have seen, died three months after the tragedy "left him pale and thin and weeping like a child, longing for death and threatening suicide."

At the time of Augustus's collapse, Mary James had written to Wilky and "pointed ominously" to Augustus "as an example of the risks of speculation." Then, when Wilky was forced to sell the Florida property at a loss and sought work in Milwaukee with Bob, his parents not only conveyed the message that they had lost faith in his ability to support himself, but also hinted that he was in danger of following in Uncle Augustus's footsteps.[36] In 1871, his father wrote to Wilky of the dangers of speculation and the temptation to "misuse funds belonging to other people." In 1872, he wrote to Henry that "I hope Wilk will turn out well after all. He must keep in his present place, or he is gone I am afraid." In 1873, when Henry was abroad for the second time, his mother exclaimed, "This is a crisis in Wilky's life when he is brought face to face for the first time with the fact that he has got to stand on his feet, and provide for himself, and that too under the deepest sense of his own infirmities and temptations."[37]

To understand the significance for Henry of this family pattern not only of debility and failure but also of the family's willingness to prophesy such failure, let us consider another letter from 1869 in which he jokes that "this degenerescence [sic]" or illness "of mine" is the "result of Alice and Willy getting better and locating some of their diseases on me."[38] Here he unconsciously reveals the extent to which he understood that family diseases or "degenerescence" could be shared with or located on others in the family. But degenerescence of other kinds can be located on family members as well. Sons can inherit the prodigal identities of fathers; nephews can follow in the footsteps of uncles who have mismanaged their fortunes and quickly go to ruin. A father employs the same language to describe the potential ruin of his son that *his* father used for him. The "suffering" of one member of the family is taken to be the "suffering" of another. The "ancient sorrow" or digestive illness with which Henry had to contend in order to become a "well man," to "march straight ahead . . . to health and work," was a "function of intense inner malaise," as Edel observes.[39] Yet it was also a malaise deeply rooted in the emotional history of the family. That the sorrow is "ancient" suggests how deeply rooted it is in multi-generational family pain. That is why the ambition that James gives voice to in the personal writings of the following decade were increasingly grandiose. It takes a good deal of work, and a prodigious amount of success, to compensate for a "sorrow" so "ancient" or deeply-embedded.

After 1872 there is a marked change in the ways in which James characterizes himself in his letters to his family. He begins to play down the negative identity of the invalid and to celebrate "an almost unbounded confidence in my power to do and dare," to be "able to work quite enough to support myself in affluence." He is able to declare that "I'm really quite my better self again . . . I am active, cheerful, sound and altogether on the right track." There are still moments when he is plagued with "strange and mysterious visitation[s]." But, throughout the 1870s, James increasingly defines his goals in terms not only of feeling "more and more apt for writing, more active and ambitious" but also of yearning for the substantial signs of "fame and fortune."[40]

In an essay on James's quest for success, Francis Ferguson claims that the willingness to define his ambitions in ever more grandiose ways was fueled by the success he experienced in the literary marketplace in the 1870s. Michael Anesko has recently extended Ferguson's observations with the discovery that James's "career parallels (and, in some respects, anticipates) the transformation of literature's status in the culture at large." Not only James but many other writers "approached their calling with an increasingly professional self-consciousness"—a consciousness that saw writing as a "source of income and status" and encouraged a deliberate and strategic approach to the marketplace. But James's ambitions were also related to the desire to avoid the fate of the fool or prodigal, and, in the 1870s, he deliberately strove to avoid this fate by adopting strategies for countering what Anesko calls Henry, Sr.'s, "vocational amorphousness" and embarrassments, particularly his practice of underwriting the publisher's cost of production. In 1873, for example, Henry, Jr., was not only more careful and deliberate than his father advised him to be in gathering together his stories for his first collection, his first entry into the publishing field. He also successfully "negotiated contracts with Osgood that would clarify his work's market value."[41]

There were times, of course, when the contrast with his father's professional history was not as complete as these negotiations suggest. He confessed to Henry, Sr., that the deal he struck with Osgood over *Confidence* was a "weak proceeding, natural to the son of my father." But throughout the 1870s, Henry, Jr., was largely successful in striking good business deals with his publishers and, in doing so, in defending himself against his father's message of professional helplessness. (Henry, Jr., had "no power to push himself into notice," we recall his father saying, "but must await the spontaneous recognition of the world around him.") This process of distancing himself from his father's vocational identity, and likewise from the vocational fate of the family, was enhanced by his decision to repudiate his life in America and settle in Europe. In 1873, William claimed that he must go to Europe to escape "one's impotence," and Henry's insistence on making his home and literary life abroad was partly intended to serve this function as well.[42]

An 1878 letter to William provides evidence of the distance he has traveled from both the weakness and inaction of his earlier years and from the negative example of yet another member of the family:

If I keep along here patiently for a certain time I rather think I shall become a (sufficiently) great man. I have got back to work with great zest after my autumnal loafings, and mean to do some this year which will make a mark. I am, as you suppose, weary of writing articles about places, and mere potboilers of all kinds; but shall probably, after the next six months, be able to forswear it altogether, and give myself up seriously to "creative" writing. Then, and not till then, my real career will begin. . . . poor W. [Wilky] gives a sorry account of his present business and says he means to leave it and look for a clerkship, in March. He seems to have a rude career; but I hope his wife eases him down.[43]

When in 1869 he referred to his back troubles as "my own career," James suggested that his invalidism was a potential vocation in life.[44] In this 1878 letter, however, James's career is distinctly established as a literary vocation, and, what is more, it is sufficiently successful that he can give himself up to creative writing and become a "(sufficiently) great man." Indeed, James has arrived at a place that allows him to make distinctions among the various phases or emphases of his career and thus to identify his "real career" as beginning with a full-scale dedication to creative as opposed to remunerative writing. But what is also significant about the letter is his implied contrast between his situation and Wilky's "sorry account" and "rude career." Not only is there a distinction between Henry's very successful career and a career so "rude" that, like his father, Wilky needs his wife to "ease him down." But there is also a contrast between the accounts to the family that, on the basis of their careers, each brother is able to provide; Wilky's "sorry account" is countered in this letter by Henry's confident report on his pursuit of greatness.

In the late 1870s, this carefully acquired confidence in his career and distance from family failure is also expressed in his reports about a different kind of intestinal drama, the weight that he is gaining as a result of eating out on a regular basis. In a letter to William from June 15, 1879, he boasts that "I am as broad as I am long, as fat as a butter-tub & as red as a British materfamilias. On the other hand, as a compensation, I am excellently well! I am working along very quietly & steadily, & consider no reasonable show of fame & no decent literary competence out of my reach." The following year, he made yet another connection between his confidence in his powers to work and his sense of physical well-being: "Perturb yourself not, sweet mother, on the subject of my headaches, of my exhausting life, of my burning the candle at both ends, of my being nipped in the prime of my powers—or of any other nefarious tendency or catastrophe. . . . I never was better, more at leisure, more workable, or less likely to trifle in any manner with my vitality, physical or intellectual. I wish you could see me in the flesh—I think a glance would set your mind at rest."[45]

In his early letters, James's discussions of his health pointed to an interrelationship among his digestive problems (and, possibly, his control of eating), his concern about his worth or integrity (often measured in monetary terms), and his desire to appear in a favorable light to his family. Now that he is established in London and sufficiently famous that he is dining out almost every night, James's letters suggest that a new relationship has been struck between health and well-being, between his sense of self-confidence and the palpable evidence of success that is written on his body. "I am in superb health," he writes home, "and so fat that my flesh hangs over my waistband in huge bags. My appearance attracts general attention."[46]

Particularly significant in these communications is his ability to defend himself against his mother's anxieties about "nefarious" traits or catastrophes—about the sort of tragedies that struck down her husband, her father, or uncle Augustus or the problems with alcoholism or fiscal irresponsibility that, even then, were plaguing Bob and Wilky. So intimately connected is his pride in his weight and his ability to function—indeed to have become a success—that his "huge bags" of flesh become the evidence (if not the means) of his defense.

Some experts believe that overeating is an "alternative form of nurturing" or compensation for what is missing in the family.[47] By this account, both the eating and the boasting about weight to his mother become expressions of James's feelings of self-worth. His well-established working habits and prospects for fame appear to have enabled him to indulge himself in ways he may have forbidden himself in earlier years. His pleasure in his digestive well-being stands in stark contrast to the metaphorical abdominal distress that his father experienced during his vastation experience in 1842: "One moment [sitting down to dinner] I devoutly thanked God for the inappreciable boon of selfhood; the next, that inappreciable boon seemed to me the one thing damnable on earth, seemed a literal nest of hell in my entrails."

James takes his reassurances to his family one step further in the 1880 letters he writes to explain his reasons for delaying a visit home:

If by waiting a while I become able to return with more leisure, fame and money in my hands, and the prospect and desire of remaining at home longer, it will be better for me to do so; and this is very possible. When I *do* come, I wish to come solidly.

There dearest parents, are part of my reasons for putting off my return; and when you see that they redound to my profit, glory and general felicity, and therefore, by intimate implication, to yours and my sister's, you will, I think easily accept them, and reconcile yourself to a little more waiting. My delay has nothing to do with my not wanting to go home: on the contrary, I wish to go keenly, and see a thousand uses and satisfactions in it; but I wish to do it in the best conditions and to return in a word with a little accumulation of opulence and honour.[48]

To be sure, James's appeal to the "profit, glory and general felicity" of the family can be explained by his desire to justify his delay in returning home. But his explanations also touch on the psychology revealed in earlier letters—James's need to control his appearance before others, even to justify his existence by appearing "solidly" and "with a little accumulation" not only of flesh but also "of opulence and honour." He wants to return as the great man, and so keen is this desire that he is willing to orchestrate his timetable to achieve the effect that he wants. What is more, he expects by the "intimate implication" of family relations that the "profit, glory and general felicity" that will "redound" to him will be theirs as well. In earlier letters he spoke of making their "universal fortunes" and being "a credit to you yet." But now he is much more ambitious in his claims for what by "intimate implication" will devolve upon them on his return. And the confident tone in which he makes these claims bespeaks the extraordinary pleasure he feels at being something of a family hero. He not only avoids the "nefarious" fates of other family members, too weak or failed to stand on their legs, but he also compensates for failures by, as he wrote in 1878, attempting to "cover" his family not with shame, as his father did in 1829, but with "fame."[49]

The problem with James's formulation of honor and success, of course, is the condition of failure and shame against which it is defined, and thus the difficulty of freeing oneself from the fear of diminishment and defeat. When James returned to America in 1881, for example, and turned to his notebooks to review the professional distance he had traveled in the past decade, he was able to claim, "I wanted to do very much what I have done, and success, if I may say so, now stretches back a tender hand to its younger brother, desire." But taking stock of his present situation, he felt exasperated and depressed by his "[p]rolonged idleness" at home; "the prospect of producing nothing for the rest of the winter is absolutely intolerable to me." Somewhat later in Paris, he again addresses the matter of work, and, although he feels a desire to write for the stage and "a woeful hunger to sit down to another novel," he is also troubled by what he considers his lapses and deficiencies:

I have hours of unspeakable reaction against my smallness of production; my wretched habits of work—or of un-work; my levity, my vagueness of mind, my perpetual failure to focus my attention, to absorb myself, to look things in the face, to invent, to produce, in a word. I shall be 40 years old in April next: it's a horrible fact! I believe however that I have learned how to work and that it is in moments of forced idleness, almost alone, that these melancholy reflections seize me. When I am really at work, I'm happy, I feel strong, I see many opportunities ahead. It is the only thing that makes life endurable. I must make some great efforts during the next few years, however, if I wish not to have been on the whole a failure. I shall have been a failure unless I do something *great!*[50]

In the Jamesian scheme, "partial triumph was equivalent to defeat." Though he has already enjoyed an impressive success as a writer, James has also increased the standards by which he gauges his success—"something *great"*—and accordingly preserves in his life the possibility of almost total failure. Karen Horney has argued that, in certain individuals, the "striving for power" is a "protection against helplessness" and the "danger of feeling or being regarded as insignificant."[51] So, too, does the great effort to work which leads to success serve as a protection against emotional pain, against "unspeakable reactions," "melancholy reflections," and an unendurable life. James confessed to his mother in 1878 that the "ferocious ambition" he had hidden "beneath a tranquil exterior" enabled him "to support unrecorded physical misery in my younger years."[52] Loyal to the family rule of blocking pain, the forty-year-old James is still using this ferocious ambition, the great efforts to work, and the dream of achievements in the literary marketplace as a way of keeping "the monster" of his shame-based emotions at bay.

I do not want to suggest, by this account, that James's literary vocation was no more than a means of escape from painful emotion and his fiction nothing more than the outpourings of a tortured personality. Henry James is one of the great novelists of the modern age, and to achieve this level of greatness he drew on powers equal to or greater than his need for emotional protection—his fertile imagination, his verbal acuity, his sense of form, his faith in the novel as an art. But these truths do not change the fact that, in order to hold his family's negative identity at bay, he rigorously defined his ambitions in terms of the failure he wished to avoid. And he used the activity of work itself as a way of controlling or escaping from the feelings that troubled him. Writing to a friend in 1905, and using an image from his childhood dream, James claims that work has been a "remedy, refuge, retreat and anodyne!" for whatever feelings of depression or debility he may experience. "From the bottom of my heart I pity you for being without some practicable door for getting out of yourself. We all need one, and if I didn't have mine I shouldn't—well, I shouldn't be writing you this now. It takes at the best, I think a great deal of courage and patience to live—but one must do everything to invent, to force open, that door of exit from mere immersion in one's states."[53]

II

[A] great, I confess, and bitter grief.
—Henry James (1908)

Central to my interpretation of James's career is the theory that, within families, categories of conflict and emotional pain are transmitted, sometimes even amplified, from generation to generation. By this account, the powerful emotion that fueled Henry James's "ferocious ambition" was the product of at least two generations of conflict over and anxiety about vocational choice and achievement, and the honor or shame with which an individual can "cover" an entire family. But categories of conflict and pain also persist within the life of an individual. When toward the end of his life he began to experience a series of professional setbacks and to suffer psychosomatic illnesses reminiscent of his early years, James brought with him not only the multi-generational legacy of family feeling about failure and shame but also the accumulated disappointments or emotional injuries of the "Treacherous Years." He brought with him, in other words, the interrelationship between the two.

These disappointments began in the 1880s with the critical and financial failures of *The Bostonians* (1886) and *The Princess Casamassima* (1886). Edel claims that in *The Bostonians* "Henry James wrote the most considerable American novel of its decade." But most Americans in the mid-1880s shared Mark Twain's assessment of the Jamesian work—"he would rather be damned in John Bunyan's Heaven than read *The Bostonians*." "The editors of *The Century*, where the ill-fated book ran through thirteen months, said they had never published a serial which had encountered such an awesome silence."[54] As a result, James wrote a letter to William comparing this failure with his father's:

I fear the *Bostonians* will be, as a finished work, a fiasco, as not a word, echo or comment on the serial (save your remarks) have come to me (since the row about the first two numbers) from any quarter whatever. This deathly silence seems to indicate that it has fallen flat. I hoped much of it, and shall be disappointed—having got no money for it I hoped for a little glory. . . . But how can one murmur at one's success not being what one would like when one thinks of the pathetic, tragic ineffectualness of poor Father's lifelong effort, and the silence and oblivion that seems to have swallowed it up? Not a person to whom I sent a copy of your book [the *Literary Remains*], in London, has given me a sign or sound in consequence, and not a periodical appears to have taken the smallest notice of it. It is terribly touching and, when I think of the evolution of his production and ideas, fills me with tears.[55]

Although he compares his career with his father's, James can see that his disappointment with the *Bostonians* is nothing compared with his father's fate, and he is still hopeful that his next book, *The Princess Casamassima*, will "appear 'more popular.' " But the *Princess* likewise did badly in the marketplace, and though the "obviously exciting and topical theme of the *Princess* pleased a number of reviewers," the response of most readers was to "depreciate" or ignore the book. Thus, only three years after writing to William and Godkin about his father's *Literary Remains*, James found himself turning to Howells to lament the failure of his own work to attract the public's attention: "I have entered upon evil days—but this is for your most private ear. It sound portentous, but it only means that I am still staggering a good deal under the mysterious and (to me) inexplicable injury wrought—apparently—upon my situation by my last two novels, the *Bostonians* and the *Princess*, from which I expected so much and derived so little."[56]

What interests me in this letter is the use of the image of woundedness to refer to the damage done to his career (and also, it appears, to his feelings) by the public's indifference to his novels. The language he once applied to his father, and that his father's father employed as well, has now been used on his own behalf. In 1885, the *Nation*'s critique of his father evoked in him a "certain wounded feeling"; in 1888, his own situation has incurred an "injury" and caused "wounded feelings." When he goes on to suggest that the damage done by his novels has affected the short pieces already accepted by magazine editors, his feelings of injury are likewise conflated with feelings of shame and his father's fate becomes fused with his own: "They [the novels] have reduced the desire, and the demand, for my productions to zero—as I judge from the fact that though I have for a good while past been writing a number of good short things, I remain irremediably unpublished. Editors keep them back, for months and years, as if they were ashamed of them, and I am condemned apparently to eternal silence."[57] In his 1885 letter to Godkin, Henry, Jr., understood that the failure of his father's works to attract a public caused Henry Senior's "spirit" to pass into "darkness and silence." In his letter to William from October 1885, he thinks of "the silence and oblivion that seems to have swallowed" up "poor Father's lifelong effort."[58] Now Henry, Jr., suggests that his own shameful fate might condemn his writings to "eternal silence" as well.

The emotional slippage between his father's fate and his own is one of the reasons that James finds his situation so "evil" and "portentous." It is one of the reasons, too, that, in pursuing a career in the theater after the failure of *The Tragic Muse* in 1890, James began to make a new round of claims for his career. We recall that in 1878 he wrote to William that, with the advent of serious creative work in the novel, he was just beginning his "real career." Yet in 1891 he claims, "I feel at last as if I had found my *real* form." So, too, did he write to Robert Louis Stevenson that the modest success he was experiencing with *The American* in 1891 was "pronounced—really *pronounced.*"[59] Such predictions about both the shape of his career and his theatrical success, says Roger Gard, were neither "particularly sane" nor "sensible."

They were rather fevered. James's tone betrays it, as did such things as the elated scorn with which he treated William Archer's advice on the theatre, at Southport. He was *too* excited by his success there—by all other accounts a very moderate one. Edmund Gosse says of the slight London failure of *The American*, "James was now cast down as unreasonably as he had been uplifted . . . we endeavored to persuade him that, on the whole he was not justified (in continuing in the theatre) but he swept our arguments aside." Surely the reasons for this, as for his euphoric persistence, were that James turned to the theatre in the hope, not only of money, but of a tangible response to his work.[60]

In part James turned to the theater out of the same motivations that fueled his "ferocious ambition" in the 1870s—to compensate for the feelings of humiliation and failure that surfaced in his letter to Howells in 1888. Indeed, the pervasiveness of these feelings throughout the early 1890s, and James's consciousness of them, provide a continual counterpoint to his on-going theatrical ambitions. He spoke of feeling like a "failure," a failure that is "humiliating," in an 1890 letter to his publisher Frederick Macmillan; he wrote to Stevenson in 1893 that "neither editors nor publishers will have anything whatever to say to me."[61] In January 1894 he began to consider for the subject of a story "the drama, the tragedy, the general situation of disappointed ambition—and more particularly that of the artist, the man of letters." Reflecting on the repercussions of such disappointment, he became increasingly specific about the feelings that arise when one's ambitions have failed: "I mean of the ambition, the pride, the passion, the idea of greatness, that has been smothered and defeated by circumstances, by the opposition of life, of fate, of character, of weakness, of folly, of misfortune; and the drama that resides in—that may be bound up with—such a situation. I thought of the tragic consciousness, the living death, the helpless pity, the deep humiliation, etc., etc., of it all." The language of exposure, humiliation, and defeat likewise recurs in the introductory notes to the volumes, *Theatricals: Two Comedies* (1894) and *Theatricals, Second Series* (1895), in which he published plays which had not had "the good fortune" to be produced.[62]

It is well-known that James emerged from his final attempt at theatrical success, the performance of *Guy Domville* in 1895, with a deeper sense of humiliation than anything he had experienced before. Writing to William, he speaks of the hours "of disappointment and depression" he endured following the incident, the "pitiful, tragic, bankruptcy of hours that might have been rendered retroactively golden," and of experiencing "the horridest four weeks of my life." "Produce a play and you will know, better than I can tell you, how such an ordeal—odious in its essence!—is only made tolerable and palatable by great success; and in how many ways accordingly non-success may be tormenting and tragic, a bitterness of every hour, ramifying into every throb of one's consciousness." He reassures William that he is a "Rock," that "when a thing, for me (a piece of work), is done, it's done," and that he has given himself up to the "better and fresher life of the next thing to come." But the language of mutilation and injury he uses to talk about his play and the anger he vents at the public for its stupidity and vulgarity belie his reassurances.[63] After all, when the only terms of well-being are work and non-work, success and failure, and when the success must be stupendous to keep failure at bay, the shame woundedness not only of a professional failure but also of humiliation before an audience is powerful indeed.

Edel has argued that with the failure of *Guy Domville*, James seems to have suffered a kind of nervous breakdown, to have experienced a pervasive sense of depression and failure of confidence. But, Edel also maintains, it was out of this pain that James discovered his source of renewal. By retreating in his fiction of the late 1890s to his "earliest experience" as a child, James was able to heal his wounds and find "new sources of power within himself." He was able to rediscover and possibly rework the means by which "he had long before armed himself for life" and emerge, triumphant, as the Master of the "Major Phase."[64] In the midst of the Major Phase, writing *The Ambassadors* and arranging for publication of *The Wings of the Dove*, he acquired an agent and began to envision new possibilities for his career. As he writes to William's wife Alice in 1900, "[n]ow that after such previous years of dropping out and languishment—by my own dire detachment from *ways*—the excellently effective Pinker is bringing me up, and round, so promisingly that it really contains the germs of a New Career."[65]

Yet evidence suggests that even as he worked through the pain of failure and loss and prepared himself for the Major Phase, James was also engaged in an act of repression. By recovering and reworking childhood solutions to the threats he experienced in the 1880s and 1890s, James remained loyal to his old formula for blocking and containing painful emotion; he became, in fact, increasingly articulate in defining this formulation. He wrote to Antonio de Navarro in 1905 the advice for managing depression that I quoted earlier in this chapter. "From the bottom of my heart I pity you," he exclaimed, "for being without some practicable door for getting out of yourself. We all need one, and if I didn't have mine I shouldn't—well, I shouldn't be writing you this now. It takes at the best, I think, a great deal of courage and patience to live—but one must do everything to invent, to force open, that door of exit from mere immersion in one's states." He wrote to Edith Wharton a similar piece of advice when he said: "Only sit tight yourself *and go through the movements of life*. That keeps up our connection with life—I mean of the immediate and apparent life; behind which, all the while, the deeper and darker and the unapparent, in which things *really* happen to us, learns, under that hygiene, to stay in its place. Let it get out of its place and it swamps the scene."[66]

Not only has James become more articulate about his method of coping with problems because of the experience of dealing with the painful emotions of the Treacherous Years, he also appears to have accumulated a good deal of "deeper and darker" emotion to keep in its place. The notebook entry he made after the unfavorable reception of *Guy Domville* hints at the process by which this flood of "deeper and darker" emotion came to be. He begins by inspiring himself to "take up my own old pen again," to consider that he may yet "do the work of my life." He then continues with an attempt to come to terms with the painful experience he has recently been through. "I only have to *face* my problems," he declares. But what follows is a gesture toward repressing his problems, not facing them: "But all that is of the ineffable—too deep and pure for any utterance. Shrouded in sacred silence let it rest."[67]

For all of James's honesty about his emotional experience, for all of his willingness to speak of feeling failed, humiliated, and unwanted, there is a limit to his willingness or ability to articulate the "ineffable" sources of that feeling. There is even a tendency to idealize as "deep" and "pure" what remains obscure or "ineffable" about his problems and, as ever, to renew his commitment to work as a means of salvation. As Habegger remarks, "the father's deep apostasy—his willed refusal to know himself and to let himself be known—was visited on his son."[68] In 1895 the son willfully refuses to know himself as well, and to romanticize as central to his genius what is deep and unapparent in his being. Inevitably that which is "ineffable" in James's life will continue to work its mysterious and sometimes destructive power.

The power of repressed affect from the Treacherous Years emerges in a letter written to Morton Fullerton the day after he made to Alice Gibbens James the buoyant prediction about his "New Career." He claimed to Alice that he did not want "to sacrifice any present and immediate period of production" for other less urgent activities. But to Fullerton he expresses this desire in a negative form reminiscent of his reflections on the fate of his father's *Literary Remains*: "I *am* face to face with it, as one is face to face, at my age, with every successive lost opportunity (wait till you've reached it!) and with the steady swift movement of the ebb of the great tide—the great tide of which one will never see the turn. The grey years gather; the arid spaces lengthen, damn them—or at any rate don't shorten; what doesn't come doesn't, and what goes *does*."[69]

Particularly significant about James's sense of urgency in this letter is the extent to which, over the years, he has reduced his sense of satisfaction in life—his sense of what is not "arid"—to his professionalism and his opportunities for production. What is more, his reasons for urgency closely reflect his sense of his father's fate when, with the negative review in the *Nation*, James felt depressed by the fact "that so ardent an activity of thought, such a living, original, expressive spirit may have passed into darkness and silence forever, the waves of time closing straight over it" and consigning his father to insignificance and oblivion. "Shrouded" in the "sacred silence" of what James was unwilling to face about his problems in 1895, then, is his desire to protect periods of production and cultivate opportunities that will not necessarily stop the "great tide" of time, but will prevent time from consigning him to insignificance. He is still cultivating opportunities to protect himself from the fate of his father.

Central to this desire is the opportunity he began to consider in 1904 for a collected edition of his work that would enable the public to appreciate him in a way that he had not been appreciated before. To "assist the public" in its chance to read and value him anew, says Michael Anesko, "James was eager to embellish his Edition with prefaces and frontispieces and to rework his earlier fictions. To captivate a publisher and the public, James was prepared to frame his artistic goals in distinctly marketable form."[70] Indeed, writing to Scribner's in 1905, James was very definite about his interest in packaging his writings, in revising and re-classifying them, so that they will "gain in significance and importance." His prefaces, too, he hopes

might count as a feature of a certain importance in any such new and more honorable presentation of my writings. I use that term honorable here because I am moved in the whole matter by something of the conviction that they will gain rather than lose by enjoying for the first time—though a few of the later ones have in some degree already partaken of that advantage—a form and appearance, a dignity and beauty of outer aspect, that may seem to bespeak consideration for them as a matter of course. Their being thus presented, in fine, as fair and shapely will contribute, to my mind, to their coming legitimately into a "chance" that has been hitherto rather withheld from them, and for which they have long and patiently waited.[71]

One wonders if there is much difference between the claims that

James makes for the Edition in 1905 and the desire he expressed in 1880 of wanting to return to America "with a little accumulation of opulence and honour." He is interested in the Edition's "form and appearance," in an "outer aspect" for his writings that "may seem to bespeak consideration for them as a matter of course." He is interested in the honor that will accrue to his fictions as a result of their new, solid, and dignified presentation. The primary difference between the two letters is that in the former James speaks of the honor he seeks for himself (and his family) and in the latter of the honor his fictions deserve. But the sub-text of the letter to Scribner's suggests that in talking about his fictions, James is talking about himself; his "form and appearance" to the world is what he has a chance to rescue from the past.

The final pages of his preface to *The Golden Bowl* demonstrate James's belief that the revision of his fictions will contribute to the act of redeeming his honor. At one point he imagines his works as mussy children in the nursery who need to be spruced up before being brought out for display to the bright lights and the peering eyes of the drawing room. Later he extends the metaphor of dress to explain that in some of his early works there is "the long-stored grievance of the subject bristling with a sense of over-prolonged exposure in a garment misfitted." He imagines these works, *The American* in particular, making "claim for exemplary damages, or at least for poetic justice." Soon after he describes the mistakes in his earliest texts as the "old catastrophes and accidents, the old wounds and mutilations." Thus his process of revision has been not only to "hang about" or "gild" about his fictions "the finer air of the better form" but also, in the process, to spruce up their appearance, correct the accidents, undo the catastrophes, and heal the wounds. In a remark that interprets his personal investment in this process, James explains that revision has "doubtless" been a way of "remaining unshamed" or, as I interpret it, of protecting himself from the shame that would accrue to his work (and to him) were he to let it appear in its original form. Given what he has already said about the mistakes of the past, given the association in the James family between woundedness and humiliation, the claim that he is striving to remain "unshamed" is deeply ambiguous. The effect of sprucing up mussy appearances and correcting past accidents suggests that the shame is already there to be covered over, compensated for, or healed.[72]

The entire history of his "operative consciousness" in the prefaces constitutes an effort to rescue his career from the shame of its smudges, mistakes, and mutilations. He not only avoids mention of various texts that would besmirch this "honorable" vision of his career, *The Bostonians* for example, but he often makes explicit efforts to defend his choice of subject matter or technique with regard to the texts he does consider.

For example, he justifies his attraction to the form of the ghost story in his preface to *The Turn of the Screw*; he defends his interest in "my Neil Paradays, my Ralph Limberts, my Hugh Verekers and other such supersubtle fry" in his preface to *The Lesson of the Master*; and he justifies his use of a seemingly unpromising subject in his preface to "Daisy Miller." In the latter he goes to great lengths to defend his decision not to use the nouvelle form for exploration of a subject, the American "down-town" or business world, which he knew nothing about: "To ride the *nouvelle* down-town, to prance and curvet and caracole with it there—that would have been the true ecstasy. But a single 'spill'—such as I so easily might have had in Wall Street or wherever—would have forbidden me, for very shame, in the eyes of the expert and the knowing, ever to mount again; so that in short it was n't to be risked on any terms."[73]

Remarkable in this passage, as well as in the Scribner's letter and the preface to *The Golden Bowl*, is James's awareness that he was motivated by a fear of making a fool of himself. He is interested in rescuing his honor from a past that, although highly respectable, did not live up to his ferocious ambition, and he is exceptionally direct in the prefaces about the attempt to rescue his career and defend himself against shame. The problem is that defending yourself against shame, no matter how great your awareness of its power, only serves to increase its power in your life. When you have reduced everything in your life to your work and staked your honor on professional success, you have created a situation in which the only way out of shame is the patent evidence of fortune and fame.

When James first received word of the financial failure of the New York Edition, the disappointment he experienced was more serious than Leon Edel suggests: "The effect . . . was as if he had faced a booing audience again, and were being told that his life work was no good, and that he was unwanted."[74] Edel speaks as if this recent failure was a repetition of an earlier failure over which James had eventually triumphed. But, we must remember, with the failure of the Edition went the failure of James's efforts to rescue his entire career from the threat of oblivion by giving his writings, and therefore himself, another chance for the recognition he felt they deserved. Unlike his failure in the theater, the failure of the Edition implied a full-scale rejection of the fictional forms—the short story, the nouvelle, and, especially, the novel—in which he had invested a lifetime of effort and expertise.

There is still more. The autobiographical discourse of the prefaces was an open invitation to the reader to appreciate James's work from his own perspective. "What has the affair been at the worse," he writes, "but an earnest invitation to the reader to dream again in my company and in the interest of his own larger absorption of my sense?"[75] By acknowledging his desire for appreciation, James thus exposed himself well beyond the point required for the publication of his collected works. Indeed, his entire autobiographical narrative in the prefaces, a narrative bent in the direction of self-justification, was itself a form of exposure, and the greater the exposure, the greater the risk of being hurt.

In October 1908, James exclaimed to Pinker that the figures from the first royalty statement had knocked him "rather flat"; it was "a greater disappointment than I have been prepared for," "a great, I confess, and bitter grief." In a subsequent letter, he clarified the nature of the shock he received. Although "I warned *myself* indeed, and kept down my hopes," he explains, "this didn't prevent my rather building on something," particularly on something that "would outweigh—a little—my so disconcerting failure to get anything from" the production of his most recent theatrical effort. An earlier remark that he had been "living in a fool's paradise" sums up the hopes on which he had been building, and a subsequent observation to Howells expresses the worst of his fears: "I've just had the pleasure of hearing from the Scribners that though the Edition began to appear some 13 or 14 months ago, there is, on the volumes already out, no penny of profit owing me—of that profit to which I had partly been looking to pay my New Year's bills! It will have landed me in Bankruptcy—unless it picks up; for it has prevented my doing any other work whatever; which indeed must now begin." He had already explained to Pinker that he felt "sickened and poisoned" by the long interruption of his "out-and-out 'creative' work."[76]

The hint of having played the fool, the worry about the possibility of bankruptcy, even the reference to the feeling of grief—each of these phrases picks up on the legacy of failure and pain not only in James's life but in the life of his family. The fool was the role he wanted to avoid by making the family's fortune, and "in the nature a fool's paradise," it turns out, is how in *Notes of a Son and Brother* he will characterize the philosophical writings to which his father devoted his entire career (372). With the failure of *Guy Domville* in 1895, James experienced a "pitiful, tragic, bankruptcy of hours that might have been rendered retroactively golden" in terms of both fortune and fame; now he imagines the literal bankruptcy that would result if the returns from the Edition fail "to pick up." Living in a "fool's paradise" with regard to professional matters and fearing that he is on the brink of bankruptcy, of course, conflates the situations of his father, his uncle Augustus, and his brother Wilky, each of whom, in his separate way, could be seen as having shamefully squandered his opportunities to fulfill the vocational expectations of grandfather William James. To characterize his disappointment as "a great, I confess, and bitter grief" picks up on and generalizes the many unresolved experiences of loss in the family that, having been passed on to Henry in the form of shame-based emotion, contributed to the pressure he felt to achieve honor and glory and financial reward. It is no wonder that he feels "sickened and poisoned" by the interruption of his creative work.

In the years in which he was working toward becoming more active and productive, James's anxieties about making it in his career, proving himself to his family, and repudiating the family's negative identity were expressed through his digestive complaints and problems with constipation. Now that he has failed to redeem the career that ought to have been given another chance, James replays the experiences of his early years as he begins to struggle with obscure bodily complaints and the hygienic regimen intended to cure them. He replays the history of the family when he collapses in the style of the family as well.

Not long after writing to Howells in December 1908, James began to experience the first symptoms of what would become a prolonged illness. Initially he thought he was suffering from heart disease, like his brother William, but like so many of the psychosomatic illnesses suffered by members of their family, this new series of complaints was mysterious and obscure. "There were some palpitations, a little shortness of breath," some digestive difficulties, "but no pain to speak of." As James reported to William on February 3, 1909, he was feeling "a little solitarily worried & depressed"; "I can't believe that the extraordinary *gain* of health (what I've never *fully* detailed & expressed to you) that has been my portion for so long has only suddenly, nervously, eccentrically, led up to or *flowered into* a *grave* trouble." Accordingly, the heart specialist James consulted in London in February "addressed himself" primarily to "James's anxieties." Comparing James's worries about illness to the ambiguities of *The Turn of the Screw*, Mackenzie "tapped Henry on the chest and said: 'It is the same with you, it is the mystery that is making you ill. . . . You think you have got angina pectoris, and you are very frightened lest you should die suddenly. Now, let me explain to you the real matters.' " He went on to suggest that whatever symptoms James was experiencing were merely "coincident" with his age. "It simply follows that if you be more judicious in your living, and give your heart less work to do, there is no reason why you should not reach the ordinary span of human life."[77]

But the "mystery" Mackenzie refers to goes deeper than James's concern for his health. For the anxiety about heart trouble itself was expressive of the anxiety and grief James experienced over the news of the Edition and, accordingly, of the ineffable fund of feeling about his problems that had been stored in his psyche. When he reported the outcome of his consultation with Mackenzie to William on February 16, James thus described as a solution to his mysterious condition a hygienic routine that would not only help him live more judiciously but also encourage him to exert control over the anxiety and depression that were intimately entwined with his sense of physical malaise. Mackenzie "definitely enjoins on me," he claims, "to exercise—i.e. to walk since that's my only form—*superabundantly and up to the limit of exhaustion*, and to reduce my 'figure.' " He also "*enjoins* upon me strongly," writes James, to continue the habit of Fletcherizing, "to practise it just as I *have* been doing (thank the powers!)."[78]

When he speaks of "Fletcherizing," James is referring to one of the most popular developments in the nutrition and hygiene movements of the early twentieth century. After 1890, writes Harvey Green, "[p]ublic awareness of nutrition grew as newspapers and magazines reported the findings of scientists and physicians, as well as the often rancorous sectarian arguments between meat eaters and vegetarians." Horace Fletcher's contribution to this growing interest in the relationship between health and nutritional management was his theory of chewing. "Fletcher reasoned that by chewing food so thoroughly that all the flavor was extracted and the remains involuntarily swallowed, people would eat less, digest their food more easily, and more efficiently use the food they ate." But Fletcher had begun his career as an expert in self-improvement by writing books on "menticulture," the cultivation of mental and emotional health. His interest in dietary reform arose from the "discovery that the best mental results could not be accomplished in a body weakened by indigestion, any mal-assimilation of nutriment, any excess of the waste of indigestion." Fletcherism, then, was a program of both dietary reform and "Physiologic Optimism." Fletcher claimed it could produce benefits ranging from an "increase of 50% to 200% in physical endurance" and "[i]mmunity from sickness" to "[r]enewal of normal confidence and laudable ambition" and "[o]ptimism, usefulness and happiness."[79]

Both William and Henry James became enthusiastic about Fletcher and his methods several years prior to James's worries about his heart. At William's suggestion, Henry turned to Fletcherizing around 1904 apparently both to control his weight and to remedy some problems with heartburn and indigestion. By 1905, he was writing to friends that he was "a *fanatic*" about Fletcher, and to Fletcher himself that his dietary regime was "my *own* conversion & redemption." "I Fletcherize—& that's my life," he wrote to his savior, "I mean it makes my life possible, & it has enormously improved my work." Because of his "salubrity" and "serenity," Fletcher himself became an "object-lesson" to James. Two or three days after returning from their meeting in London to the "quiet living & sane nutrition" of Lamb House, James is so full of "the measure of what" he owes Fletcher that "my existence scarcely affords room for the operation of further benefits." For Henry, Fletcherizing was the means by which he could sustain the sense of health and well-being necessary to his work at this crucial stage of his career. Accordingly, he insisted on maintaining his regime at the expense of his social life in Rye. "Here I spend fifty minutes (I spent 'em tonight)," he wrote Mrs. Humphrey Ward, a fellow Fletcherizer, "over a cold partridge, a potato (three potatoes) and a baked apple—all with much bread (indispensable with soft things); which means that I munch unsociably and in passionate silence, and that it is making me both unsociable and inhospitable (without at the same time making me in the least ashamed of so being. I brazenly glory in it.)."[80]

In one of the several letters he wrote to Fletcher during this time, however, James identifies a possible drawback to the food faddist's program of nutrition control:

I find I must be on my guard against real *under*-feeding—into which I tend rather easily to fall—as the result of an old hatred of the whole act & business of eating, the source for me, in the past, of so much misery—black to look back upon. That underfeeding fixed in me at one time certain very bad, quite horribly bad, *weakened* abdominal conditions, & I find that these tend to lie in wait for me again unless thoroughly due nourishment keeps them at bay. My inclination is to make Fletcherism perhaps a little *excessively* reduce quantity—it does so legitimately & triumphantly reduced [sic] it when this virtue in it is not made an over-ridden horse. I have to be sure, in a word, to eat *enough*.[81]

James makes an explicit connection in this letter between the "business of eating" and the bodily "misery" in the past that was associated with his struggles to free himself from the family legacy of failure and shame. He also suggests that this connection has inclined him in the direction of behavior we now associate with eating disorders—attempts to gain control of painful aspects of one's life through such compulsive eating patterns as over-eating or self-starvation.[82] Thus he unintentionally predicts the dangers he would face in 1909 when a crisis in confidence gave rise to anxieties about health, and his doctor would prescribe a routine of rigorous exercise and "complete mastication and insaliva- tion."[83] He unintentionally predicts the dangers inherent in a hygienic scheme that would play into his desire to keep "the deeper and darker and the unapparent in its place. Let it get out . . . and it swamps the scene." Evidence suggests that around the time he received his first royalty statement for the Edition, James had begun to slip into "long & protracted (systematic) under-exercise & *underfeeding*," possibly to control the gout that had resulted from too much "meat & . . . port-wine" in his diet, but also to control his feelings of grief over the fate of the Edition.[84]

Initially, the regime James established after seeing Mackenzie worked well for him. In 1905, he had been able to recover his "serenity & improvement" at "any return of *malaise*" by observing the "difference between Fletcherizing on really *enough* (of quantity) & on too little." Throughout the spring and summer of 1909, he appears to have achieved a similar balance between Fletcherizing and walking, and, in July, he met with Fletcher himself to thrash "things out together"—to discuss his eating, that is—"in a way that will have really been of great use to me for the rest of my days—of this I am confident." But a letter written in the fall suggests that the regime has broken down. Although the heart trouble is "very distinctly & confirmedly better & better," he explains, the experience of the last 3 months has been very trying with regard to his digestive conditions. The Fletcherizing, he claims, has "proved [a] *cul de sac.*" But "I am worrying out my salvation," he adds, "very interesting work & prospects, I think, much aiding." The fact that he replaces the phrase "working out" with the substitute, "worrying out," in this letter puts special emphasis on the anxiety he is investing in his recovery. It also suggests that his anxiety has become greater than the capacity of his hygienic routine to contain it.[85]

The loss of a scheme by which emotional "salvation" can be achieved must itself have been a source of worry. But James's professional history in 1909 reveals that problems with his career were accumulating as well. Edel points out that in October James received another discouraging royalty statement, "$596.71—hardly reassuring for his old age." In no previous year, he told his agent, had he so "consummately managed to make so little money as this last." Earlier in the year, when two American periodicals rejected "The Velvet Glove," he wrote to Edith Wharton that "as I seem to be living on into evil days, your exquisite hand of reassurance and comfort scatters celestial balm—and makes me *de nouveau* believe a little in myself, which is what I infinitely need and yearn for." In July, after thanking his agent for placing "The Bench of Desolation," James claimed that "clearly I have written the last short story of my life—which you will be glad to know." In August he reports that he is "having a very good & propitious working time & deep in my theatrical jobs—deeper & more interested, & really with more horizon, I think, than ever in anything."[86] But even this characteristic optimism was not sufficient to hold off despair.

The severe collapse James experienced in January 1910, then, was not the delayed reaction to the news of the New York Edition that Edel has claimed it to be. Rather, it was the result of a gradual process by which James became unable to withstand the accumulation of injuries to his pride and his prospects, unable to calm his anxieties about his health, and unable to depend on the dietary regime on which he had almost religiously counted. Like his father, he moved beyond his capacity to cope with the anxieties inspired by his failures and beyond his characteristic ability to muster his optimism and envision projects for the future. Accordingly he moved closer to a state of total anxiety and despair. Indeed, when the collapse finally came, it appears that James had tried to compensate for his previous disappointments with Fletcherizing by Fletcherizing to extremes. "His own method," his secretary wrote to William, "has been to eat little or nothing and go for immense walks." His method had been, in other words, a program of too much exercise and something close to self-starvation, a program that appears to have become increasingly compulsive as he became increasingly depressed. James apparently made one final effort to stave off the inevitable when, on January 4, he once again appealed to "all the powers and forces and divinities to whom I've ever been loyal and who haven't failed me yet—after all: never, never yet!"[87] Shortly thereafter he collapsed.

He wrote to Hugh Walpole in January that his illness was "obscure." Two weeks later he described his condition to a friend as a "digestive crisis making food loathsome and nutrition impossible—and sick inanition and weakness and depression permanent." He wrote to William in February that his diagnosis of this "angry and at first most obscure crisis," this "most persistent and depressing stomachic crisis," is "to myself, crystal clear." The "condition of more and more sickishly *loathing* food" and the attendant "increase of weakness and emptiness—failure of nourishment" was caused, he believed, by his earlier unwillingness to "*dis*Fletcherise." "*I hadn't intermitted that* [his Fletcherizing] *jealously and intently and intensely enough after the mortal warnings of last (the later) summer and the autumn that I wrote you of—and a greater vigilance—of intermission and violation was all the while insidiously required.*" Thus, he concludes, all that is needed is to "*dis*Fletcherize" and improvement would be guaranteed.[88]

But his doctor was treating him as a "case of 'nerves,' " and when his condition did not improve and nephew Harry arrived on February 24, James "had begun to speak candidly of his 'black depression' " and 'his beastly solitudinous life.' " There was a brief period of improvement, and, feeling he had "got hold of something," James tried to continue his Fletcherizing in secret. Then there was a new collapse. "There was nothing for me to do," wrote Harry to his parents, but to sit by his side and hold his hand while he panted and sobbed for two hours until the Doctor arrived, and stammered in despair so eloquently and pathetically that as I write of it the tears flow down my cheeks again. He talked about Aunt Alice and his own end and I knew him to be facing not only the frustration of all his hopes and ambitions, but the vision looming close and threatening to his weary eyes, of a lingering illness such as hers. In sight of all that, he wanted to die. . . . He didn't have a good night and the next day the same thing began again.[89]

Edel goes on to say that the doctor Osler "found nothing serious wrong" with him, but, persisting in his indictment of Fletcherizing, Henry rejected William's belief that he had experienced a nervous breakdown. "My illness had no more to do with a 'nervous breakdown' than with Halley's comet: I *had* no nervous breakdown—& no reason to have one. . . . I *became* agitatedly nervous (like our poor Alice of other years, a little) under the depression & discouragement of relapses & sufferings, & of Skinner's well-meaning bunglement."[90]

But his letters increasingly suggest that beneath the focus on Fletcherizing, and the need to find manageable explanations for his problems, James finally discovered the presence, though obscure, of psychological causes. In doing so, he unconsciously clarified the relationship between his practise of undereating and the pressure of his negative feelings. To Jessie Allen he spoke of the "black despair" into which he had toppled: "I do feel that I have definitely turned the corner and got the fiend down, even though he still kicks as viciously as he can yet manage." To Mrs. Edith Bigelow he writes of having had a "perfect Hell of a Time" through fifteen "long weeks of dismal, dreary interminable illness (with occasional slight pickings-up followed by black relapses)." He writes to Hugh Walpole on May 13, 1910, that "I am utterly unfit for visits—with the black devils of Nervousness, direst, damnedest demons, that ride me so cruelly and that I have perpetually to reckon with." He claims to W. E. Norris a few days later that his illness has involved "a development of nervous conditions (agitation, trepidation, black melancholia and weakness) of a—the most—formidable and distressing kind." In June there are more references to the "nervous possibilities still too latent, too in ambush, for me to do anything but cling for as much longer as possible to my Brother and sister. . . . I feel that the completeness of the change là-bas will help me more than anything else can—and the amount of corners I have already turned (though my nervous spectre still again and again scares me) is a kind of earnest of the rest of the process. I cling to my companions even as a frightened cry-baby to his nurse and protector—but of all that it is depressing, almost degrading to speak."[91]

In his continual references to a threatening demon or "nervous spectre," James not only picks up on and expands on language he used to describe his psychosomatic ailments in the 1860s and 1870s and repeats the language of the dream reported to Lady Ottoline Morrell. He also approximates the figurations his father and brother gave to the emotional dangers experienced in their own nervous collapses. Recall that his father was reduced to an infant-like state during his terrifying encounter with the "damnèd shape squatting invisible" of his own shame-bound self; that William "became a mass of quivering fear" when he believed he would assume the shape of an "idiotic" youth "with greenish skin" in an asylum;[92] and, that following his bankruptcy, Uncle Augustus was left "pale and thin and weeping like a child." To these unconscious identifications with his family we add James's conscious identification with the fate of his invalid sister Alice.

The emotional imperative of the James family system has come full circle. Having put extraordinary effort into the project that, once and for all, was meant to rescue his honor and to redeem his family from shame, James became unable to withstand the emotional force of his failures. His problematic regime of Fletcherizing and walking failed to stave off the power of several generations of family shame and, in the end, he collapsed in the style of the family and on behalf of the family as well. He then had to cope with the emotional force of both conscious and unconscious identifications with the psychosomatic illnesses of his family. No wonder that he soon began writing the Family Book that would pick up where the "history" of his "operative consciousness" in the prefaces left off—with the personal history of his imagination. In the autobiographies, James probed the sources of his identity as a boy growing up in his original family and, in the end, attempted to justify the special nature of the writer, "that queer monster the artist," that he had become.[93]

3

Strategies of Self-Protection and Vocational Success in *A Small Boy and Others*

Sharp again is my sense of not being so adequately dressed as I should have taken thought for had I foreseen my exposure.
                                                    —Henry James (1913)

In *Notes of a Son and Brother* Henry James claims that he considered writing his autobiography long before he actually embarked on the project in the fall of 1911: "I am fully aware while I go, I should mention, of all that flows from the principle governing, by my measure, these recoveries and reflections . . . none other than the principle of response to a long-sought occasion, now gratefully recognized, for making trial of the recording and figuring act on behalf of some case of the imaginative faculty under cultivation" (454). We can trace James's vision of this "long-sought occasion" as far back as his preface to *The Portrait of a Lady* where he briefly considers the possibility of writing "the history of the growth of one's imagination." Early in 1910, James began a project for *Harper's Bazar* that, in depicting the turning point of his life, showed signs of becoming that history of his imaginative growth.[1] But he soon fell ill, and it was not until he began to recover from his emotional illness and the death of his eldest brother—William died in August 1910—that the desire to write his autobiography would be fully realized.

James claimed to his nephew in 1913 that the narrative he envisioned during his period of recovery from illness and grief began not as a book about his imaginative development but as a collection of letters and reminiscences. He began "to 'dally' " with the idea of doing something with his memories of William "and the rest of us" when he was visiting his sister-in-law Alice in the fall of 1910.[2] He returned to England the following summer with the intention of writing the "Letters of William James with Notes by Henry James." The project was to be a Family Book based on a collection of early letters. But the history of James's efforts to get started on the Family Book reveal that his personal needs superseded his commitment to family from the start. Once he established himself in his rooms, with his amanuensis poised for dictation, he felt uncomfortable with the idea of beginning with the letters. "I find the question of the Letters to be copied or dictated baffles *instant* solution, but shall have been able to judge in two or three days," he wrote to Theodora Bosanquet on November 2: "I shall rather like to begin with something that goes very straight so as to get the easier back into harness."[3]

Without detailing the precise nature of his work, James reported the success of this effort to get "back into harness" towards the end of November: "I now have got thoroughly into the vein & current; so much so that I hope really to go very straight & uninterruptedly & quite swiftly." A month later he reports again that "the only thing is to *let* everything, even *make everything*, come & flow, let my whole consciousness & memory play into the past as it will, & then see afterward about reducing & eliminating." Conveying a similar message to Alice in January, James adds that much of the material he has let flow is about his own boyhood. Then in June he announces that the completed narrative is focused largely on himself: "I have done more than *100,000* words about our (and above all *my*) very early (American & foreign) boyhood and early youth alone."[4]

For James the process of letting "everything" flow obviously satisfied a pressing desire to tell the story of his artistic development. Robert Sayre contends that James's decision to focus on his own childhood and to remember the distant past became an "effort to regain his creative powers" following the years of depression and loss. Leon Edel claims that the recollection of childhood "held in it the same form of release from discouragement and depression he had experienced a decade earlier when he had written out of his fantasies a series of novels and tales of children." Similarly defining that involvement as therapeutic, Eakin argues that James "derived strength for the present from the insight he acquired into the resources of his ego" in the past.[5]

When he admits in *A Small Boy* that he is "reconstituting . . . the history of my *fostered* imagination," James points to a motive for writing about his childhood that is closely related to his need to gain insight into "the resources of his ego" and renew his creative powers (65; my emphasis). Particularly in the early portions of the narrative, he seeks to discover the ways in which his inner life was fostered—nurtured, encouraged, developed—by his parents, his father especially. He seeks to uncover the ways in which his inner resources were a paternal gift, perhaps even a paternal legacy.

But James was clearly divided in this endeavor. For *A Small Boy and Others* simultaneously addresses an issue that, having haunted him all his life, unconsciously expressed itself in his breakdown—the extent to which his identity was negatively shaped by his father and, to a lesser degree, by his father's family. Throughout the narrative, but particularly in its later chapters, James expresses a nagging fear that his father's eccentricity points to some basic deficiency or deficit of character within himself. If this is my father, he seems to ask, then who am I? And he expresses the fear that his development had not been fostered after all.

Accordingly, much of the tension of *A Small Boy and Others* resides in James's tendency to probe his past yet pull back from what is revealed there, to indulge joyfully in reminiscence and revelation yet deliberately to confuse and conceal as well. For all his confidence about and pride in the autobiographical act, James retains his lifelong concerns about the capacity of self-revelation to expose painful parts of his life and shameful parts of himself, and at times these concerns emerge as much in what he reveals about his father as in what he reveals about himself.

I

[R]econstituting as I practically am
the history of my fostered imagination,
for whatever it may be worth.
—Henry James (1913)

In the opening pages of *A Small Boy and Others*, James often recreates what might be called a collective consciousness of his and William's earliest years in the family. He speaks of "our childhood," of "our parents," of "our father's family," of "our very first preceptions [sic]," and recalls two occasions which he and William shared together (7–10). But even in these moments of fused consciousness or shared experience, James begins to define himself as subject of the story by carefully teasing the thread of his own experience from the weave of the familial or fraternal fabric. When he says that he is interested "in identifying the scene of our very first preceptions [sic]," he goes on to add, "of my very own at least, which I can here best speak for" (7). He then launches into a contrast between his brother and himself that not only exempts William from sustained consideration—"He was always round the corner and out of sight" (8)—but also enables Henry to articulate the nature of his own identity.

Critics and biographers have long pointed out that this recreated identity is a negative one. William is active, accomplished, successful, Henry passive, inept, and ashamed. "There may be during those bewildered and brooding years," he says of imaginative individuals like himself, "so little for them to 'show' that I liken the individual dunce—as he so often must appear—to some commercial traveler who has lost the key to his packed case of samples and can but pass for a fool while other exhibitions go forward" (8). James then devotes much of his autobiographical account to reflection upon his failed youthful identity. I was "blankly innocuous," he says in one early passage (11); he expresses concern in another that he had nothing "to distinguish me by" (26). To the end of *A Small Boy and Others* and well into *Notes of a Son and Brother*, he continues to characterize himself as somehow deficient or defective: "I quite recall being ashamed . . . it was only I who didn't understand," "the shame of my sad failure," "my own case must have been intrinsically of the poorest," "my general dazzled, humiliated sense," "I passed for generally 'wanting,' " "my general failure of acuteness," "I must have . . . been ashamed at such inner penury" (50, 55, 67, 111, 128, 129, 149, 217).

James's talk about being a failure in *A Small Boy* and *Notes* takes on added significance when viewed against the backdrop of his father's professional identity, or lack thereof: "I remember well how when we were all young together we had, under pressure of the American ideal . . . felt it tasteless and even humiliating that the head of our little family was *not* in business." So humiliating did the father's non-conformity seem to the young Henry that, as he further recalls, he made "my own repeated [and unsuccessful] appeal to our parent for some presentable account of him that would prove us respectable." His brother Bob was apparently confident enough about his father's credentials to declare not only "that our parent 'wrote' " but also that "he had written *Lectures and Miscellanies James*." But Henry must have lacked Bob's confidence. When a school friend "crushingly" reported that "the author of *his* being . . . was in the business of a stevedore," he hung "back with the fatal truth about our credentials," or lack of them. Experiences like these prompted him—and, he suggests, the other children as well—to make to their father this "constant appeal": "What shall we tell them you *are*, don't you see?" Their father would respond, "Say I'm a philosopher, say I'm a seeker of truth, say I'm a lover of my kind, say I'm an author of books if you like; or, best of all, just say I'm a Student" (278–79).

Intentionally or not, this discussion reveals his father's unwillingness to take seriously his children's anxieties and concerns, as I mentioned in Chapter 1. It also highlights James's memory of how thoroughly he identified his youthful sense of social and psychological discomfort with his father's inability to fit into the "American ideal" of the professional man. A father, James suggests, is the author of a son's being, biologically, socially and psychologically, and clearly that father's "tasteless and even humiliating" lack of acceptable vocational identity became the son's humiliation as well (278). Indeed, the passage is rife with memories of how energetically and self-consciously the young Henry tried to protect himself from this negative paternal legacy. Not only did he implore his father for a respectable account of himself, for something that would be presentable to those who challenged their credentials, but he identified as "abject" and "ridiculous" the playful and amorphous answer his father supplied (278). Then, when given the opportunity, he refused to offer the information that his father was a writer of lectures and miscellaneous essays, perhaps because the vocation of writer was not yet deemed sufficiently respectable in mid-nineteenth-century American culture, perhaps because, as I suggest in previous chapters, James intuited the secret shame his father felt over his own lack of clear vocational identity and success.

A scene towards the end of *A Small Boy* further defines the consequences for James of his extreme sensitivity to the relationship between the vocational identity of his father and his own sense of self-importance. The setting is the Institution Fezandié in Paris, and James, then about age ten, is the object of his tutor's patient "attention, one morning . . . in some corner of the villa that we had for the moment practically to ourselves." Suddenly a newly arrived pupil is ushered in by Madame Fezandié, and as soon as he learned that this pupil was "the son of M. Arsène Houssaye, lately director of the Theátre Français," James's tutor so intensified his interest in the boy "that I knew myself quite dropped, in comparison, from his scheme of things. Such an origin as our little visitor's affected him visibly as dazzling, and I felt justified after a while, in stealing away into the shade" (209).

Once again James makes a patent connection between a father's significance and a son's; once again he confirms that significance by attention to the intense interest of a third person, the tutor, in the boy's credentials. Once again, or so it is implied, his father's lack of signifi- cance is the cause of the boy's. His tutor quickly drops the young James "from his scheme of things" when the son of a celebrated father appears on the scene and the young James, feeling his "insignificance," steals off to sit—perhaps to hide?—in the shade (208).

Other passages in the autobiographies enrich our sense of how the small boy assessed the danger of having a father who was unable or unwilling to take on an acceptable social identity. James says that his father's unwillingness to join a church "involved, to my imagination, much the same discredit that a houseless or a cookless would have done" (133). It involved the same disregard for the forms of identity, and the same "discredit" or shame, that the family would have incurred living without servants or, what is worse, living in the streets. Insignificance in the world of James's autobiography thus connotes a fearful peril, even "a fatal truth" (278). He intensifies that peril when he says of his father's lack of interest in business that "our common disconnectedness positively projected and proclaimed a void; disconnected from business we could only be connected with the negation of it, which had as yet no affirmative . . . side" (279). In other words, insignificance is tantamount to living in a social and psychological "void." The psychological equivalent of homelessness, insignificance constitutes an emotional destitution and emptiness, a personal nothingness or non-being.

The autobiographer's attempt to convey a sense of the depths of his youthful abasement and potential non-being is further intensified by his memory of the continual tragedies that befell the members of his extended family. "[O]ur father's family" he says in chapter 1, "was to offer such a chronicle of early deaths, arrested careers, broken promises, orphaned children" (10). Soon after this declaration, he speaks of young family members "originally so formed to please and to prosper" who then vanished "untimely," who became "mysterious and legendary, with such unfathomed silences and significant headshakes" (26). Indeed throughout the story of his early New York upbringing (chapters 1–20), James returns again and again to his often confused but nonetheless compelling memories of uncles and cousins who were "dissipated" and "exposed," "obscurely afflicted . . . and untimely gathered," "slave[s]" to their "passions" and "not to be trusted," "succumbing to monstrous early trouble," "young together" and "luckless together," and who, after showing considerable promise, inevitably became "a theme for sad vague headshakes" and "sharper" sighs (28, 30, 76, 84, 83, 108, 111).

His analysis of the fate of certain relatives, Uncle J. J. and the Barkers, in particular, clearly connects this pattern of tragedy to the family's departure from the example set by their grandfather, William of Albany. James claims that their "rupture with my grandfather's tradition and attitude" left them without "*the* American [the "only"] resource of those days"—business. And he imagines that the members of his extended family thus "went forth into the wilderness without so much as a twinkling taper" to light their way (109).

By naming business as the resource unavailable to his family, James is not suggesting that it was money they were lacking. What they lacked were the personal strengths and solidities that would have enabled them to fulfill their youthful promise and survive, both emotionally and psychologically, into adulthood. What they lacked was some ability to become prepared, and to prepare others, for life. When he says, for example, that the "bright and empty air was as void of 'careers' for a choice as of cathedral towers for a sketcher," the reader completes the equation that implicates the small boy in the family's behavior—"as void of 'careers' " for *a boy growing up and looking to his future* as "cathedral towers for a sketcher" (30). He, too, is one of the many who was going forth "into the wilderness" of adulthood in America without a guide or a light to mark the way.

The following passage from chapter 4 performs a kind of summative role in these stories of "broken fortunes" not only because it reveals the source of much of the boy's sense of family history, his father's stories, but also because it depicts the James family history as something in which, through his fondness for the stories, the boy himself is implicated:

The truth was indeed that we had too, in the most innocent way in the world, our sense of 'dissipation' as an abounding element in family histories; a sense fed quite directly by our fondness for making our father—I can at any rate testify for the urgency of my own appeal to him—tell us stories of the world of his youth. He regaled us with no scandals, yet it somehow rarely failed to come out that each contemporary on his younger scene, each hero of each thrilling adventure, had, in spite of brilliant promise and romantic charm, ended badly, as badly as possible. (29)

As this passage suggests, James tends to recall these and other episodes of family history in terms of the "thrilling adventure" they provided his young and absorptive imagination. Somehow there was charm and romance to these stories of dissipation and decay, especially since they came to him through the medium of adult interpretation—both the stories, that is, and the headshakes, and sighs—and thus were exaggerated in import or shrouded in secrecy.

But there is more to these stories than their romance. Clearly the fates of his aimless, dissipated, mysteriously failed or otherwise doomed relatives are intertwined with the destiny of the boys in the family, in particular of a boy who took his uncles "as the principal men of their time," and who continually heard thrilling accounts of their early history from a father who himself was "void of 'careers' " and failed to look after his financial interests (103, 30). Surely his own observations and the histories provided by his father create a kind of negative example to follow, a void or abyss into which he too could fall. He too could "end badly, as badly as possible," without the opportunity of first being a "hero" of "brilliant promise." Given his ineptness and failure, might he then sink so far into oblivion that his story would not even be told? Would he become a secret within a secret, a void within a void? The novelist who was so keen in portraying the psychology of shame in his stories penetratingly defines the psychological peril faced by a small boy whose family is steeped in failure, secrecy, and shame.

James articulates this sense of imperiled boyhood in an autobiography that itself runs counter to the genre of tragic histories within the family. For even as he conveys his intrinsic sense of worthlessness, James shows that, without quite knowing it, the small boy possessed a trait that would eventually ensure his survival and success. He defines this trait as the "wonder" of his "consciousness" or the imaginative faculty which was nurtured by his passive, indirect way of "taking life" (4, 8, 163). As he says in an oft-quoted passage from chapter 2 of *A Small Boy:*

> For there was the very pattern and measure of all he was to demand: just to *be* somewhere—almost anywhere would do—and somehow receive an impression or an accession, feel a relation or a vibration. He was to go without many things, ever so many—as all persons do in whom contemplation takes so much the place of action; but everywhere, in the years that came soon after, and that in fact continued long, in the streets of great towns, in New York still for some time, and then for a while in London, in Paris, in Geneva, wherever it might be, he was to enjoy more than anything the so far from showy practice of wondering and dawdling and gaping: he was really, I think, much to profit by it. (17)

The use of the word "profit" here is crucial. For if James's is a success story, its plot depends, at least initially, on reversing the "American ideal" of success that makes profits or takes "producible form" (17). First in New York and then "in London, in Paris, in Geneva," the boy's success consisted of his ability to acquire image upon image, impression upon impression, or, as James says, to "seize" his imaginative "property . . . at the absurdest little rate" (158). Eakin explains that "the seizing of his own property becomes a metaphor for the formation of identity" that midway through *Notes of a Son and Brother* enables James to discover what can be done with his impressions and to become a writer.[6] Thus even as James chronicles the relentless series of humiliations and failures that threatened to destroy him psychologically, even as he defines the negative pressure of his family's fate, he chronicles the process by which an alternative identity was quietly and secretly being formed and his "being" was being saved. Indeed, as I will soon discuss, the story suggests that his boyhood ineptness allowed the young Henry not only to survive but eventually to flourish in a world where brighter, seemingly more promising relatives, male relatives in particular, ended in collapse. As William Goetz observes, the autobiography is a success story: "James's personal success (with that of his brother William) constitutes one of the dramatic resources of the narrative, especially since it is set off against the calamities befalling other people around him."[7]

Initially, James suggests that this successful process of identity formation was nurtured by his parents' early recognition and appreciation of his essential being. Indeed, there is one strand in the autobiography that, for a time, shows James's attempt to develop a strong, nurturing sense of parental, especially paternal, presence in his life. Limited primarily to his early chapters, and thus to his account of his early years in New York, this strand begins with a vague memory of paying a social call with his father who conveyed "me presumably for fond exhibition" (9); it continues in the passage from chapter 2 in which, recalling his freedom to wander and gape, he concludes that "my elders" must have had "some timely conviction . . . that the only form of riot or revel ever known to me would be that of the visiting mind" (16); it goes on to a memory of having accompanied his mother to a meeting which she apparently believed would be imaginatively enriching for her second son—"Was it that my mother really felt that to the scrap that I was other scraps would perhaps strangely adhere" (25–26); and to memories of his father who was, he recalls, "again and again accompanied in public by his small second son: so many impressions come back to me as gathered at his side and in his personal haunts" (40–41). The cumulative effect of so many examples of "my parents' positive cultivation of my society . . . and thought for social education" is the impression that, although the boy himself felt failed and inept, his parents took pains to nurture his imaginative life and thereby to build on the core of his identity (53).

James suggests that this parental care went even deeper when he defines his father's "incomparable" inner life as the foundation or "*fond*" for whatever social sophistication he (and William) may have developed in the "extraordinarily unfurnished" world of early New York (34). It was, of course, because of the "lack of filling in" or "destitution" in a family "disfurnished . . . of the actualities of 'business'" that "we had been thrown so upon the inward life" in the first place (35, 36). James also suggests that this situation is not what, as a boy, he needed or would have preferred. But like their house in New York, his father's inward life is presented in these early chapters as a probable "anchorage of the spirit" on which a boy could rely (57). The autobiography thus pays tribute to the spiritual resourcefulness, to the psychological foundation, his father's inwardness provided for his son. As James says of the parental "medium" in which "we were most immediately steeped":

it is quite for me as if the authors of our being and guardians of our youth had virtually said to us but one thing, directed our course but by one word, though constantly repeated: Convert, convert, convert! . . . We were to convert and convert, success—in the sense that was in the general air—or no success; and simply everything that should happen to us, every contact, every impression and every experience we should know, were to form our soluble stuff. (123)

The nurture provided by parental advice and example is reinforced throughout the early chapters by James's frequent references to physical nurture and a kind of early American social security. Initially he describes "the sweet taste" of the family's "Albany experience"; then he evokes "the small warm dusky homogeneous New York world," that mid-century "small and compact and ingenuous society" in which he and William were raised, and eventually he claims that it was within this society that he and William enjoyed a "general Eden-like consciousness" (6, 38, 42). According to R. W. B. Lewis, this "allusion, suitably, was to the feeling experienced while the boys were consuming vast quantities of fruit—from the great heaps of fruit, of peaches and grapes and pears, deposited at the waterside piers and showing up on every street corner."[8] It was to the experience described throughout the early chapters of *A Small Boy and Others* of consuming "vast" quantities of other kinds of food—the pears in his grandmother's Albany garden, the molasses, griddle-cakes and sausages on Fourteenth Street in New York, and so on. What did the "stacked boxes and baskets of our youth represent," he says, "but the boundless fruitage of that more bucolic age of the American world. . . . We ate everything in those days by the bushel and the barrel, as from stores that were infinite; we handled watermelons as freely as coconuts" (42).

We have seen that James's "Eden-like consciousness" is nurtured by the abundance of impressions of people, places, and things to which his boyhood self is continually exposed. The repeated images of physical nurture thus serve as a metaphor for his ongoing imaginative growth and development. The autobiography, after all, is the story of the boy's "*fostered* imagination," of an imagination that was as abundantly nurtured and promoted as food was provided for his young life. It is an account of how he acquired the "fund" or "small hoard of memories maintaining itself in my own case for a lifetime" (59). How fitting that after a breakdown which repeats the history of his father and other male relatives in the family he should re-imagine his early life with his parents, his father in particular, as deliberately nurturing his inner life. How fitting that, after starving himself through his program of Fletcherizing, James should imagine himself both literally and figuratively feasting on the abundance of midcentury American life.

All these threads of James's youthful personal history, the core identity of inwardness, the sense of failure and shame, and the ability quietly to thrive, come together in a series of passages or scenes in which we witness him using both his inner life and his conversion strategy to cope with threats around him and, in the process, to develop a relationship to life that guarantees survival and success. It is apparent from the text, of course, that the small boy became an artist by learning to convert his outwardly passive relationship to life into an imaginative relationship of considerable energy and power. Less apparent perhaps is the extent to which James presents his habitual inwardness as a survival strategy in a family characterized by anxiety and nervousness, dissipation and doom. Let us look, for example, at an oft-quoted passage from chapter 13. Here James recreates the occasion on which he accompanied his father to his Uncle Augustus' estate to mediate a crisis in the family. One of his aunts (the mother of Minny Temple) had unwilling left her husband, "wasted with consumption, near death at Albany," on the insistence of her family, and Henry James, Sr., had been summoned as "the person in all his family most justly appealed and most anxiously listened to" in the family's attempt to keep the couple apart. Mrs. Temple was herself "gravely ill" with consumption and, in spite of her having "passionately rejected" the family's decree, Henry, Sr., agreed "to come and support her"—and the family, too, it appears—in this crisis (105).

James recovers his sense "of being for the first time in the presence of tragedy, which the shining scene, roundabout, made more sinister—sharpened even to the point of my feeling abashed and irrelevant, wondering why I had come." (Why, indeed, did his father wish to expose him to this difficult situation?) Whatever the reason, James remembers being "scared and hushed" by the "wail of" his aunt's "protest and her grief"; he remembers "stealing" onto the verandah, beyond the "reach" of his aunt's misery. Suddenly the disobedience of a young cousin threatened to intensify an already tense situation. James's uncle Augustus "expressed the strong opinion that" his daughter Marie should go to bed. When her objection brought some harsh words from her father, Marie rushed for "refuge" to the arms of her mother. James then heard from Marie's mother an expression that brought all the emotion of the family situation to a head: "Come now, my dear; don't make a scene—I *insist* on your not making a scene" (105–7).

James highlights this passage because of the epoch-making understanding at which the artist-to-be had arrived. The "so vivid, so portentous" expression "seemed freighted to sail so far. . . . Life at these intensities clearly became 'scenes'; but the great thing, the immense illumination, was that we could make them or not as we chose." What also emerges from his analysis is an almost imperceptible description of the coping mechanisms of the frightened, embarrassed, yet highly attentive child who had been exposed to this family crisis by his father.

By focusing on the "scene" before him and realizing its artistic possibilities, the small boy not only deflected his attention from the crisis before him but converted his personal discomfort to artistic revelation. The "passage, gathering up *all* the elements of a troubled time, had been itself a scene . . . and I had become aware with it of a rich accession of possibilities" (107). At the same time, artistic awareness has made painful emotion more manageable and bearable. Among the discomfiting emotions that needed to be managed, perhaps, was Henry's ambivalent reaction to his father's display of "coercive patriarchal authority." "Did James ever realize," asks Habegger, "that the dying Mrs. Temple . . . had to undergo a harsh ordeal as a result of Henry Sr.'s intervention?"[9]

The dynamic implicit in James's description of the Linwood visit becomes more explicit in a subsequent discussion of his doomed male relatives, first his Barker cousins, one of whom became "a theme for sad vague headshakes . . . and died prematurely," and then his uncle John James and his son who were "young together . . . luckless together," in a "combination" as "strange as the disaster was sweeping" (108, 111). When he attempts to explain the small boy's inapt response to the "whole queerness," James claims that "I can only have been inapt, I make out, to have retained so positively joyless a sense of it all, to be aware of most of it now but as dim confusion, as bewildered anxiety" (111). Well he might recall feeling "confusion," bewilderment, and "anxiety" in the midst of the crises that afflicted the family. Well he might have developed a strategy for managing the emotion and protecting himself: "What happened all the while, I conceive, was that I imagined things—and as if quite on system—wholly other than as they were, and so carried on in the midst of the actual ones an existence that somehow floated and saved me even while cutting me off from any degree of direct performance, in fact from any degree of direct participation, at all" (111–12). Here James's strategy for survival is patent. To imagine things "wholly other than they are" was to cut himself off from any direct involvement, any "performance" or "participation." It was also to free himself from the pain of his anxiety and confusion.

James comes even closer to showing how he survived emotionally painful situations when, in chapter 19, he comments on his memory of William's habit of rebuffing him: "I take refuge easily enough in the memory of my own pursuits . . . I also plied the pencil, or to be more exact the pen . . . I was so often engaged at that period, it strikes me, in literary—or, to be more precise in dramatic, accompanied by pictorial composition—that I must again and again have delightfully lost myself" (148). I attend later to the repetition of this move on the part of the autobiographical narrator who takes refuge from difficult memories. For now I wish to call attention to the association between problems with

William and the habit of losing himself "again and again." It is not merely by imagining things as "wholly other than they are" that the boy is able to lose himself. It is through the actual practice of art that the life-saving detachment takes place and, as such, brings James one step closer to his literary career.

I do not want to suggest that, in his version of the past, James's genius depends solely on his habit of retreating from the threatening anxiety of family problems, nor that James himself provides a straightforward analysis of this dynamic. His descriptions are often anything but straightforward, and equations are often made between family difficulties and the boy's response only by association and suggestion. But the association of discomfort and crisis with emotional and artistic detachment occurs frequently enough to become a definite pattern. And the elements of this pattern are themselves drawn together and summarized by James's famous dream of the Louvre in chapter 25.

The small boy's first visit to the Louvre assumes a particularly prominent place in the mature James's memory. It was there that he felt himself "most happily cross that bridge to Style constituted by the wondrous Galerie d'Apollon." It was there that he "inhaled little by little, that is again and again, a general sense of *glory* . . . not only beauty and art and supreme design, but history and fame and power, the world in fine raised to the richest and noblest expression." But the Louvre was also the scene many years later of a dream that in many of its details replicates the nightmare James recounted to Lady Ottoline Morrell. In what he calls the "most appalling yet most admirable nightmare of my life," James as dreamer routs a mysterious "visitant," an "awful agent, creature or presence, whatever he was, whom I had guessed, in the suddenest wild start from sleep, the sleep within my sleep, to be making for my place of rest."

The triumph of my impulse, perceived in a flash as I acted on it by myself at a bound, forcing the door outward, was the grand thing, but the great point of the whole was the wonder of my final recognition. Routed, dismayed, the tables turned upon him by my so surpassing him for straight aggression and dire intention, my visitant was already but a diminished spot in the long perspective, the tremendous, glorious hall, as I say, over the far-gleaming floor of which, cleared for the occasion of its great line of priceless vitrines down the middle, he sped for *his* life, while a great storm of thunder and lightning played through the deep embrasures of high windows at the right. (196–97)

Commenting on the significance of this passage, Thomas Cooley observes that "impulses deep within" the small boy "irrepressibly asserted" his "right to a central place not only in the temple of art and culture but of 'history and fame and power' . . . Instead of merely guarding the door to the temple, that [small scared] consciousness had expelled forces threatening to expel it and had aggressively taken possession of the interior." Cooley agrees with Leon Edel that the threatening figure might well be identified with the talented and aggressive presence of his elder brother, whom he routs in order to attain a position of superiority.[10] But coming after a narrative in which the small boy is threatened not only by William but also by his entire family, and threatened most of all by the emotions of bewilderment, failure, and shame, it seems more likely that, when read as a climax to his story of the past, the dream of the Louvre symbolically summarizes the whole of his youthful strategy for repressing emotion and forcibly asserting his reliance on that part of himself, his imaginative consciousness, that offers strength, safety, and repose. It would be some time, as the passage suggests, before he could aspire to the "temple of art" and its associations with glory that the Galerie d'Apollon represents. But the glory which the autobiographer celebrates as the boy's ultimate goal becomes, in the context of recreated childhood perils, an enormous compensation for abasement and pain. The promise of glory, in other words, constitutes the opposite of the psychological devastation that would result if the "awful agent, creature or presence" had subdued him. As James wrote in his letter of 1905, do "everything" you can "to invent, to force open, that door of exit from mere immersion in" your feelings or "states."

According to Lady Ottoline Morrell, James's earlier version of this dream represented a recurrent nightmare of his childhood and, in chapter 2, I interpreted this version in the context of James's young life. Because it replicates the conversion strategy James describes in earlier passages in *A Small Boy*, the strategy by which emotional threats are converted to imaginative acquisitions or performances, I have here read the Galerie d'Apollon nightmare in the context of James's personal narrative of the past. But Eakin calls our attention to the fact that, in the Louvre passage, James reflects a state of mind more nearly contemporaneous with the experience of his autobiographical narrator and thereby enables the dream to function for James "in two [other] distinct contexts: as a memorable psychological event in the inner life of an older James who dreamed a dream 'many years later' and, for an autobiographer older still, as definitive textual evidence proving the truth of his thesis [in the autobiography] about [the success of his artistic education during] his early years."[11]

The first context is the period of James's depression in 1910. James says of the dream that "I recall to this hour, with the last vividness, what a precious part it played for me . . . on my awaking, in a summer dawn many years later, to the fortunate, the instantaneous recovery and capture of the most appalling yet most admirable nightmare of my life" (196). Comparing this information to some cryptic marks in James's diary, Edel speculates that the dream may have occurred on July 21, 1910: "Since the dream contained a vigorous moment of self-assertion and putting to flight of a frightening other-self (or brother) it may have helped restore to James that confidence and faith in himself which had crumbled in his life when he received the news of the failure of the Edition."[12]

Edel's formula is, of course, a little too neat; it does not account for the fact that James continued to suffer setbacks of his nervous condition throughout the following years, nor does it account for the fact that the dream was apparently one in a series of recurrent nightmares. But James's dream of the Louvre does repeat the language of psychological drama James used in his 1910 letters to describe his nervous illness. (He calls his nervous symptoms a "fiend" or "visitant" which was continually threatening to subdue him.) Thus the dream can be read as an emblem for the process by which, in his collapse of 1910, James struggled to oust the nervous spectre of his breakdown and, as such, repeated the psychological dramas of his earlier years. In turn, the dream can be read as an emblem for the autobiographical act through which, like his dreamer, James successfully meets a threat, his failure and depression, by affirming the function of art in his life. Art in this case is the art of the autobiographer, and, as Eakin suggests, "the ornate structure [of the Galerie d'Apollon] is, in fact, the perfect emblem of James's autobiographical text, which, similarly elaborate, houses the workings of the boy's imagination in the splendor of a work of art."[13]

Seen this way, the elaborate autobiographical text reflects the mature Jamesian consciousness which has generated the complex web of reminiscence. Thus, as many have noted, James intends his autobiography to demonstrate not only the success of his coping strategies as a developing writer but also the identity of the autobiographical narrator and performance of the mature Jamesian consciousness. James never mentions the palpable sign of his success as autobiographer in the form of the book in which his reminiscences appear; rather, he locates success in the "I," or the sign by which his consciousness is present to him and demonstrates its riches. "The truth is doubtless, however, much less in the wealth of experience than in the tenacity of my impression, the fact that I have lost nothing of what I saw," he says in demonstration of the power of memory and the abundance of consciousness (60). "I have never since renewed the old exposure without renewing again the old emotion. . . . *That*, with so many of the conditions repeated, is the charm—to feel afresh the beginning of so much that was to be" (198), he says in demonstration of his deep affinity with the past and delight in his formative beginnings. Here speaks an autobiographical narrator who is delighted to find that his memory is so forthcoming and abundant; here speaks a narrator who fondly displays for exhibition—as if for proof of success—every shred of evidence testifying to the richness of memory and imagination.

William Hoffa suggests that James's autobiography "is just as much about the autobiographer's reaction to the process of telling his story, about the present re-experiencing of his early life" as it is about the past.[14] As such, *A Small Boy and Others* readily demonstrates the difference between the autobiographical narrator and the boy he recreates. Unlike the boy, the autobiographer knows what consciousness is for. He now possesses the key to the packed case of wares and, something of an exhibitionist, he happily displays them to his audience. In fact, James's autobiographical narrator has such a range of experience and depth of perspective, such an assurance of the power of his artistic consciousness that, however accurately he is able to recreate his boyhood discomfort and pain, he nonetheless views that pain from a position of maturity and detachment. Read in this context, his language of embarrassment and shame becomes a rhetorical gesture intended to soften the impression of autobiographical self-indulgence: "I confess myself embarrassed by my very ease of re-capture of my young consciousness; so that I perforce try to encourage lapses and keep abundance down" (156).

The problem with this theory is, of course, implicit in the psychological drama of the Louvre nightmare and its rich indeterminacy. Critics claim that the dream enacts James's ability to triumph over forces that threaten him. But, let us recall, these forces are generated from within; they are the equivalent in old age of the stuff of his youthful identity—abjectness, failure, shame—and thus of the fears of repeating the fate of his father and other members of his family. The routing of these emotions in his life required a forceful ("ferocious," said James) act of will and, at the same time, a powerful act of repression. Thus for me the dream functions as an emblem of the autobiographical act in a slightly different way than it does for Eakin. Representing as it does the mature Jamesian consciousness, the dream is also an emblem of the repression upon which not only James's recovery from depression but also the autobiographical act and the identity of his autobiographical narrator (the mature Jamesian consciousness) is constructed.

Let us turn now to James's efforts to rout unmanageable shame from his autobiographical act. Let us turn to those chapters in *A Small Boy* in which James tries to come to terms with his memory of his father's alarming approach to their education and successive travels abroad. We need first, however, to review James's attitudes towards autobiography and self-revelation.

II

[Y]ou mustn't give my *Small Boy* away.
—Henry James (1913)

The image of the Jameses that emerges from letters and biographies is that of a family that failed to foster a climate of personal privacy. Letters from one member of the family were passed to other members or read to gatherings of friends; details of William's and Henry's illnesses, Alice's collapses, or Bob's deficiencies were readily shared in correspondence with other members of the family, even with family friends as well. Henry, Sr., was aggressive in his appraisal of the failings of others, and William was apparently a ready and willing critic of his siblings, his younger brother Henry in particular. The members of the James family were excessively invested in one another's affairs, indeed in one another's personalities, and the absence of limits on family intrusiveness had a powerful effect on the children.

Early documents suggest that it was in the context of this intrusiveness that Henry, Jr., developed his love of privacy and habit of self-protection. As Thomas Sargeant Perry wrote: "those unhappy [James] children fight like cats and dogs. The other evening I went there, and stayed about an hour and a half, during 3/3 of the time" Henry "was trying to obtain solitude in the library, with the rest of the family pounding at the door, and rushing in all the time. He so far forgot himself at one time as to try to put and lock me out of the house. It was a terrible sight, and I can assure you I pitied poor Harry [Henry], and asked him to come and stay with me."[15]

James's desire literally to lock himself away from the other children had its counterpart in his reluctance to share his youthful compositions with the family. "[T]he only difference there is between Willy and Harry's [poetical] labours," wrote Wilky in the late 1850s, "is that the former always shows his productions while the modest little Henry wouldn't let a soul or even a spirit see his." James himself reveals that once he began to submit manuscripts for publication he protected himself from scrutiny by requesting his correspondence be sent to T. S. Perry's address: "I shall take the liberty of asking the *Atlantic* people to send their letter of reject. or accept. to you. I cannot again stand the pressure of avowed authorship (for the present.) and their answer could not come here unobserved. Do not speak to Willie of this."[16] We also know that James had for years kept his "ferocious ambition" hidden from the family, as he admitted to his mother, and only exposed this ambition when he had attained a respectable amount of success.

James's early experiences in his family, says Edel, "may well explain, in part, the reticence and secrecy with which Henry surrounded his literary efforts both early and late. There had been too many prying brothers, too much merciless criticism and childish lampooning."[17] It may also explain the fact that, in his initial theorizing about literature, James argued for the absence of the author in the text. "[A]rt requires, above all things, a suppression of one's self," he wrote about Whitman in 1865; it depends upon "a subordination of one's self to an idea."[18]

To be sure, James's youthful arguments against Whitman reflect his father's repeated injunctions against the aggrandizement of the self. They also reflect the idea, patterned on Matthew Arnold, that the artist must remove himself from the world in order to extract "its latent meaning" and hold "it up to common eyes." And they are related to what would become a life-long effort to define an aesthetics of the novel and to establish it as a serious literary form. As he wrote in his critical review of the first-person novel *John Godfrey's Fortunes* (1865), "to write a good novel is a work of long labour, of reflection, of devotion; and not in any degree an off-hand piece of business." But James's strictures against self-revelation in literature likewise reflect his discomfort with the tendency in certain kinds of narratives—first-person narratives or novels that "run on"—to expose the personality of the writer. The "merit of most fictitious autobiographies," he derisively explains in the same review, "is that they give you a tolerably fair reflection of the *writer's* character."[19]

William Goetz observes that throughout his career James spoke of the first person as if it had the potential to "refer to the reality of its author" and not, as post-structuralists contend, to its status as a linguistic sign. James wrote in 1910 that the "I" is one of the "signs by which I know myself" and his comments on the work of other writers—George Sand, for example—reveal his belief that the use of the "I" in autobiography exposes, for better or worse, the author (and the author's family and friends) to the insatiable curiosity of the public. But James also approached the first-person or autobiographical form in fiction as if in itself "the use of the 'I' partially obliterates the distinction between fictional and nonfictional discourse."[20]

In his late critical writings on autobiographical form in the novel, James explains that from an artistic point of view the use of the first-person, which he found manageable in short pieces, was unacceptable in the "long piece" or the novel. "The first person," he says in his preface to *The Ambassadors*, not only endows the hero "with the double privilege of subject and object," thereby sacrificing "certain precious discriminations," but also foredooms the novel to formal "looseness" or the "terrible *fluidity* of self-revelation."[21] A few years later, he explains to H. G. Wells that "that accurst autobiographic form" must be avoided if the novelist is to achieve the proper distance from his material:

> There is, to my vision, no authentic, and no really interesting and no *beautiful*, report of things on the novelist's, the painter's part unless a particular detachment has operated, unless the great stewpot or crucible of the imagination, of the observant and recording and interpreting mind in short, has intervened and played its part—and this detachment, this chemical transmutation for the aesthetic, the representational, end is terribly wanting in autobiography brought, as the horrible phrase is, up to date.[22]

On the basis of these writings, James's objections to autobiographical form in the novel stem from his belief that the novel should not only be formally self-contained and "rounded," to use his own term, but that it should also provide a detached perspective on the world. In these and other writings James uses water imagery to describe the threat to authenticity and form that is posed by the use of the first-person narrator. In a letter written in 1913, James laments the "heart-breaking leak" or autobiographic looseness that "so nearly play[s] the devil with the boat" of Wells's novels. Because of her proclivity for self-exposure, George Sand is "liquid" and "loose."[23] Self-revelation, he says in a passage I have quoted before, is a "terrible fluidity." Leaks, liquidities and fluidities neatly express the ease with which a narrative can get formally out of control, and the unmanageability that occurs when they do so.

But James's use of water imagery in his late writings on autobiographical prose points to a concern with self-revelation that goes beyond the need for formal control and authenticity. Recall that in 1908, around the time he wrote the preface to *The Ambassadors*, James counseled Edith Wharton to adhere to a routine by which "the deeper and darker and the unapparent" can be prevented from "swamp[ing] the scene." Recall, too, the remark he made to T. S. Perry in 1912 on the occasion of the large dinner party thrown in honor of Howells's seventy-fifth birthday. "Fancy deliberately *stirring up* such an exhibition," he says of the dinner's organizer, "pulling with a wanton hand the string to let loose the flood of shame otherwise for the time confined."

In the latter passage, as I argued in Chapter 2, shame is a given amount of emotion just waiting to be released. Exposure of the self is clearly a condition for the loss of control over this emotion, for being swamped by a "flood of shame," just like the loss of routine during times of emotional crisis is a condition for the release of other kinds of negative affect. Control is the solution, loss of control the danger, and the problem with emotional crises or with public events is that, by setting you up for exposure, "wanton," irresponsible people can trigger your shame.

Through his use of water imagery in his late letters, through the link that his imagery provides between emotional and formal dangers, James connects his personal need to control the shame he acquired from his family with his theory of autobiographical form. In an autobiography or first-person narrative there is no obvious "wanton" hand to release the "flood of shame," no one like the colonel to organize an extravaganza that intensely focuses on the self. But the use of the "I" does put the self before the public, in a sense, and is likewise potentially exhibitional and exposing. Because it also encourages a proclivity to run on with one's narrative, the use of the "I" tempts the autobiographer to expose himself even further.

For all his distrust of autobiographical form, James began in the 1890s to move increasingly in the direction of personal expression, a direction that many readers have interpreted as a defensive reaction to or retreat from the disappointments and failures of the Treacherous Years. James's stories of misunderstood or unappreciated writers in the 1890s were, by his own admission, "drawn preponderantly from the depths of the designer's own mind." The "states represented, the embarassments and predicaments studied," he insists, could have been "intelligibly fathered but on his own intimate experience." Edel believes that James likewise expressed his feelings of "depression and mourning" after the failure of *Guy Domville* in his fictions in the late 1890s about threatened or victimized children. Throughout this period, James also began to develop a highly rarified literary style appropriate to his growing interest in the "poor sensitive gentleman," the "supersubtle fry," or the men of imagination who found their ultimate fictional expression in Lambert Strether of *The Ambassadors*. "Especially after the decline of his popularity and the unfortunate theatrical adventures," says John Halverson, James "apparently decided more than ever on the rôle of the writer's writer." James himself declared after the failure of *The Tragic Muse*, "[o]ne must go one's way and know what one's about and have a general plan and a private religion . . . One has always a 'public' enough if one has an audible vibration—even if it should only come from one's self."[24]

After the turn of the century, James's process of turning inward also found expression in his continual experiments with autobiographical writing in a variety of non-fictional genres—biography, travel writing, literary criticism, even the philosophical essay. In "Is There Life After Death" (1910), he defined the workings of his individual consciousness—the process of "feeling one's exquisite curiosity about the universe fed and fed, rewarded and rewarded," of "carrying the field of consciousness further and further"—as the "highest good" of which he could "conceive." He found that as a "man of imagination" he now valued more than ever his ability to say "I" and found himself "cling[ing]" more than ever to the "signs by which I know myself."[25] We see, accordingly, that even in his literary criticism of the period James dramatizes the process of his imaginative consciousness as it plays over his subject; he continually figured this process within his writings as an "adventure" on which he, the writer-critic, had embarked. The "beauty of this adventure" in "Honoré de Balzac" (1902), to take one example, was his interest in reviving a relationship with a much-loved writer from his past. The source of his adventure in his introduction to *The Tempest* (1907), to take another, was his interest in seeing the man William Shakespeare behind the artist.[26]

More than anything else, it was his biography of the American sculptor William Wetmore Story (1903) that provided James with his first sustained opportunity to present in the first-person a drama of memory and consciousness for himself, in this case as Story's biographer. Driven by his discovery that in Story's life "there is no *subject*—there is nothing in the man himself to write about," James determined "to *invent* a book, patching the thing together and eking it out with bare irrelevancies" and, in doing so, to "invent an attitude (of general evocation and discursiveness) to fill out the form." Thus James became the "careful chronicler" and the "so fond an embroiderer" of Story's life who portrays himself going in "pursuit" not only of the meaning of Story's past, and of their vanished anglo-American world, but also of associations from his own childhood that are called up by Story's life and letters. When the book came out in 1903, Henry Adams informed James that "you have written not Story's life, but your own and mine,—pure autobiography."[27]

Written after his return to America in 1905, *The American Scene* continues the experimentation with autobiographical form begun in the Story biography. Here James objectifies his role as perceiver and evaluator of his subject, America at the turn of the century, by frequently referring to himself as the "restless analyst" or the "story-seeker," the "ancient contemplative person" or the "returning absentee"; in doing so, he makes himself, first as observer of American life and second as composer of the narrative, as much the subject of the narrative as the American scene itself. Once again James uses the narrative as an occasion to look back on his own childhood and recover relevant fragments of his personal past; he uses this occasion as an opportunity to comment on the passage of time, on the changes in American society that have transpired since his youth, and on the effect of these changes on his identity as a writer who got his start on American soil. As Gordon Taylor puts it, *The American Scene* is a "methodical" work of autobiography "in which James repeatedly brings the remembered and reimagined past to bear on the present moment of his encounter with an altered America." Like the Story biography that came before, *The American Scene* is also "about its own composition and its own composer, as well as about—as a *way* of being about—its more literal subjects."[28]

Next came what Mutlu Blasing calls James's "autobiography of an artist"—his prefaces to the New York Edition of his fiction (1907–1909).[29] James himself describes the prefaces as notes representing "the continuity of an artist's endeavor, the growth of his whole operative consciousness and, best of all, perhaps, their own tendency to multiply, with the implication, thereby, of a memory much enriched." Given his interest in the highly complex mind of the "man of imagination," James has clearly embarked in these prefatory notes on a project with enormous appeal. "Addicted to 'stories' and inclined to retrospect," he says, the artist "fondly takes, under this backward view, his whole unfolding, his process of production, for a thrilling tale, almost for a wondrous adventure, only asking himself at what stage of remembrance the mark of the relevant will begin to fail. He frankly proposes to take this mark everywhere for granted." As he puts it in his preface to *The Ambassadors*, "There is the story of one's hero, and then, thanks to the intimate connexion of things, the story of one's story itself."[30]

James also enjoys commenting in the prefaces on the composition of the autobiographical account itself, and in one case, this self-reflective disquisition on the origins and development of the fiction spawns the idea for yet another autobiographical narrative, the story of the writer behind the stories. James could explain, for example, how the image of the "single character" that inspired *The Portrait of a Lady* happened to have been "placed" in the "back-shop" of his mind if he "could do so subtle, if not so monstrous, a thing as to write the history of the growth of one's imagination." He does not pursue this project in the prefaces themselves, of course. But he does indulge himself momentarily in imagining the shape that such a narrative might take and thereby anticipates the autobiographical volumes—the chapter on Minny Temple, in particular—he would write several years later: "One would describe then what, at a given time, had extraordinarily happened to it [one's imagination], and one would so, for instance, be in a position to tell, with an approach to clearness, how, under favour of occasion, it had been able to take over (take over straight from life) such and such a constituted, animated figure or form."[31] Not only has James extended in the prefaces the range of the autobiographical writing he began with *William Wetmore Story and His Friends* but in this, the final phase of his career, he has also envisioned as the capstone of his extended experiment in autobiographical prose a personal history of his life as an artist. As he said in the autobiographies themselves, "Fed by every contact and every apprehension, and feeding in turn every motion and every act," the story of the "man of imagination, and of an 'awfully good' one" at that would "become as fine a thing as possible to represent" (454–55).

But there is clearly a difference between writing about one's vision of America and the growth of one's "operative consciousness," even about the shape of an autobiography to come, and telling a long, first-person account about one's personal past. How did James determine to go one step further and, after three years of loss, write about his life without incurring the "terrible fluidity" of autobiographic form and "self-revelation" alike? How did he effect the necessary control over his revelations when, as he wrote to his family, his plan was simply to let his memory flow? How did he attempt to achieve the narrative objectivity and control that he was able to effect in his earlier autobiographical narratives by centering the narrative in his own observing and drama-tizing consciousness and reacting to subjects largely distanced from (or, perhaps, selectively related to) his personal history? As he says in the prefaces, "There is the story of one's hero, and the story of one's story itself"; "if one's a dramatist one's a dramatist, and the latter imbroglio is liable on occasion to strike me as really the more objective of the two."[32]
 We see the answers to these questions in at least two places, the first being the fragment of an autobiographical account, "The Turning Point of My Life," written early in 1910. Here James attributes to an old friend, probably William Dean Howells, the notion not only that "every man's life had had its 'turning point' " but also that James experienced "one of these momentous junctures in question" during his year in law school (1862). Because he produced a number of stories during this time —"small sickly seed enough, no doubt, but to be sown and to sprout up into such flowers as they might"—James considers the possibility that at law school he "stood at the parting of my ways" and, consciously committing himself "to my particular divergence," began his career as a writer. We then see James self-consciously begin to define the direction this narrative of artistic beginnings would take.
 First he acknowledges that by defining his turning point his friend has created an opportunity for him as a writer by "giving me the ancient, the classic thrill known to all those who felt the ground made firm for talking about themselves." The autobiographical act is then figured as a "smiling Opportunity" standing "before me" and, as the fragment comes to an end, James claims that the best use of this opportunity, the "real bliss of publication," involves not the "things" one has rejected but "those one has kept in." Given the language of the prefaces—his

description of images having been placed in the "backshop" of his mind, of figures taken "over straight from life" for the uses of his fiction—James appears to define the "things" one has kept in as the accumulations, the possessions, the treasures of memory and consciousness acquired in his youth. Eager to embrace the "Opportunity" to write about himself, and to write about the act of composition, James apparently planned to dramatize the operation of his remembering consciousness and focus on the things of the past that, having "richly accumulated," remain perhaps "too tightly packed" in his mind.[33] Itself a turning point in James's career as a writer of autobiographical prose, the "Turning Point" fragment places James on the threshold of the full-scale history of the imagination that he began with *A Small Boy* almost two years later.

In his 1911 letter to Wells, James had given additional thought to the problem of writing an autobiography before embarking on the task he set himself that fall. Here he explains that the much-desired "detachment, this chemical transmutation for the aesthetic, the representational, end is terribly wanting in autobiography brought, as the horrible phrase is, *up to date*."[34] The way to avoid the "heart-breaking" autobiographic "leak" he criticizes in Wells's fiction, then, is to avoid the tendency to bring one's history of the past up to the present and contemplate one's recent past or contemporary circumstances. Instead James depends on the sort of detachment he began to establish in the "Turning Point" essay when he defined his subject as the "things" that had been taken in by his youthful imagination. In the autobiographies themselves, he also establishes a chronological distance between author and actor, between subject and object, to achieve this necessary objectivity. At times he even refers to his younger self in the third-person and creates that self in the figure of a character, a small gaping boy. "I have but to close my eyes in order to open them inwardly again," writes the autobiographical narrator about a memory of his boyhood self: "I at any rate watch the small boy dawdle and gape again. . . . He is a convenient little image or warning of all that was to be for him" (16–17).

Having thus achieved a distance between present and past selves, James then limits himself as autobiographical narrator only to what he sees about the small boy himself, or, to put it another way, to what the boy himself sees. He may identify with the small boy and directly reexperience the small boy's feelings, but he rarely moves beyond his memory of or reaction to that which the boy's situation evokes.[35] In this way James can both return to the comforts and trials of childhood and let his narrative unfold as the flow of his memory dictates; he can use a method I call *controlled association* and, going on "with something . . . very straight," delight in the form and shape of memory's consciousness of the past, indeed in the shape and texture of every particle of the past. He can cling to the signs of the "I" and its manifold consciousness. Yet he can also avoid a totally unmanageable formal looseness and, at the same time, the dangers of that form of associative reminiscence in which one follows "those networks of association which will cause him the great unease." After all, to pursue the free association of ideas, says John Sturrock, is deliberately to court embarrassment and pain.[36]

That James is clearly invested in this kind of controlled association becomes clear not only in those passages where he tells us that he dare not pursue this or that memory for fear of getting out of control formally. "I feel that at such a rate I remember too much," he says in chapter 8 of *A Small Boy*; or, as he later puts it, "I lose myself, of a truth, under the whole pressure of the spring of memory proceeding from recent revisitings and recognitions" (54, 131). James's interest in control also becomes clear in those passages where he consciously defines the emotional limits of his memory. One particular recollection about his father, for example, "would again half prompt me to soundings were I not to recognize in it that mark of the fitful . . . which was to devote us for some time to variety, almost to incoherency, of interest" (166). James is not likely to make the mistake he attributes to his younger self in *A Small Boy and Others* on the occasion, sprung on him by his father, of having to pose for his daguerreotype: "Sharp again is my sense of not being so adequately dressed as I should have taken thought for had I foreseen my exposure" (51). We might say that, highly conscious of the state of exposure presented by the autobiographical act, the act of placing the "I" directly before one's audience, James takes care to present himself suitably or to be "adequately dressed."

We witness James's desire to control the extent of his exposure and the adequacy of his dress in those portions of *A Small Boy* in which he moves from the story of his early nurturant years in New York and to the years of his father's experiments in education and travel. To prepare for this discussion, we must return briefly to those early chapters in *A Small Boy and Others* in which James recalls the memories of his parents' positive influence on his life, his father's in particular. Earlier I made a point of emphasizing those places where James recalls explicit moments of encouragement, nurture, and support. Yet other passages, or alternative readings, suggest that the certainty of these early memories are qualified by his ignorance of and wonder about his parents' real motives for doing what they did. His "infant participation" at a dance he attended with his mother is a "riddle," he explains: "Was it that my mother really felt that to the scrap that I was other scraps would perhaps strangely adhere" (27, 25–26)? He also wonders why he was given so much freedom to wander as a boy: "What I look back to as my infant license can only have had for its ground some timely conviction on the part of my elders that the only form of riot or revel even known to me would be that of the visiting mind" (16). As autobiographer, James seems to be supplying what his memory cannot—the belief that his parents understood the nature of his personality and made deliberate efforts to foster it. Indeed, in these early pages James is affirming his identity as author and autobiographer by emphasizing the possibility that he was parented attentively and with his true interests at heart. (In therapeutic terms, he is *re*-parenting himself.) Perhaps as he suggests in the passage quoted above, his mother really understood that "scraps" or impressions would "adhere" to his consciousness "to the extent thus of having something to distinguish me by, nothing else probably having as yet declared itself—such a scrap for instance as the fine germ of this actual ferment of memory and play of fancy, a retroactive vision almost intense of the faded hour and a fond surrender to the questions with which it bristles?" (26).

Throughout these early chapters, however, we begin to see that something is missing in the picture of parenting that James's memory provides. In chapter 2, for example, his "wonder" is excited by "the number and succession" of schools which he and William attended: "we couldn't have changed oftener, it strikes me as I look back, if our presence had been inveterately objected to" (11). Later in chapter 2 he recalls that his father's "presence is in fact not associated for me, to any effect of distinctness, with the least of our suffered shocks or penalties" (40). Two pages later he notes that, during their European travels, whenever their father would leave home to scout out "some improvement of our condition, some enlargement of our view," he would "breathlessly . . . reappear, after the shortest possible interval, with no account at all to give of the benefit aimed at, but instead of this a moving representation, a far richer recital, of his spiritual adventures at the horrid inhuman inns and amid the hard alien races which had stayed his advance" (43). Shortly thereafter James notes that, because he never liked "fussy challenges," his father had never in all his life "taken personal cognisance" of the property that after his death was "of importance to us all" (43). He talks about the many times he was allowed to "dangle so unchidden" at "wild evenings" or theatrical entertainments as a boy and about the "complacency of conscience" without which "every felt impression" would be unable to "live again" (93). He talks about the "vague and small" experience of school "in contrast with the fuller and stronger cup meted out all round to the Albany cousins" (99).

What these bits of memory begin to add up to is a story that runs counter to the history of his fostered imagination, a story of parental abandonment or neglect, and it is highlighted by James's attraction to, even envy of, the orphaned cousins whom he believed to be "more happy, through those numberless bereavements that had so enriched their existence" (99). William Veeder claims that James idealized his orphaned cousins in order to compensate for the emotional abandonment he experienced from his parents: "James thus idealizes a negated role, a position of lack (father*less*, mother*less*, home*less*) so that he can defend against, can in fact negate, the negating forces of experience."[37] What is more, their envied presence in the narrative continually underscores the possibility that, without parents, his orphaned cousins were receiving better care than were the "intensely domesticated" children of Henry, Sr. The hands that sowed *their* "aesthetic seeds," James says of himself and his siblings, were "[c]areless at once and generous," and it is the carelessness of his parents' approach to their development that begins to concern him as the narrative progresses (11, 95). In the chapters on their New York schools and European travels, in particular, James is faced with the problem of explaining the fact that his father would continually uproot his children and expose them to yet another city and yet another educational possibility. He is faced with the problem of recollecting qualities in his father that undermine the grounds of his father's nurturing presence in his life and the grounds of his own identity.

It would take too long to review every passage in which James tries to account for his father's manner of educating his children at home and abroad by subjecting them to a seemingly endless succession of schools, governesses, and tutors. But I will mention a few. In the first of such passages, James begins by recovering his memories of the school which he and William attended in 1854–55, shortly before the family left for Europe. Quickly his memories of the "establishment of Messrs. Forest and Quackenboss" give way to a consideration of his parents' approach to education—"we wholesomely breathed inconsistency and ate and drank contradictions" (127, 124)—and that consideration gives way to a debate on the value of such an unprogrammatic approach. A hypothetical critic takes up the case against his father's "failure of method" in educating his sons; "think," says this critic, "of all the things that the failure of method . . . didn't put into" your consciousness. James as autobiographical narrator defends his father's approach by defending the ability of his youthful sensibility to profit from anything to which it was exposed: "[H]ow in the world, if the question is of the injection of more things into the consciousness (as would seem the case,) mine could have 'done' with more: thanks to its small trick, perhaps vicious I admit, of having felt itself from an early time almost uncomfortably stuffed" (124–25).

The problem is that James's ability to entertain both sides of the question continually undermines his attempt to prove that he "mastered" the "waste involved in the so inferior [educational] substitute of which the pair of you were evidently victims" (125). He justifies his father's method, for example, by claiming that Henry, Sr., cared "for our spiritual decency unspeakably more than for anything else, anything at all that might be or become ours." But at the end of the sentence he adds, "had he but betrayed more interest in our mastery of *any* art or craft" (126). His father believed, James explains, that "the effect of his attitude . . . could only be to make life interesting to us at the worst" (126). But shortly thereafter James not only refers to William and himself as a "defeated Romulus" and "a prematurely sacrificed Remus"—the Roman twins thrown into the Tiber by their father—but he also qualifies the "success" of his father's belief that the boys "had in their very sensibility an asset . . . a principle of life and even of 'fun' ": "Perhaps on the other hand the success would have been greater with less of that particular complication or facilitation and more of some other which I shall be at a loss to identify" (127).

The qualifications continue in the chapters devoted to their travels in Europe. Here, in a passage quoted earlier, a memory of their movements "would again half prompt me to soundings were I not to recognize in it that mark of the fitful, that accent of the improvised, that general quality of earnest and reasoned, yet at the same time almost passionate, impatience which was to devote us for some time to variety, almost to incoherency, of interest" (166). Again, after launching a passionate defense of his father's approach to their education in Europe, he admits, "It *had* indeed again an effect of almost pathetic incoherence that our brave quest of 'the languages,' suffering so prompt and for the time at least so accepted and now so inscrutably irrecoverable a check, should have contented itself with settling us by that Christmas in a house, more propitious to our development, in St. John's Wood" in England (171). When he claims that "I gather, as a rule, much more the extreme promptitude of the parental optimism than any disproportionate habit of impatience," he follows with the admission that the "optimism begot precipation [sic], and the precipitation had too often to confess itself" (173).

James insists that, unlike William, he had as a boy "no such quarrel with our conditions"; he insists that what William believed was their "poor and arid and lamentable time" in Paris was for him "really a revel of spirit and thought" (170–71). But the reader's willingness to be persuaded by these claims is undermined by the fact that, as Eakin notes, James as autobiographical narrator has by now expended a good deal of "rhetorical energy" explaining his father's carelessness, inconsistency, and incoherence—and justifying his father's effect on his life.[38]

101

What is at stake for James in all of his explanations, equivocations, qualifications, and justifications? Certainly more than the discomfort he feels from the memory of his father's carelessness and incoherence alone, considerable though that discomfort is. Certainly more than the possibility that he and William might have received a better education, significant though that possibility is. What is at stake is the identity of the autobiographical narrator who, in the absence of another, more substantial account of his youth, is asking his reader to appreciate the value of his autobiographical act and the worth of the consciousness that constitutes his identity. James is haunted by the possibility that at the core of all that celebrated inwardness and spiritual richness was a lack of selfhood that prevented Henry, Sr., not only from caring properly for his son's development but also from passing on to his son a solid, substantial, and acceptable identity. James thus wants to convince himself that "deep down" in his small patch of "virgin soil" he had in him "the root of the matter," and that "the fashion after which it struggled forth was an experience as intense as any other and a record of as great a dignity" (124).

James's investment in writing an acceptable, self-justifying life story is nowhere more patent than in his discussion of the material consciously omitted from *A Small Boy and Others*, omitted for the sake of the negative impression it might make on the reader. In comparison to the bulk of material included in the text, this omission might be considered slight and insignificant. But measured in emotional terms, this material was sufficiently painful to James that, as I discussed in chapter 1, it shaped the version of his youth that he shared with William Dean Howells and informed his response when William proposed a quick turn-about in his sabbatical plans. It was so painful to James that late in life he enlisted the help of family and friends in keeping certain facts of his boyhood hidden. As he wrote his boyhood friend, T. S. Perry, he was ashamed of the fact that between 1855 and 1860 his father had taken the family to Europe not once, but twice, and he was uncomfortable with the problem of recording that fact in his autobiography:

And apropos of those pages precisely I desire to ask of your discretion & fidelity a small (inarticulate) service—which when you turn them over you will understand. I seemed to myself to have had in the foregoing volume, & to still have in this sequel, to enumerate so many choppings & changes & interruptions & volatilities, (as on our parents' part, dear people,) in our young education, that the aspect of it grew in a manner foolish on my hands, & when it came to our having rushed back from Europe, when I was 15–16, for a year at Newport, only to rush again back *to* Europe, Switzerland &c, & begin once more (with the return to Newport &c,) I found I positively *had* to simplify . . . it seemed to represent my dear Father as *too* irresponsible & too saccadé in his generous absence of plan & continuity.[39]

As the letter to Perry reveals, the family's actual pattern of travel was impossible to represent if James hoped to sustain some manner of formal coherence in his narrative. Lewis points out that the cuts were also "made in the interest of dramatic effect—the lapse into unconsciousness which brings the first volume to a close, the curtain rising on a large change of European scene in the second." But James is also concerned lest his narrative present his father as even more impulsive and irresponsible than he, as autobiographer, had already portrayed him, and an old family injunction stipulated that, like William did in the *Literary Remains*, the son was to rescue the reputation of the father. Lewis calls this approach an act of "filial piety," but James's comments to his nephew Harry about his cuts and omissions suggest that, like his grandfather, the son wishes to "ward off the shame and reproach" of a confused and irresponsible man.[40] "There is one thing about your father's early life in respect to which you mustn't give my *Small Boy* away," James is reported to have said, and in a tone more anxious than that of his letter to Perry, "I've covered over the fact, so overcome am I by the sense of our poor father's impulsive journeyings to and fro and of the impression of aimless vacillation which the record might make upon the reader—that we didn't go to Europe twice, but once. I've described our going abroad the first time, and am saying that the year '60 found us back at Newport." After recording this conversation, Harry then offered his own observations: "Uncle H. evidently has a very lively consciousness of his father's vacillations and impulses—as if the possibility of going home or going to Europe, going from one place to another, were always in the air and often realized to the disturbance of his, Uncle H.'s equanimity. He is also evidently self-conscious about the fanciful and inconsequent explanations and reasons which his father used to give to people, who expressed surprise or made inquiries."[41]

As he did with Perry, James enjoins his nephew to keep his editorial decisions secret for fear of what the facts will reveal about his father. Indeed, he is "overcome" specifically by his father's "aimless vacillations" and "the impression" they will make upon the reader, and Harry's impression confirms that these memories were a source of real anxiety for his Uncle Henry. But James is equally concerned about the light that the historical record would cast upon his autobiography. When he says to Harry that he "mustn't give my *Small Boy* away," James implies that a breach of secrecy would disclose something shameful about the book, the *Small Boy*, that he has "covered over." He implies that a breach of secrecy would disclose something shameful about his small boy, about himself as small boy, about himself as autobiographer. He does not identify what that shameful something is; indeed, connected as it is with the history of his family, this something is too amorphous and deeply buried to be named. But we feel its presence in James's anxious memories about his father, his need to obscure the historical record, and his insistence on keeping secrets. We feel it in his need to justify the secrecy and the omissions alike.

Henry James wishes to persuade his reader that as a man, a writer, and an autobiographer, he has moved beyond the feelings of failure and shame that haunted the small boy whom he features in *A Small Boy and Others*. He wishes to persuade us that the generous, nurturing side of his father so often in evidence in the narrative was sufficient to foster in his son a solid confidence in not only the power but also the respectability of his imaginative and reminiscing consciousness. He wishes to persuade us, finally, that in *A Small Boy* he has truly revised, even reversed, his father's stories of the "arrested careers" and "broken promises" that depicted the fates of other male members of his father's family. But James's frequent explanations, justifications, qualifications, insistences—and, finally, his revelation about his omissions and his concern for secrecy—both complicate and undermine the history of his fostered imagination that he begins to present with such confidence and enthusiasm at the start of *A Small Boy*.

Like the dreamer in the nightmare of the Galerie d'Apollon, like the boy in the dream recounted to Lady Ottoline Morrell, James as autobiographer has attempted to rout from his story of the past the spectre of family pain and shame. But the force of all that which had been left unresolved in his life, of that which could leak out and give him away, was too persistent and powerful to be utterly routed or contained. Indeed, the series of self-justifying letters he wrote to Harry in the summer of 1912, when he finished writing the bulk of *A Small Boy*, suggests that the unconscious feelings that informed much of the autobiography were at work in James's response to his autobiographical act and his relationship to his family as well.

4

Biographical Consequences of the Autobiographical Act

I am . . . so sick and so paralyzed with disgust at the appearance I have thus gone
on hideously presenting.

—Henry James (1912)

The narrative of *A Small Boy and Others* reads as if the transition James
made from writing a Family Book to generating an autobiography came
as easily and smoothly as the process of letting his memory flow. "In the
attempt to place together some particulars of the early life of William
James," he claims in the opening sentence of the autobiography, ". . . I
found one of the consequences of my interrogation of the past assert
itself a good deal at the expense of some of the others. For it was to
memory in the first place that my main appeal for particulars had to be
made" (3). Once the bulk of this narrative was written, however, the
transition from memoir to autobiography became more difficult. James
now faced the task not only of determining what to do with his material
but also of explaining his decisions to Alice and Harry James, the
relatives who believed that he was writing a book about William and the
family.

The first task, determining what to do with his material, involved his
decision to write not one volume of reminiscences but two and, as he
decided soon after, to publish the story of his childhood before going on
with the Family Book of letters. The second task involved a series of
long, often tortuous letters to William's family in which he attempted to
justify his ultimately self-serving decision, to placate the family—nephew
Harry, in particular—and to assure himself of the family's support. Thus
James enacts in this fevered correspondence between June and September 1912 a struggle as old as his history in the family—to remain loyal
to the family, or to maintain the appearance of doing so, yet to assert the

needs or priorities of the self. He enacts another family dynamic when, following a family crisis, he falls seriously ill and uses his illness as a means of both personal renewal and personal defense. As such James also re-enacts the story of the autobiographical narrative he is in the process of writing. In *Notes of a Son and Brother* disability both expresses the young James's conflicts with his family—or, to be more exact, the vocational conflicts engendered by his family—and enables him finally to dedicate himself to art.

I

It sickens me "all the time" to have had for
you so long that odious appearance.
—Henry James, 1912

We begin this discussion with a reconsideration of the autobiographical narrative James had completed by June 1912: but for a conclusion, all of the material that comprises *A Small Boy and Others*. We begin, too, by directing our attention away from James's relationship with his father and focusing it instead on his presentation of his elder brother William, the ostensible subject of the narrative. Edel has argued that the sibling rivalry between William and Henry is enacted in the dream of the Louvre recorded in chapter 25 of *A Small Boy and Others*. When James routs the frightening spectre who is haunting him, Edel suggests, he realizes his lifelong desire to retaliate against and triumph over his critical elder brother.[1] But the routing of William James that is enacted in *A Small Boy and Others* happens not on the level of the dream, in which James features a battle within himself, but on the level of the autobiographical narrative overall. "I never for all the time of childhood and youth in the least caught up with or overtook him," James writes of William in chapter 1, "He was always round the corner and out of sight" (7–8). James then uses this testimony to William's active superiority as an opportunity to avoid featuring William directly. Bright, active, accomplished, William is upstairs when Henry is down, running off when Henry is quietly gaping, and the result is that we are left to focus on Henry himself. Thus we see that James's self-characterization reflects both an emotional truth about the past and a psychological strategy in the present. His recollection of himself as an inactive, inept little boy somewhat disguises his egotistical move and deflects our attention away from his almost exclusive self-focus.

The task of usurping William's place in the Family Book enables James to devote his reminiscences about the family and their milieu to the story of how *his* imagination was fostered. Many of the impressions of Albany, New York, London, and Paris so lovingly recorded by James as autobiographer must have been absorbed by William and the other children in the family, just as the others undoubtedly consumed the bountiful supplies of peaches and pears, hotcakes and molasses. But just as he seized on those impressions and made them his own—his "property," so to speak—as autobiographical narrator he now claims ownership of the memories these impressions became. He claims ownership, in particular, over a hoard of memories acquired during the times when his father sought out his second son's company alone and allowed the small boy to accompany him on excursions. William, he says, "must have had in *his* turn many a mild adventure of which the secret—I like to put it so—perished with him" (41). Now that he is sole survivor of the family, Henry's secrets—the secrets of his father's attentions, the secrets of his impressionistic adventures, the secrets of his inner riches—can be exhibited to the world without corrections or contradictions from William. In order to protect his version of the past and the integrity of his identity as a man of imagination, he can also determine which memories will remain concealed and which secrets will go unchallenged.

The entire process of letting his memory flow in the fashion *he* desires can, in fact, be seen as Henry's response to the memory of William's criticisms and corrections, perhaps even to his envy of William's reminiscential powers. In chapter 6, he begins a lengthy discourse on memory by writing first of the "many young impressions" gathered "at his [his father's] side and in his personal haunts" (40–41). These recollections lead him to the realization that their father must "have offered his first born at least equal opportunities" and then to the regret that the "secret" of his brother's "mild adventure[s] . . . perished with him." James then recalls the many times he envied his brother the memory of "impressions I sometimes wished . . . that I might also have fallen direct heir to." Yet William, he adds, "professed amazement, and even occasionally impatience, at my reach of reminiscence—liking as he did to brush away old moral scraps in favour of new rather than to hoard and so complacently exhibit them." Thus, James concludes, "If in my way I collected the new as well I yet cherished the old; the ragbag of memory hung on its nail in my closet, though I learnt with time to control the habit of bringing it forth. And I say that with a due sense of my doubtless now appearing to empty it into these pages" (41).

I find this passage nothing short of remarkable. Not only do we see James besting his brother by asserting his claim to memories of his father's companionship, even as he defers to the possibility that his brother enjoyed similar adventures. But having suggested that William was impatient with Henry's reminiscential impulse and that he, the younger brother, "learnt with time to control the habit" of bringing forth the "ragbag of memory," James goes on to claim that, now that William and his impatience have perished, he as autobiographical narrator is "doubtless now appearing to empty it,"—"the ragbag of memory"—"into these pages." The "appearing" and the deprecatory designation of memory as a "ragbag" constitute James's attempt to disguise the obvious—he is emptying onto the pages of the so-called Family Book a storehouse of personal memories that for him are charged with signifi- cance. Additionally, when at the beginning of *A Small Boy* he evokes the memory of his father's autobiography, he creates the appearance of having been given his father's blessing on his enterprise; his father can even be seen as setting a precedent for the second son by writing his own autobiography.

Let us then consider how, in spite of the sorrow he felt at the loss of his brother, Henry has nonetheless benefited from William's death. For one thing, it gave James the "long-sought occasion" to write the history of "the imaginative faculty under cultivation." "The idea of some pretext for such an attempt had again and again, naturally, haunted me," he says in an oft-quoted passage in *Notes of a Son and Brother* (454–55). What is more, it was William's widow Alice who, by encouraging him to write his reminiscences, indirectly provided Henry with the "pretext" to make this attempt. By writing the autobiography, he also freed himself from the need "to control the habit of" reminiscing and proceeded to tell the story of *his* fostered imagination without the fear of being countered and corrected by William. So too does he wrest the shared memories of the past for himself in order to reassure himself of the validity of his way of being in the world, and he does so in opposition to William's identity and William's theories that their childhoods were an educational wasteland.

In spite of James's tendency to undermine his own self-portrait, as I discussed in Chapter 3, *A Small Boy and Others* constitutes an act of self-assertion in which Henry at last achieves what he always sought—mastery over his family. "He can reshape their characters even as he re-writes their letters and alters their travels,"[2] and he can do so in a way that puts his own small boyhood self and his exhibitionist autobiographical narrator at center stage. At one point in the narrative, James says that he takes "refuge easily enough" from the memory of "W. J.'s eclipses"—indeed from the memory of being "an actively rebuffed suitor"—"in the memory of my own pursuits, absorbing enough at times to have excluded other views" (147–48). In a sense, then, *A Small Boy and Others* is a refuge from his memory of William's overbearing superiority into the affirmation of his own pursuits and individual way of being. It is a refuge in which, for all his deficiencies, the overshadowed younger brother and the autobiographer can emerge as the unchallenged hero at last.

Henry's usurpation of William's role in the autobiography did not concern James in his correspondence with his literary friends. When he commented on *A Small Boy and Others* to H. G. Wells, for example, he talked of the difficulties of interesting the reader in the "cheeky" story of his boyhood, not the fact that he made room for himself by elbowing out his eldest brother.[3] But William's family was another audience altogether. Alice and Harry James were closely involved in the original plans for the Family Book, and they believed that the book was to be a tribute to William based on his early letters. Before Henry left for England in the summer of 1911, the family provided him with a number of letters, and they continued to send more in the months ahead. The ownership of the project was thus shared by several members of the family, to a certain extent, and when James calls *A Small Boy and Others* a "labour of loyalty and love," he undoubtedly refers not only to the family members he survived—to his mother, his father, his three brothers, and his sister—but also to those surviving members who themselves felt a personal investment in the work (4).

Indeed, James's 1912 correspondence with Alice and Harry suggests that he wrote frequently about the Family Book not only because he was excited about the project, and wanted them to share in its progress, but also because he felt accountable to William's family. He assumes—correctly, I think—that Alice would play the supportive, nurturing role traditionally required of James family women and give him her unqualified support. But Harry, William's eldest son, was the executor of William's estate, and, just as William felt responsible for his father's literary remains, Harry felt responsible for William's. Harry would see to it that his father's letters were published, if not by his Uncle Henry, then by himself. Harry had also adopted some of his father's condescension towards and impatience with James. Thus it is Harry, as a kind of stand-in for William, whom James is most capable of offending and whom he most seeks to please.

The beginning of their correspondence on the Family Book, and the first hints of their eventual misunderstandings, appear in James's letters to Alice and Harry late in 1911. This was the period, we recall, when James was discovering that the letters were an obstacle to the composition process and his determination to let his memory flow. It was also the period in which he was best able to affirm the understanding that was reached by the family over his handling of the family letters. As he writes to Alice in November, "I am entirely at one with him [Harry] about the *kind* of use to be made by me of all these early things, the kind of setting they must have, the kind of encompassment that the book, as *my* book, my play of reminiscence and almost brotherly autobiography, and filial autobiography not less, must enshrine them in." To Harry he then writes something of the same:

I am absolutely at one with you as to your idea of the atmosphere & setting that should flow round & encircle all these things—& that should (& shall) be filled with all the evocations that I can summon up of the old figures & feelings & times, all the personal & social & subjective (& *objective*) furniture of our family annals. Seen this way & in the light of my own "genius," the whole subject matter opens out to me most appealingly & beguilingly, & if you will but trust me so to *keep* seeing it & doing it, I think something altogether beautiful & interesting & remarkable & rare will be the issue.[4]

The family has agreed, in other words, that though the letters themselves are the focus of the project, James's retrospective vision should provide the context and atmosphere for the letters. "I am at one with" Harry on this matter, he writes to Alice, and to Harry he reiterates, "I am absolutely at one with you." Apparently Harry assumed that, as James's creation, the Family Book would be much more than an edition of letters or a factually-oriented biography. He understood that his uncle would use his literary gifts to recreate the past and place the letters in the appropriate "atmosphere & setting." But already there is a question of territoriality that compromises their understanding; James feels the need to insist that it is "*my* book, my play of reminiscence," a book to be seen "in the light of my own 'genius.' " Even his definition of the book as a "brotherly" and "filial autobiography" anticipates the more clearly focused autobiographical emphasis that emerges in the months to come. Perhaps it is his desire to insist on his ownership of the book that raises the question of trust in a letter that suggests that trust had already been established. "[T]rust me," he says to Harry, and something "remarkable & rare will be the issue."

James did not report in detail about the "issue" of his reminiscential genius until April 1912. Then he wrote a long letter to Harry describing his progress on the book. But the April letter never arrived—perhaps, as Harry believed, it went down with the Titanic—and its disappearance posed serious problems for James. He apparently feared that the gap in their correspondence would undermine his nephew's trust in him and, as a result, he wrote two long explanatory letters to Harry in early June.

The first of these letters, written on June 5, is devoted to an expression of James's emotional distress over the lost letter. I quote at length:

Forgive this process, used under stress and as a stopgap till I can recover a little from the dismay of horribly learning, by your delightful letter of May 20th. from

Chocorua, that you have never received my very long and very important letter of about two months ago—a letter telling you everything and wholly wiping out the reproach of my too long previous silence. Now that yours arrives with the miserable news that you have been all this time without that, I am staggered and discouraged, and must take a little longer to come round. For the purpose of that very long letter, the longest I ever wrote you, or, almost, ever wrote anyone, was to touch on every possible point that currently interests us and "post" you, so to speak, as to everything you and your mother could wish to know about me. I shall have to return to these things, but probably just for the present only by a little at once. The black mystery meanwhile is what has ever become of my letter, the only one I remember ever to have lost, knowingly, in all my long postal relations with the U.S. I haven't the exact date, but the explanation isn't the Titanic, for I must have mailed it, and by my own hand, I am sure, a clear fortnight before the Titanic horror. It is utterly inexplicable, and I had been for some little time wondering before your present letter came—wondering that I hadn't yet heard from you in response, as I had gone into various things as to which you would have been moved, in all probability, rather promptly to answer. And now I must go into them all again—and, disconcerted and discouraged, shan't be able to do it so well. Also I can say but comparatively little this morning, as I am taking, under pressure, time off from my morning's work—and am moreover quite sick with the thought of your natural view of my cruel dumbness; so sick and so paralysed with disgust at the appearance I have thus gone on hideously presenting.

This insistent refrain of apology and regret is then repeated at the beginning of his June 11 letter as well: "I dispatched you a few days ago an at best sadly mechanical cry of distress over the miscarriage of my long letter to you . . . & still can't *not* go on thinking with horror of all that time during which I only seemed to you brutally dumb. It sickens me 'all the time' to have had for you so long that odious appearance."[5]

Though more blatant and exaggerated, these letters reflect the same sensitivity to shameful appearances that emerged in James's apprehension over his reader's response to *A Small Boy and Others*. But here James is neither ashamed of his father nor fearful of what his father's behavior might say about himself. He is ashamed instead of his own selfish behavior within the family, or at least by the appearance thereof. I am "quite sick with the thought of your natural view of my cruel dumbness," he says; he is "so sick and so paralysed with disgust at the appearance" of indifference or neglect he has presented to Harry. He is even sickened by the thought of having presented to Harry the "odious appearance" of a silence so cruel as to be thought brutal.

However much he was guilty of it himself, selfishness, we recall, was the primary sin in Henry, Sr.'s, theology, and Mary James let it be known that selfishness in the form of overt self-assertion or self-indulgence was unacceptable to her as well. In the 1860s and 1870s, in fact, James wrote a number of letters to his parents in response to direct or veiled accusations that he had been abusing his parents' generosity, playing fast and loose with family funds, and in general indulging his selfish desires at the family's expense. The repeated use of the language of apology and appeasement in these early letters not only demonstrates his well-developed sensitivity to behavior codes in the family but also clarifies the psychology of James's 1912 letters to Harry.

He writes to his father on May 10, 1869, "To have you think that I am extravagant with these truly sacred funds sickens me to the heart, and I hasten in so far as I may to reassure you." To his mother he writes on June 8, "When you speak of your own increased expenses etc. I feel very guilty and selfish in entertaining any projects, which look in the least like extravagance. My beloved mother, if you but knew the purity of my motives!" Several years later, living on his own in Paris, a rebuke from his mother over his indifference and neglect once again brings the customary confessions and apology, though his tone here is decidedly less fevered and anxious: "I was much distressed by your further mention of your resentment at my failure to acknowledge the draft from Houghton some weeks since. It was certainly a most culpable omission and I cannot think how it came about. The draft reached me so as a matter of course that I treated acknowledging it too much as a matter of course. I didn't appreciate, either, that *you*, sweet mother, had had all the trouble procuring it. I am covered with shame, I thank you most tenderly and I assure you that I will never sin in the same way again!"[6]

In these letters, the young James seeks to exonerate himself of the sin of selfishness (taking more than his fair share of family funds) and, in doing so, to work his way back into his parents' good graces. His method is to acknowledge his "sin" and "shame," as if the expression of self-abasement is capable of gauging the extent of his regret. He also refers to the acute unhappiness he feels at the possibility that his mother thinks badly of him. Feinstein comments on the success of this strategy following yet another letter in which James tried to reassure his mother of his honorable motives. "My lovely mother," Henry wrote, "if ever I am restored to you sound and serviceable you will find that you have not cast the pearls of your charity before a senseless beast, but before a creature with a soul to be grateful and a will to act." Feinstein observes that in response "his mother assured Henry that he could do what he wished. He was so successful at the politics of invalidism that he got her to apologize for having questioned his motives."[7]

In letters to Harry many years later, we see an intensified version of these earlier exercises in apologetics and self-flailing. Not only is the apologetic language in these late letters more hyperbolic; not only is

James now "sick" and "*paralysed* with *disgust*" and conscious of having presented an "*odious* appearance" to a member of his family (my emphasis) but his language is intended to address accusations that come from James himself. After all, it is not clear that anyone but Henry himself has inflicted a reproach, the reproach he claims, for "my too long previous silence." It is not clear that Harry took the "view of my cruel dumbness" that Henry believes himself to be guilty of. Through the selection of adjectives of intensity, through the repetition of his emotion in both letters, through his exacerbated awareness of deserving a reproach, James expresses a sense of personal distress far in excess of the regret one might feel over a lost letter. Clearly more is at stake.

The "dismal thing," James writes on June 5, "is your loss of my statement as to my recent work and its aspect and prospect." James has seemed insensitive, then, to the requirement that Harry be kept posted on the Family Book's progress. What is more, some changes have taken place. The book "goes, it goes," he insists; his "great dream is to finish the Book by the autumn's end." He has found that packets of William's "sundry letters," recently dispatched by Harry, are "most welcome" and "very usable." He is sure that there is "no want of material now" for the Book. But the surprising news, and the reason he wishes to talk to Harry, is that "the Book will have absolutely to have two volumes." What is more, the material he has written so far is largely unusable for the project thus far conceived. As he says on the fifth, "I am working much better than when I began, and even at the rate at which it *has* gone I have produced 100,000 words all about our quite extreme youth, not to say our childhood, only; though doubtless about my own—save that I don't distinguish or differentiate, and that it's all one, with everything together." But on the eleventh he reveals that his treatment of William's and his childhood is not so inclusive after all:

Mountains of interruptions meanwhile seem to have risen up against my telling you all I want to, and need to, about my work on the Book, so far as I have got on with it. It has come on more steadily than swiftly, with my hampered physical condition . . . I have done more than *100,000* words about our (above all *my*) very early (American & foreign) time, boyhood & early youth, alone; all of which has drawn me on & on—& of which, if I leave out big chunks of it, I hope I shall be able to make perhaps some independent Reminiscential use. But I must go on & on, & then see; then judge & decide.

Finally the truth emerges—the book about early childhood that does not differentiate between William and Henry is about "above all *my* . . . boyhood & early youth, alone." If we think back on those youthful letters to his parents, if we consider the fact that James turned to apology when he was accused of abusing family funds, the intensity of his discomfort in 1912 becomes more explicable. The problem with abusing family funds is that you are taking something that potentially belongs to someone else, and Henry knew that William would use these funds for travel when he returned from abroad. He thus had to justify his use of "truly sacred funds" by continually appealing to his needs; yet he had to mitigate any impression of selfishness in these acts of self-justification by confessing his feelings of shame and self-abasement.

It appears then, that as autobiographer, Henry believes himself to have appropriated something equivalent to the family income, the furniture or property of the family annals. It appears that his exacerbated sense of shame and self-disgust in his letters to Harry stems from the knowledge of selfishness inherent in this autobiographical appropriation. We recall that, when William had an opportunity to pay tribute to a recently deceased member of the family he did so by editing and writing a lengthy introduction to his father's unpublished writings. Henry, however, appropriated for his own story the opportunity to memorialize William and publish his letters. His own concerns in *A Small Boy* were so pressing that he virtually crowded William out of the story or reduced him to the invisibility of the plural pronouns "we" and "us." However genuinely it reflects his feelings, then, James's language of self-abasement and shame in his letters to Harry is also intended to diminish the appearance of egotism in his act of self-appropriation.

But there is more to be said about James's strategy in these letters. "Between 1866 and 1873," Feinstein explains, "sickness became a means," even a "weapon," by which Henry could seize his "share of family resources."[8] Now in 1912 he also attempts to justify his selfishness and mollify his family by similarly appealing to the fragility of his health. Speaking of his "hampered physical condition" in his June 11 letter, he insists, "don't think of that as *un*hampered—it will always be hampered now, the process of emergence being continually a fight." He claims in a letter from July 16 that he has experienced "pulls up & breaks, sometimes disheartening ones, through the recurrence of bad physical conditions." But, he continues, "I have really now reached the point at which the successful effort to work really *helps* me physically—to say nothing of course of (a thousand times) morally." In the same way that family funds helped him work himself back to good health in the past, then, his indulging himself now in the "costly" but nonetheless salutary process of following the "very process & action of my idiosyncrasy, on & on into more evocation & ramification of old images & connections" steadily helps him physically and morally back to health.[9]

In June 1912 James had determined to set aside his autobiographical material for a separate volume on his early childhood and continue his work on the book he had originally planned with William's family. Writing to his agent in early August, James tries to clarify the nature of those two volumes, but manages instead to create a certain confusion: "What I really make out is that I seem to have sufficient material, quite, for *two* books, two distinct ones, taking the place of the one multifarious and comprehensive one that I originally saw." The first of these volumes "will have to detach and disengage itself from the 'family book', and, for literal practicability, for workable form's sake, stand upon its feet as 'Early (or Earlier) Letters of W. J.' " His method, he goes on, will be

. . . to produce and present, to comment and accompany, or in other words duly and vividly *biographise* them, by themselves. *They* will make the first book—and a very charming and interesting one—especially as I shall be thus free to extend my measure of time, that is the degree of the Early and the Late, in the matter, to the great increase of our facility in dealing with the Correspondence of his mature years: this in itself, to our sense, so very rich and voluminous, and to which also comment and picture and history, as an accompaniment, will be so applicable. (Let me add that *these* two Divisions, into largely Earlier and largely Later, are not what I meant above by the two different Books. These volumes will make, as I see them, but two instalments of One. I reserve tackling the question of the second, the other, Book, to another occasion—though it is practically what I have already written some 130,000 words of!).[10]

What James seems to be suggesting is that his first book, devoted to the "Early (or Earlier) Letters of W. J.," will be divided into "two instalments," one devoted to the early letters, the other to the "largely Later" letters. The second book, it turns out, will be reserved for the "130,000 words" he has already written, the material on his very early boyhood and youth. Clearly James is sufficiently uncertain about the form that the voluminous material should take that, at this point, he is giving mixed messages to his agent.

In trying to clarify matters to Alice on August 26, James only confuses the matter, and the family, more. "The 'Family Book,' *as a vehicle for William's Early Letters*," he writes:

has had wholly to break down—after drawing me along into the delusion that I might make the whole thing *one*. It was becoming far too copious & complicated to *be* One, at all; absolutely it will have to be *two*—but with the Early Letters, as a publication by themselves, the 1*st* now to be thought of. It has been an immense relief to see the case thus beautifully simplified—for I shall accompany the Letters with as much 'Family', all along, as *immediately* concerns them, & with thereby the light so much more completely focused on William himself. (I am in very auspicious treaty with the Scribners for the volume—'Early Letters of William James, with Notes by Henry James,' and with the "Notes" (the simplest and best name for *my* part) I can do *everything* I want.

He goes on to consider the idea of serializing parts of this volume of the "Early Letters"—what became of the Late Letters is unclear—and to ask Alice to look for more letters written by William during the 1860s and early 1870s. He explains that much of what he had written for the " 'Family Book' is useable," in this context, "& being used."[11]

Harry, it turns out, was in Canada during the end of the summer. After hearing from his mother upon his return, he understood that the Family Book had broken down, perhaps that Uncle Henry was giving it up altogether. Harry cabled his concern to his uncle in September and, responding to the cable, James finds that he has a complicated situation to unravel and to explain. First, he tries to clarify the idea, communicated in his August 26 letter to Alice, that the entire project would take two volumes, not one. Second, he has to communicate an important, more recent plan which, he says, has cleared up the problems with "the Family Book *as a whole* . . . in the most helpful way."[12]

That plan emerged in early September when he suddenly realized that the autobiographical material he had written earlier that year was a book in itself. As he wrote to his agent, "I find myself much interested in the fact that in going over more searchingly my work of the past winter I can't help recognizing in it—that is in a mere portion of it, for the moment—the stuff, already highly finished and, as it were, deliverable—of a beautiful little book of about 70000 words, complete in itself, carrying the record concerned in it up to my *twelfth* year (!!!) and of the most enchanting effect."[13] Perhaps Harry's cable prompted James to review this material and to see, from the distance of several months, a unity of composition that he failed to recognize before. Perhaps he had written enough of his personal narrative to see that William's letters belonged in a book that, for chronological reasons, should be published after the story of the small boy. Whatever the cause of his recognition, James felt elated to realize that all the work of the previous winter would not have to be deferred for some other use, and that he would not have to wait for the volume on William's letters to publish another book. "The mere getting it out & clearing my foreground," he writes to Harry, "will make enormously for the confidence & comfort of my present work."[14] But he still had a lot of explaining to do.

The explanatory letter James did, in fact, write Harry on September 23–24 is one of the longest in his three-year exchange of letters about *A Small Boy* and *Notes*, and it is the last of such letters to be written until, following a prolonged illness, James was again able to report on his work in the spring of 1913. Because it concludes a lengthy period of confusion and misunderstandings about his reminiscential writings and reflects James's intense desire to exonerate himself with his nephew, the letter provides a good deal of useful information about James's thinking about the books that became *A Small Boy and Others* and *Notes of a Son and Brother*. It likewise reveals the enormous stress James felt from his family's misreading of his motives. Regarding the books themselves, James is pleased to announce to Harry that, but for a conclusion, he is

> ... in possession of a *finished* Family Book No. I—or First Series of Instalment of the Same (not that I dream of so *calling* it, naturally;) finished, that is, as soon as Miss Bosanquet has done finally & beautifully re-copying it; which she is fast getting on with. This is, in its essence & inevitably, autobiographic—the autobiography of a very small boy, but reflecting everything imaginable & unimaginable in my whole environment, family scene & consciousness; which means of course constant reference to, & speaking for, your Dad: though I can only *most* of all, of course (as the sentient & observant organism,) speak for myself.

He goes on to insist that because "the more juvenile record couldn't, can't, with propriety, felicity or logic, come out *after* the less juvenile," the book about his father, beginning "with our time in Geneva from the end of 1859," must necessarily come second. Of this he reports that he has finished "(as a slight illustration) a dozen pages of mere *introduction* of Minny Temple, 15 of evocation of our 1*st* meeting with John LaFarge at Newport, about as many as to William Hunt &c, & about Miss Upham's old table at Cambridge (these being, as examples, but trifles, however.)" He insists that in packing in as much "citation of other letters," his father's in particular, his "design is to follow more or less every hare I can start."[15]

What is more, James wants to give the "2 Books titles of an *associated* sort or sense, with something in common or mutually referential." Having "provisionally settled on (for the forthcoming:) *A Small Boy and Others*," James proposes as possibilities for the second volume *A Big Boy and Others* and *Notes of a Son and Brother*. He arrived at these possibilities after rejecting two other titles that reflect his sense of the self-focus of volume one, "*Earliest Memories: Egotistic*" and "*Earliest Memories: Altruistic*." James also insists that the associated nature of the two volumes "will of necessity involve their *both* being published by Scribners—it would be an enormous embarrassment if the second were not to be."

As in his June letters, James's attempt to convey this information to Harry is intermixed with an extended apology about their previous misunderstandings and miscommunications. James begins, "I have your long letter, so eagerly awaited after your cable, & I try to rally enough from the effect of it in these few hours (it came this a.m.) to answer it more or less tonight. For this effect has been to penetrate me with the sense of how effectively I seem to have succeeded in making you misunderstand me—& at the very time of my life when I have wanted you to understand me most. It is clearly my fault altogether, & I will do my best to explain."

Throughout this protracted explanation, James walks a fine line between reassuring Harry that he cares intensely for the family and enlisting Harry's support for his decision to pursue his own course of action. James writes that "I curse my want of precautionary expatiation (which takes time & freshness) when I see that I so awkwardly expressed myself as to lead you to suppose that I am 'giving up' the Family Book instead of being each day more & more immersed in what I see as constituting the only possible & workable form of it!" Again he writes, "I could shed bitter tears over my having so clumsily or so superficially expressed myself as to lead you to suppose that I am not becoming at every step of my process, more intensely 'Family' even than at the step before. When I ask myself how I came to do so—to *be* so alarming & misleading—I can but suppose it was because of my too sketchily discriminating between the 470 pages of type I have rounded off & completed & the very much larger segment mass in which your Dad's Letters are the *Feature*, even though so embedded in all the circumjacent picture." Thus he attempts to reassure Harry, who now must consider publishing his own edition of William's letters, "don't for a moment doubt of their [William's letters] immense *intrinsic* attractiveness, vividness, value." But, he insists, his plan is the "only way to get the Family Bible (as I am moved to call it) realized in its *quantity*"; "indeed it will be only a mercy if I don't find myself floated on to *three!*" books.

Throughout these passages, James continually tries to assure Harry of his loyalty to the family and his regard for its importance. He calls the book the "Family Bible," and the process of writing it "intensely 'Family.'" At the same time, he displays an insistent narcissism that, much like his father's philosophy, reveals his preoccupation with himself and belies his altruistic concerns. He mentions first the primacy and power of his writing process: "This whole record of early childhood simply *grew* so as one came to write it that one could but let it take its way." Then he celebrates the "miracle" of "how the memories revived & pressed upon me, & how they *keep* a-doing of it in the 'letters' book." Because the first book is "a very charming & original & unprecedented one of its kind," he claims that "there isn't a line of it, now that it is done . . . that I am willing to sacrifice." He insists, "[t]his Book it *now* seems to me highly important to publish first and at once"; it "is in fact highly *urgent* for me that the volume in question should appear as soon as possible."

Throughout the letter James reminds Harry of how seriously he has been affected by their misunderstanding. "I try to rally enough from the effect of" Harry's letter, he claims at one point, and at another "I could shed bitter tears." But the effect of these emotional claims, finally, is to remind Harry of just how considerate and self-sacrificing he, Uncle Henry, has been:

I groan over the thought of the alarm & delusion into which I must indeed have bedevilled you by my inadvertence of expression, when you add that you would have been, for it, all ready to come straight over. Truly you must have mistrusted me & deeply must I have misled you! There is a bitterness in that—when I think how, all this year, through all difficulties of condition, & they have again & again been extreme, though now at last, thank God, much abated, I have had but the one thought of filling the measure of your content, *that* of all of you, to the brim. It has been *the* thing that has kept me going!

We see in this letter James's skill at inflicting guilt on someone for doubting his motives. We see, too, that he is able to elicit apologies from the person he had supposedly wronged, and thus exonerate himself of any wrongdoing:

. . . the reading of it [*A Small Boy*] by you all as soon as possible, & not least by your Mother, will, I feel, keep you in patience & renewed trust (a trust that will immensely sustain & steady me—for I feel not a little "rattled" by this sense of my having let myself in, through my reckless not dotting of more i's, for the pouring forth of so much explanatory & apologetic statement—& I haven't any margin for nervousness.) I thus want you to have the First Book in your hands, as a gage & sample, as soon as possible; & after that to let *me rip*!

The marginal comments that Harry wrote on the manuscript copy of this letter suggest that he, too, was feeling frustrated by his exchange with his uncle and, like his uncle, misunderstood. When James suggests that Harry believed him to be giving up the Family Book, for example, Harry wrote, "No—I didn't say any such thing."[16] But the pattern of communication established between uncle and nephew apparently required the suppression of Harry's frustration, his uncle having made it clear that expressions of confidence and support alone were acceptable. Harry thus tries to clarify the origin of the misunderstanding with his uncle and, like his uncle, expresses regret: "This misunderstanding would be totally ridiculous if your letter didn't fill me with real dismay and grief at the shock this part of my letter seems to have given you." He then follows with the reassurances his uncle needs: "so complete and implicit is my confidence, so great my hope and impatience, that I don't ask anything more or make any suggestion about the first volume [*A Small Boy*] as you've now described it. All I want is to be able to read it as soon as possible!"[17]

Harry's comment about the severity of the "shock" he had given his uncle was only too accurate. Before his letter arrived in Rye, Henry fell ill with an affliction caused, he claims, by a "a bad chill, a bad 'shock,' or a 'bad worry.' "[18] In June, James wrote of being "so sick and so paralyzed with disgust" over the appearance he had made to Harry; he spoke in his September letter about being " 'rattled' " by the effect of having to go into "so much explanatory & apologetic statement" and without "any margin for nervousness." Has his anxiety over the autobiographical act literally made him sick? In the past James paid an emotional and physical price to get his share of the family resources even as he maintained the angelic appearance of the scrupulously dutiful and appropriately shame-ridden son. Now, in the present, he may have paid a similar price not only for taking more than his share of family reminiscences, even breaking a taboo against competing with William, but also for having to maintain to Harry the appearance of remaining as scrupulously dutiful, as "intensely 'Family,' " as ever. Here in his old age James still suffers from the psychological legacy of the family system created by Mary and Henry James, Sr., namely the difficulty of reconciling the claims of the self with the claims of the family, of achieving autonomy within a family that penalizes an individual for asserting the self.

II

I have had many illnesses, to my shame be it said.
—Henry James (1912)

The illness that afflicted James in September 1912 was *herpes zoster* or shingles, a painful viral disease in which a rash with small clusters of blisters forms on the skin. In James's case, the "evenly spaced skin eruption, from which the ailment takes its name, appeared across the chest and round to his back; since it follows the line of a cutaneous nerve, it was painful in the extreme."[19] In the letters James wrote during this period, voluminous letters detailing every aspect of his illness and treatment, he describes the illness as a "horrible kind of visitation," a "horrid ailment," an "interminable visitation," and "a beastly little nightmare." Later when his recovery was still uncertain, he claimed that he was "good for very little yet—so long-drawn, so violent & vicious & really cruel, has been this horridly persistent assault."[20]

James experienced this illness in what he saw as two phases, the first emerging in September and lasting for several months, the second appearing in January and taking the form of "a horrible gastric and stomachic crisis grafed upon my poor ravaged herpetic tract." Moreover, he twice characterized the entire illness as a continuation of the debilitating breakdown he experienced in 1910. To Alice he claims that it is "all part and parcel, with an absolute logic and continuity, of what began for me 3 years and 18 days ago," and to Harry he writes that "[t]his hideous herpetic episode & its developments have been of the absolute continuity" of "my long illness of Jan. 1910" and "now makes its (I hope) dire but departing climax."[21] Thus his recovery in the spring of 1913 would herald for him the end of not simply the shingles episode but more than three years of illness and debility.

We have already seen that illness was a phenomenon that played an important role in James family dynamics. Pertinent to this discussion, however, is the specific role that illness played in the relationship between William and Henry in their formative years. According to Edel, the rivalry between William and Henry was the central feature of their relationship, and this rivalry clarifies certain features of James's auto-biographical act. But Feinstein observes that the brothers shared a relationship that, though embattled, was also exceptionally close. "[O]ne brother was always in the other's consciousness," he explains. When abroad, William would wish that Henry was "by my side" to "rejoice" with him in the Parisian theater and to react to the paintings of Titian and Veronese. Years later in *A Small Boy and Others*, Henry would portray their first aesthetic adventures in Paris as intimately entwined.[22]

This complex fraternal bond or relationship of "rivalrous fusion" was specifically represented in the 1860s and 1870s by the "shared sympto-mology" of their back and bowel problems.[23] The letters that flowed back and forth across the Atlantic detailed symptoms and offered sympathy, sometimes suggestions for cures, and by allowing the boys to appeal to their shared suffering, the letters also served the role of smoothing over the tensions between them. Perhaps these epistolary discussions of illness were a permissible way of focusing on oneself, on giving oneself some attention in a family that disapproved of self-preoccupation and selfishness. Perhaps they were a permissible way of expressing negative feelings, as I argued in chapter 2. The intimacy of these disclosures may also have been a way of alleviating the loneliness that develops in a family that shames you for being a self.

Henry and William continued their epistolary attention to bodily functions and illness into old age. They corresponded on the benefits of Fletcherizing in 1904 and 1905 and on the state of Henry's health in 1909 and 1910. When Henry developed shingles in 1912, he continued to write letters on the state of his health, now to William's family. Like the letters he had been writing on the autobiographies, the illness letters were voluminous outpourings indeed, so much so that James occasionally apologizes for what he calls his "flood of egotism." Or, as he puts it in another letter, "[f]orgive my thus sprawling on you—it is a kind of inevitability of my so practically complete solitude in respect to material and intimate, or 'family', matters."[24] Henry appears to know what sick persons inevitably discover, that sickness contracts one's world to a stifling self-focus, and the reports James provided on his illness were a means of both expressing and alleviating that preoccupation with himself and his pain.

But these 1912 illness letters were written in the aftermath of some painful misunderstandings about James's work on the so-called Family Book, and, like the early letters between William and Henry, they played a role in shaping the relationship between William's family and Henry. By refocusing the family's attention away from the book—or, should we say, the books—and onto James's condition, the letters allowed for renewed expressions of caring and affection. "And my conditions here have been admirable," he writes to Harry, "—save for yearning in vain for some member of 'my family' to commune with." They also became a means by which James could legitimately ask to be alleviated of the responsibility of accounting to Harry for his thinking about the volumes. "Be easy with me," he asks in October, "till I can pull round and really write. The arrest and interruption of work is too sickening—but I really believe that when I get on again it will be to a still better tune than before."[25]

Especially salutary, he explains, is the assurance that Harry will once again proclaim his unqualified trust in his uncle's judgment. "I wish I could persuade you," he writes in November,

to a little greater confidence, through all these heavy troubles of mine, in my proceeding with the utmost consideration for—well, whatever you want most to be considered; and I shall feel this confidence most, and most happily and operatively profit by it, if you won't ask too much in advance, or at any rate now for some time to come, to formulate to you the *detail* of my use, of my conversion into part of the substance of my book, of your Dad's letters; . . . But let me off—your letter in fact explicitly and mercifully does, dearest Harry—from any specified reassurances now; I am not fit to make them, and the sense of having so much to report myself is, frankly, oppressive and blighting. Don't *insist*, but trust me as far as you can; . . . The degree in which the element of his [William's] Letters shall figure in either of the parts is entirely within my discretion; and to attempt to give you pledges about that now would fill me with a sad sense rather that, for some reason, you wish me to get the minimum benefit of that blest material, rather than the blest maximum (compatible with the interests of the whole various Book) that I supposed, so fondly, to be at the bottom of your entrusting me with the Letters at all."[26]

By now, James's logic is fairly predictable. Because he is ill, he needs Harry's confidence, but because he is ill, he is not in a position to earn that confidence through a detailed explanation of his plans for William's letters. The "sense of having so much to report" in itself is "oppressive and blighting" and, anyway, were he to make the attempt to provide "pledges," James would have to conclude that Harry did not have his uncle's, or the book's, interests at heart. He would be filled with a "sad sense," as he says, "that, for some reason, you wish me to get the minimum benefit of that blest material, rather than the blest maximum (compatible with the interests of the whole various Book)." Predictably, this manipulative appeal to Harry's sympathies will obviate the need for James to account for the Book and, in the end, will lead to a new round of misunderstandings over his reminiscential project.

The passages quoted thus far from James's letters in the fall of 1912 show that once afflicted with shingles he significantly shifted the subject of his correspondence with his family. Now he is unable to work at all, let alone report on his work, and the outpouring of information and misery in these letters seems not only to console James in the absence of work but also to provide a substitute for, if not an extension of, the autobiographical texts on which, he claims to Pinker, he was working so well before the "horrible attack."[27] As he was doing in *A Small Boy and Others*, James is writing autobiographically. He is telling tales about himself, long detailed accounts of his illness, his difficulties with his physicians, the loyalty of his servants, his frustration with his inability to work, and so on. As if to suggest a link between his autobiographical account and his lived experience, he occasionally refers either to his illness or to the letters about them as if they were formal texts. On January 5, he calls his most recent difficulties "the second edition, as it were, of my illness." On February 25 he speaks of the details he has provided Harry as "my already sufficiently full chapter." And the second phase of his illness, as we have seen, constituted the "dire but departing climax" of three years of intermittent suffering."[28]

Enriching this interplay between the autobiographical text he was writing and these intensely personal letters is the fact that illness, the main subject of the letters, plays an important role in the autobiographical volume James was close to completing. Along with his passivity and ineptness, sickness in *A Small Boy and Others* is one of the negative aspects of his identity. It threatens to link the boy's fate with that of his doomed relations, and it constitutes one more reason for the small boy to feel ashamed. Yet "sickness, solitude, and confinement," says Eakin, are often portrayed as "enabling conditions" as well; they provide "a secure environment where the activity of the imagination, frequently associated with eating, can operate freely without interruption."[29]

In the first of the scenes of illness in *A Small Boy*, James portrays his boyhood self as practically reveling in the occasion in which, sick with malaria, he was confined to his bed in London. It was 1855 and James was twelve years old:

[P]resent to me as ever is the apprehended interest of my important and determinant state and of our complicated prospect while I lay, much at my ease—for I recall in particular certain short sweet times when I could be left alone—with the thick and heavy suggestions of the London room about me, the very smell of which was ancient, strange and impressive, a new revelation altogether, and the window open to the English June and the far off hum of a thousand possibilities. I consciously took them in, these last, and must then, I think, have first tasted the very greatest pleasure perhaps I was ever to know—that of almost holding my breath in presence of certain aspects to the end of so taking in. (158)

So significant was this experience, and so central to the growth of his imagination, that James used his memory of that London summer as an opportunity to comment on the act that was central to his way of being, the act of "taking in." "We seize our property by an avid instinct wherever we find it," he says, and "I must have kept seizing mine at the absurdest little rate, and all by this deeply dissimulative process of taking in, through the whole succession of those summer days" (158). Eakin claims that these experiences of "taking in" gave the small boy "a sense of possibilities and power . . . the seizing of his own property becomes a metaphor for the formation of identity." Because of the opportunities they provide for "taking in," both this London scene and another scene set in Geneva depict illness as having played a positive role in James's development.[30]

A Small Boy ends with the memory of yet another illness, and, coming as it does at the end of the narrative, this illness figures in a way that is even more momentous. Earlier in the final chapter, James claimed that the bout of typhus he experienced in Boulogne in 1858 signaled the "marked limit of my state of being a small boy. I took on, when I had decently, and all the more because I had so retardedly, recovered, the sense of being a boy of other dimensions somehow altogether, and even with a new dimension introduced and acquired; a dimension that I was eventually to think of as a stretch in the direction of an essential change or of living straight into a part of myself previously quite unvisited and now made accessible as by the sharp forcing of a closed door" (224). The memory of the illness itself shows the young James in the midst of this process of change; feeling weak and frightened by his illness, he also apprehends "something suddenly queer" in the atmosphere around him: "something had begun that would make more difference to me, directly and indirectly, than anything had ever yet made." As he leaves his bed and gropes for the bell on the other side of the room, he is lost "in the strong sick whirl of everything about me." He swoons, he loses consciousness, and this "lapse of consciousness" then becomes a "considerable gap" that brings this portion of his story to an end (236).

It is difficult to know exactly what James is trying to say in this passage. Is he, as Eakin suggests, experiencing a "pre-vision of the cost and consequences of the small boy's own development?" Is he simply overwhelmed by the possibility of change itself, by the anticipated transition from boyhood to adulthood? Whatever the reason, James has depicted illness as the condition which both facilitates this transition and hinders it and, as such, he not only summarizes the psychological situation of the small boy throughout *A Small Boy and Others* but also anticipates the climactic events that in *Notes of a Son and Brother* lead to his choice of vocation. Finally, he presents illness as one of the remembered and seemingly negative conditions through which, in the wake of his nervous breakdown, he "derived strength for the present" and a renewal of his literary powers.[31]

Crucial to our understanding of the role of illness in James's autobiographical act is the knowledge that this final, climactic material in *A Small Boy* was written *after* James had been afflicted by shingles. On November 25 James wrote that the volume was "in Scribner's hand all but about 25 or 30 pages of Finis, which, however, can be got off to him within 10 days after my finally shaking off this horror." In early January he proclaimed that the "first Book (of the Two) is really *done*," and on January 19 he announced that he had received the proofs of *A Small Boy and Others*.[32] Sometime before the onset of the second phase of his illness, James had felt well enough to dictate the final chapter of his story.

The timing of these events allows for a reading of James's autobiographical act that posits an especially intimate relationship between the lived present in James's life and the recorded past. The autobiographical text in which illness plays a prominent role anticipated a severe illness in the life of the autobiographer who, among other things, was tracing the history of illness in his past. Yet the recurrence of illness in James's life as an elderly man may have encouraged him as autobiographer to develop further the role of illness in his narrative not only by concluding *A Small Boy* with the story of a serious illness experienced in his youth but also by defining this illness as pivotal in his development. At the same time, of course, James was using the letters to his family to interpret the significance of his present illness as well.

Once he fell ill with shingles, James's first concern in his correspondence was to update his family on his condition, indeed to convey to them how severely he has been afflicted. "I am in the 5*th* week of my weary, dreary—my in fact at the worst quite dreadful, *visitation* of this accurst ailment of Herpes Zonalis," he writes to Alice on October 29, "& yet this is the 1*st* time I have been able to sit up, like a Christian, to a letter." He goes on:

> I am good for very little yet . . . so long-drawn, so violent & vicious & really cruel, has been this horridly persistent assault . . . (I have had it badly—*very*, I gather; & it's really, in its badness, quite a horrible thing—for intense excruciation! As I daresay you know, it consists of the violent inflammation of the ends or tips of a whole set of nerves round 1/2 of one's body (from middle of chest or trunk, right or left, to well under the corresponding shoulder-blade behind. "When you have it *all* round," says popular wisdom, "you *die*"—& that I can guarantee as absolutely inevitable. "If it were round the right side now too," I said to myself at its worst hours, "most *certainly* shall I die: it would be an impossible thing to survive & bear." For the horrid eruption of blisters & welts & *sores* over all the compromised part into which it breaks after 2 or 3 days of the pain does nothing, necessarily, to relieve it or ease it down—it (the accurst pain) goes on with no loss of heart.)[33]

Not only is James concerned with the misery and pain that the illness causes but he is also distressed by the interruption of his work. Indeed the worry about work becomes such an incessant refrain in his letter that his discourse about illness is often indistinguishable from his discourse about work. The ailment itself is "horrid" and "accurst," but his inability to work "had been really the heaviest burden" of all; his illness "in its badness" is "quite a horrible thing" but, like his body, his work too has been "blackly blighted." The "curst interruption and arrest, for the time, of work . . . is the thing in the world that has most power to cast me down. It makes me see everything in black, while it lasts; or in other words makes me dismally nervous."[34]

In part, the intensity of his language is due to the fact that he wants to justify to the family, to Harry in particular, the reason he has been unable to move forward with the Book. But more is at stake than his relationship to Harry; more is at stake, in fact, than his genuine desire to complete both the autobiographical project and the Family Book. We recall that James often figured his destiny as pivoting on two poles or possibilities. One possibility was work and the glorious opportunities for creativity and success it provided; the other was the illness or disability that in the late 1860s and again in 1910 threatened to undermine the prospect of work and render him an invalid and a failure. With work, therefore, goes emotional well-being and a self-respecting identity; with illness come the feelings of failure and shame that undermine that identity. "I have had many illnesses, to my shame be it said," writes James to his agent in November 1912 and, as such, his efforts to recover from his illness and return to work express his need to rout the spectre of shame from his life and recover his "better self."[35] James's inability to increase his income through the publication of new writing intensified this emotional struggle.

Eakin has already suggested some of the ways in which the writing of his autobiographical account enabled James to heal himself in the present. Not only did he present "sickness, solitude, and confinement" as "enabling conditions" for the small boy's imagination but James also "derived strength for the present from the insight he acquired into the resources of his ego" in the past. Other theorists' discussions of the role that stories of sickness play in the lives of individuals struggling to recover from illness or disability compliment Eakin's understanding of the healing power of autobiographical writing and, as such, provide another link between James's letters and autobiographies.

Howard Brody begins his study, *Stories of Sickness*, with the claim that "the experience of sickness might be bound up in some intimate way with a person's self-respect" and that an individual's capacity to tell stories about his or her illness is likewise intimately related to the healing process. Storytelling is "a mode of self knowledge" that changes "the meaning of the experience for the sufferer" and restores "the disrupted connectedness of the sufferer with herself and those around her." It is a mode of self knowledge that allows the sufferer to bridge the gap that has been created in one's life by the illness. Given the association of illness with stigma and shame, illness narratives allow an individual to revise her life plan in a way that similarly reaffirms the self and provides hope for the future. Such narratives are particularly important when, as Thomas Couser observes, an afflicted person becomes sensitive to the loss of subjectivity and the dehumanizing effects of medical care: "just as patients wish to vanquish the illness that alters their lives, they may also wish to regain control of their life-narratives, which are yielded up to 'objective,' and perhaps indifferent, medical authority. . . . As patients seize, or at least claim, more authority over their treatment, they may also be more inclined to narrate their stories, to take their lives literally into their own hands." They may assert "the impulse," in other words, "to reestablish one's subjectivity in the face of objectifying treatment."[36]

We saw that in *A Small Boy and Others* the young James had to overcome a forbidding series of obstacles in his struggle to develop an identity that one day would prove his worth; we saw that, in many respects, this process of development was something that he facilitated entirely on his own. When the young James goes on to suffer his famous "obscure hurt" in chapter 9 of *Notes of a Son and Brother*, he receives no help from the dismissive physician he consults in Boston and is left to work out a *"modus vivendi"* for himself (416). Yet according to James as autobiographer, this personally and privately constructed way of life is what enabled him as a young man to begin his vocation as a writer and facilitate his own recovery. As Eakin says, "It is not hard to see why the autobiographer was drawn to the story of a young man who managed both in spite of and because of illness and disability to achieve a full realization of his creativity."[37] Put another way, it is not hard to see why an autobiographer who himself was suffering from illness would wish to tell the story of a suffering younger self who managed *on his own* "to achieve a full realization of his creativity."

The letters that James wrote to his family between October 1912 and February 1913 enabled him to create a narrative of his illness similar in many ways to the story of the autobiographies and thus to articulate a philosophy of healing crucial to his recovery in 1913. Indeed, James casts his most recent experience with illness as a narrative of heroic suffering and self-reliance in which his so-called medical advisors become well-meaning but bungling adversaries and the healing that occurs remains entirely in his, the patient's, hands. What is more, the suffering he is forced to endure confers on him a kind of distinction and the promise of a distinguished destiny. In this way, James not only articulates the nineteenth-century romantic notion that illness is the sign of a privileged sensibility, a notion that was implicit in his letters from the 1860s, but also offers a secularized version of his father's belief that sufferings "are the best possible means toward a certain Divine End."[38]

The narrative in which his philosophy begins to emerge most clearly and dramatically comes in a letter written to Harry on November 25. James had begun the letter by attempting to convey to Harry the "dire terms" on which he has had to endure the herpes infection. "The sharpest piece of actuality with me," he goes on, "has consisted in an episode so strange that I scarce know how to give a proportionate account of it—and must in any case, at best, let a brief and imperfect echo suffice for you." The no-so-brief tale he then related to Harry is so full of interest and drama that I quote it at length:

My state was such a fortnight ago, about Nov. 10*th*, that I definitely demanded of Skinner [his local doctor] that he should procure in some way a Consultation; for which, poor depleted man, quite at his wits' end, he professed himself but too anxious, only with the fatal drawback of there being no one, no other medical authority whatever of the least value, within reach or range for such a purpose. Just after this it was by a remarkable chance revealed to me that a genial and highly recognised London Neurologist with whom I had had several years ago a very pleasant and happy relation, not as a Doctor but as a Reader and Appreciator (of The Wings of a Dove) was the great expert and exponent of the mystery of this fell Herpes; the man in the whole profession who is supposed to know most about it and to have made the discoveries, or ascertained the truths, on which the present advanced knowledge of it now rests. The thing was therefore to get at *him*, as I had the existing benefit of being thus in his critical good graces. (He and his wife had been greatly struck with a chapter in the W of a D. in which a visit of the interesting heroine to a great London Doctor, in a case of life and death, is portrayed; and were so good as to marvel at the initiated "psychology", on the Doctor's part, of the whole picture; this making them flatteringly appeal to me as to "How I knew such things.") So, Skinner eagerly lending himself to my proposal, I wrote to my friend (whose name, in the light of the dénouement I don't think it fair to give, and you'll have in New York no use for it,) that, he consenting, I should be very carefully and protectedly motored up to town to him, by Skinner of course, on a certain Sunday morning; should then get a chance for an examination and consultation and pronouncement from him at a reasonably noon-like hour; and should thereafter, having frugally partaken of food, be motored back to this place in the p.m., reach it by 7 or 8 o'clock again, and tumble into a well-earned bed and whatever extension of rest might be involved. The reply from my kind admirer was of the most genial and helpful: he refused to consent for a moment to coming up; was only eager to come down both *as* an Admirer and an Adviser, and would do so on the next Saturday afternoon, spending 24 hours with me and returning to his urgent duties on the Sunday evening. This accordingly took place; he arrived in time to dine with Skinner (under this roof) while I remained recumbent and expectant; and had all the hours following for examination, converse and circulation—the last-named exclusively of course with Skinner. He is a charming, intelligent, communicative man . . . and struck me as complete master and possessor of his subject: all the more that I wanted to think him so, since he abounded in the most cheerful and helpful reassurances. He departed, therefore in a cloud of glory, leaving me a mystic Remedy, a wonderfully-distilled concoction of a Pain-killer, which I was to take twice nightly for a number of days to come, that is till the pain should be completely killed. (For the formidable, the miserable nights of all this period are not to be properly laid bare to you now!) I addressed myself at once of course to the consumption of his Cure—but with a queer bewilderment and wonder dawning even from the first night and making me ask myself after what strange fashion it was supposed to act. For, to make a long story short, it began to bedevil me from the first into a state of the saddest aggravation—which the good man's great authority, none the less, forbade one to take, openly, for so flagrant as it seemed. After three days so markedly exasperated, however, that there seemed room for doubt, I expressed my confusion and alarm—only to be overridden by the earnest and unconvinced Skinner (who, in spite of his name, has been throughout, so far from showing himself as the least in my Skin!) I therefore went on to a fourth and fifth ingurgitation of the dread dose (the same two cachets a night)—with the waiting catastrophe of the worst regular set exacerbation of anguish that I have had since the first of my illness. I took the 9th. and 10th. doses Friday night as aforesaid—and passed that period in hell, as I may also mention. From then on to an hour ago I have lain prostrate and, as I say, ravaged; with a sense of being more directly *damaged* (so that on the Saturday afternoon I had a miserable scare, unrelieved by anything that either Skinner or his assistant Button either were able or could consent to do for me, in respect to damage *final*, or, as it were, permanent and irretrievable,) than it could seem well credible that even the wildest aberration of malpractice might bring about. But I am nonetheless "better" now; I have emerged, and had my bath, and am in the little upstairs green room, ticking this queer tale out to Miss Bosanquet with a volubility that at once relieves my sense of outrage (or what would *be* my sense of outrage if my good friend hadn't come down in such a cloud of generosity and good intentions,) and shows me yet again that I am so *very* yearningly fit for better, for fruitful activities, or should find myself so, could I only get out of this hole. However, my intention is now absolutely and invincibly to do so.

James goes on to define his course of action. He will rid himself of "my practically poisonous 'medical advisors,' " renounce all medication or, as he puts it, throw "[p]hysic utterly to the dogs," and attempt "by hook and by crook" to prolong the amount of time he is able to get out and walk. In spite of his strong determination, this plan unfortunately failed to bring about immediate healing.[39] In January he experienced a painful relapse of his illness and, given the complications of this relapse, he was forced once again to consult his physicians, this time with some positive results. But his self-diagnosis was nevertheless fully established in the harrowing story of late November, and the recurrence of his illness only served to strengthen it.

Looking briefly at the story itself, we see that the "great expert and exponent of the mystery" of herpes, the man who had read with great sensitivity the text of *The Wings of the Dove*, had miserably misread the text of the writer's illness. And James dramatically constructed the story of this misreading to show that his eventual suffering and disillusionment were equal to the powers of discernment and healing he had supposed the doctor by reputation to possess; they were equal, in fact, to the suspense and hope that built within as the doctor, once contacted, insisted on coming to Lamb House to examine the "recumbent and expectant" writer. The fact that the doctor was an admirer of James's work and therefore seemed particularly solicitous of James only increased the sufferer's impression that he was "complete master and possessor of his subject."

The doctor's cure, of course, was a miserable failure. His "wonderfully-distilled concoction of a Pain-killer" so aggravated James's condition that for days he lay in bed "prostrate" and "ravaged." But the results were not without their benefits. The greater the mismanagement of his physicians, the more fixed became James's determination to manage for himself the process of healing, and the "ticking" of his "queer tale out to Miss Bosanquet with a volubility that at once relieves my sense of outrage" constituted one of the first steps in this process. The aggravated suffering also strengthened James's conviction that he was "fit for better, for fruitful" activity. "My feeling is in the fact," he says in January, "that I *must* be reserved for some decent destiny yet to have successfully struggled with so much misery and withstood so malignant a combination of enemies"; when "I get that well under—as I *shall* again—" he says of his intestinal complications, "I shall have triumphed indeed; and shall have done it all myself."[40]

These convictions were also bolstered by the retrospective view that was inspired by his illness and by the memory, accordingly, of earlier experiences of self-healing. The day after dictating his outraged comments to Harry, he wrote Pinker that "[t]here has been no illness of my life from which I haven't, in the last desperate resort, had to do it all, essentially, for myself: I have had many illnesses, to my shame be it said, but not a single one, I don't hesitate to say, out of which I haven't had, at a given moment of supremely manifested helplessness on their part, to take the affair straight out of my 'advisers'' fumbling and aggravating hands, and just personally and independently *get* myself well."[41] As if to strengthen the image of self-reliance he wishes to impress upon his relatives, upon his agent, and undoubtedly upon himself, he occasionally casts his struggles in military terms. We saw that on January 5 he described his recovery process as a struggle with a "malignant . . . combination of enemies." He then wrote Harry of having waged a "fierce fight—of which the great battle indeed is over and with only minor engagements and skirmishes, thanks to an extraordinarily malignant enemy, still going on."[42]

We have seen this kind of language before. In the letters in 1910, to cite one example, he figured his depression as a "nervous spectre" or a "fiend" (just as he often described his experience of shingles as a "nightmare" or "visitation"). But the language of January 1913 more clearly takes on a military cast and, in doing so, suggests that his physical suffering makes of him the kind of masculine hero that, throughout his life, he much admired but was never able to become. He wrote to Viscount Garnet Wolseley in 1903 that to read his autobiography, *The Story of a Soldier's Life*, "has all been to me a piece of intimate (and rather humiliating) experience." He goes on to express envy for Wolseley's "retrospective consciousness" of certain battlefield experiences.[43] Perhaps it was out of shame for his less than traditionally masculine experience that in *Notes of a Son and Brother* James then tried to figure himself as a hero like Wolseley by "measuring" his "obscure hurt" against the "wounds" of the young men fighting in the Civil War and concluding, with characteristic indirection, that "one was no less exaltedly than wastefully engaged in the common fact of endurance" (426).

James's letters do not indicate precisely when between 1912 and 1913 he wrote the Civil War section of *Notes of a Son and Brother*. Had he completed it by January 1913 the autobiographical account may have inspired James to suggest to Harry that his struggle with shingles was the equivalent of a military encounter and his badge of courage no visible medallion but the richness of consciousness instead: "I catch myself in the act of speaking thus as if I hadn't laid up the very thickest stores of experience—which are what, barring uncanny accidents, I mainly take account of."[44] But, whatever his timetable, James's attempt to portray himself as a man of courage undoubtedly played a compensatory role in his life at age seventy. It enabled him to put a positive construction on his disability in the past and his illness in the present and thereby to affirm his personal strength and capacity for healing.

I wish now to consider the variation on his epistolary narrative of self-healing that appears in a letter James wrote to his sister-in-law Alice in January 1913. Not only does this variation enrich our understanding of his attitudes towards healing but it also adds to our knowledge of his relationship with members of his family, the women in particular. Of crucial importance is the fact that the role that Alice played in a similar healing process—or, should I say, that Henry allowed her to play—constituted a departure from the dependency on women modeled by his father, Henry, Sr., and his eldest brother.

James wrote this January 17 letter after he had experienced what he called "the second and larger, and infinitely more atrocious, phase of my illness." He reviewed what he had narrated at length to Harry in the communication of November 25: the bungling of the Herpes specialist, identified here as Dr. Head; the bewildered ignorance of Dr. Skinner; the resultant aggravation of his condition; and the reiteration of his faith in self-healing and the distinction it should confer upon him: "*All* my getting better has been through my own poor groping and arduous effort; and so, essentially, it will be still. It has taken no end of doing, and will still take a good bit more; but I am fully capable, and every measurable advance, even of a step or two, is immensely supporting. I really feel in fact, after so stiff an ordeal, that I am still 'reserved' for some sort of a destiny; to have resisted in such a degree seems a practical gage of that." James goes on to describe his present living conditions and the efforts he is making to get back to work. Towards the end of this letter, however, he recalls a slightly earlier period of his recent history of afflictions, the spring of 1910, in which he likewise made a vow to get better. The inspiration for this reminiscence was Alice's news that she and Harry had considered coming to England to look after Henry:

As to this I should not be able to express myself properly, till I can sit up and bend over to writing again with my own hand; but if anything could have exceeded my unspeakably touched state at the passage through your mind of such a dream, it would have been my distress and dismay at any attempt to your translating it into action. The mere dim vision, dearest Alice, of your faring forth across the wintry sea, at this black season, to minister to me, and then having to fare back again, to your intensities of required and beneficent presence, at home, would simply have broken my heart—just literally have terrified me into prompt dissolution. No, never dream *that* way—once you shall have measured my own impossibility of allowing it even *as* a dream. You absolutely saved my life, as I was so repeatedly to assure you afterwards, when you came out to me in those dire weeks of the spring of 1910—that is what you entirely and utterly did during the time following your arrival, and after William had gone to the Continent; during the interval before we joined him there, in fact during the dreadful Nauheim period too, and afterward till we got to Geneva: when it was that I began in a measure to get hold of myself again. Unforgettable the morning I crossed the lake with you, from the hotel, in the little steam-launch, to make the so difficult arrangement for dear William at the Dentist's—when you told me of the Cable announcing Bob's death, which you had so admirably kept to yourself for the day or two, in consideration of both of us. That moment made for me somehow a date, determined my sense of my power, and above all of the intensity of my resolution, to get comparatively better. The resolution took effect, with whatever weary obstructions and difficulties were still to come and drag themselves out, from that moment; and though the difficulties and hindrances have been such a formidable matter as to comprehend, in their long-drawn long-drawnness, even this most tiresome sequel—all part and parcel, with an absolute logic and continuity, of what began for me 3 years and 18 days ago, I have never lost possession, *really*, for an hour, of the foothold which your tenderness and devotion intensely *made it possible* for me, at that crisis, to take. I am still, in spite of everything, in possession of it now, and absolutely capable (with the familiar old dodge of my own peculiar patience,) of seeing myself through in my own way.[45]

The variation in this story of healing comes in James's acknowledgment of the role that Alice played in his recovery from depression in 1910 and the role she continues to play in the present. "Angel and Heroine" that she is, says James, Alice not only "saved" his life in 1910 by coming abroad and ministering to his afflictions but she did so, in part, by taking on herself the painful news of the death of Robertson James that might have further damaged both Henry and William.[46] James then claims that it was his awareness of Alice's sacrifice that led to his determination to get better, and, even now, his memory of her "tenderness and devotion" provides a foundation or "foothold" for his recent efforts at recovery.

What is different about this account when compared to his letter of November 25 is James's acknowledgment that, however individual an effort, his healing process is greatly facilitated by the care of another member of the family. That this other member is a woman is, of course, entirely in keeping with the expectations of the family in which he was raised. Feinstein has noted that a family of invalids and neuresthenics like the Jameses required at least one individual to be the strong caretaker of the family. In the nuclear family of Henry James, Sr., that person was the mother: "Others were expected to be short of energy, but Mary remained stalwart and ever ready to shoulder her caretaking tasks." Even when she was ill, William reported, she would not be deterred from her tasks: "Mother is recovering from one of her indispositions, which she bears like an angel, doing any amount of work at the same time, putting up cornices and raking out the garret-room like a little buffalo."[47]

Mary James's ability to be a physical caretaker extended to the realm of the emotions as well, at least for her husband. She defended her husband's religious beliefs and provided for him a constant source of emotional comfort; in doing so, she behaved according to her husband's opinion that, as a "form of *personal affection*," woman exists "simply to love and bless man" and to make available for man "the satisfaction of his own want, the supply of his own lack."[48] When their second son came to describe this relationship in *Notes of a Son and Brother* in 1912 and 1913, his portrait of his mother was similarly indistinguishable from the idealized image of selfless womanhood in Victorian culture. She "*was* each of us, was our pride and our humility," he claims, "our possibility of *any* relation." But, in a passage to which I return in chapter 5, James defines her "complete availability" for their father in a way that leaves us doubting the value of his mother's availability and his father's dependence. She "was a support," he claims, "on which my father rested with the absolute whole of his weight" (342–43). Expressed in a passage written sometime between 1912 and 1913, the memory of his parents' relationship may have served as a cautionary reminder of his father's emotional dependence on his mother. And it may have informed James's claim that Alice's sacrifices in 1910 "determined" his "power" and "resolution" to get well.

In this passage James also clarifies his relationship with his sister-in-law Alice and distinguishes it from the relationships the James family men established with their women. Like Mary James, Alice Gibbens James had been the caretaker of her family, and like her mother-in-law she had learned this role in the family in which she was raised. She was a woman of large intelligence and sympathy, and she and her brother-in-law Henry had liked one another from the first. Henry apparently knew that his sister-in-law possessed a good deal of "nurturing strength," as Feinstein calls it; he knew when he wrote his illness letters to Alice that, as he remarked to his nephew Harry, "her charity and sympathy will . . . take in" all of his "information about my physical state" with which he once "drenched her"—"almost *ad nauseam*."[49] But, unlike his father (and probably his elder brother), Henry drew the line on the sympathy he absorbed from the women of the family. He even attests to the fact that in 1910 his awareness of the burden she assumed to spare William and himself forced him to try to lift that burden and get well.

That he was not married to Alice James, of course, facilitated this process, as did the fact that James had avoided romantic relationships of any kind with women. But in the history of the James family, in the history of James's healing process, his January 1913 statement about his relationship with Alice is important nonetheless. She has given enough of herself, he seems to be saying; certainly she has given enough to assure him of her devotion and to provide the comfort implicit in that assurance. The letter also suggests that, in setting these limits, Henry has Alice's needs at heart. He knows how difficult the Atlantic passage would be "at this black season"; he knows that her "beneficent presence" is needed at home. But he obviously has his own needs at heart as well. Her sacrifice would have "broken my heart," he says; it would have "just literally terrified me into prompt dissolution."

Perhaps James is saying not only that he is fully "capable" of facilitating his own recovery but also that his recovery would have been impeded if he behaved too much like his father and depended for his recovery on the sacrifice of someone else, particularly a woman in the family. He thus writes out of concern for Alice's well-being and out of his fear of dependency as well. We only need to think of the many James family letters in which a woman was given the responsibility and credit for healing one of the James family men in order to gauge the extent of these fears.[50]

We cannot know, in the end, what factors led to James's recovery throughout March and April of 1913. Perhaps the illness had finally run its natural course; perhaps James's determination to get well and to make the most of his recovery facilitated this process; perhaps the favorable reviews of *A Small Boy and Others* played a salutary role as well. What we do know is that, as he had been doing in his autobiographies, James created a narrative for himself, an autobiographical account, that put a positive construction on his illness and affirmed his own powers of healing; he interpreted his illness in such a way that he returned to his work on the autobiographies, or Family Book, with his "genius" not only intact but also enriched. My reading of *Notes of a Son and Brother* in the following chapter develops more fully what I have articulated here—that once again there was fruitful interchange between the formal record of the past and the informal outpourings of the present, and that once again the interpretation of illness or disability in his autobiographical account informed his approach to healing in the letters he writes in the present, or the other way around. Whatever the case, we move in our consideration of *Notes of a Son and Brother* to an understanding of how the youthful Henry James used adversity to overcome adversity, used his wounds to heal himself, at least temporarily, and how the elderly James continues to make emotional self-protection a part of his strategy as both memorist and autobiographer. We turn, too, to a fuller consideration of James's troubling treatment of the women in his family, in this case his mother, his sister, and his cousin.

5

Divided Messages in
Notes of a Son and Brother

I like ambiguities and detest great glares; preferring thus for my critical no less than for my pedestrian progress the cool and the shade to the sun and dust of the way.

—Henry James (1914)

A Small Boy and Others was written throughout a period of relatively good health in the winter and spring of 1912. James's testimonials to the composition process suggest that once he decided simply to let his memory flow the book proceeded swiftly and surely, and with few interruptions. But the composition of *Notes of a Son and Brother* was a very different process. James's correspondence in June 1912 suggests that along with the material that eventually went into *A Small Boy*, some seventy thousand words before the conclusion, James had written an additional thirty thousand words or so, and his September 23–24 letter to Harry provides details about some of the completed material.[1] But his progress on *Notes* was cut short by his shingles attack at the end of September and, according to his correspondence, months passed before he was able to work with any regularity.

His commitment to include family correspondence in the book posed additional problems. He acknowledged in November that he had yet to discover how both William's and their father's letters would figure into the "substance" of *Notes of a Son and Brother*. Although by January he was able to proclaim that "[a] very considerable lot of 'Notes of a Son etc' is done," and to imply that he had solved his organizational problems, James also acknowledged the receipt of an additional packet of letters that he was especially eager to work into the book, the correspondence between Ralph Waldo Emerson and Henry James, Sr.[2] A significant and irresistible packet of cousin Minny Temple's correspondence also became available to James when the book was nearly complete.

The narrative itself reflects both this intermittent approach to its composition and the need James felt to incorporate a wealth of family correspondence into a limited space. The entire autobiographical project, we recall, was originally conceived as the "Letters of William James with Notes by Henry James." But in the end, only three of the book's thirteen chapters (2, 5, 12) were devoted to James's presentation of William's "numerous and highly characteristic" letters (267). Another three chapters (6–8) feature Henry, Sr.'s, letters to a variety of correspondents, among them Julia Kellogg and Ralph Waldo Emerson. Chapter 11 is devoted to the Civil War letters of the younger brothers Garth Wilkinson and Robertson James, and the volume concludes with the letters that Minny Temple wrote to her friend and admirer, John Chipman Gray, shortly before her death from tuberculosis in 1869.

Thus a large percentage of the book is made up of either James family correspondence or the autobiographical narrator's reflections on the correspondents, and some readers have recognized in *Notes* a distinct shift away from the autobiographical focus of *A Small Boy and Others* to the portrayal and commemoration of family members. But James's correspondence reveals not only that he was conscious of the need to unify these seemingly disparate portraits of others but also that he planned to do so by incorporating "my own text" or autobiographical account into the book.[3] He provided this unifying thread by beginning *Notes of a Son and Brother* with the story of his educational experiences in Geneva and Bonn in 1859–1860, then turning in later chapters to the process by which he went from being a diffident youth with literary aspirations to becoming a professional writer (9, 10, 12).

Eakin argues that there is more to James's autobiographical account in *Notes* than the chapters which, by focusing on the young Henry James, provide chronological links for the material that emerges in family letters from the late 1850s and 1860s: "If we set aside for the moment the four chapters (6, 7, 8, and 13) that feature Henry James's father and Minny Temple, which were expanded or added to incorporate sets of letters he received during the course of composition, the outline of Henry's own story in *Notes* emerges much more clearly. It is the narrative of an identity crisis, posed in terms of vocation and developed in two distinct phases: the first of these concerns William James as he faces the choice of a career . . . and the second places Henry in a parallel position." This "deliberately schematic" analysis of the organization of *Notes* enables Eakin to conclude that, in spite of appearances to the contrary, "[m]ost of the material about others in *Notes*—and William's case is no exception—develops the themes of James's story of himself." It develops, in fact, the story of the "identity crisis" that ushered in the young James's vocational commitment.[4]

By interweaving his "own text" with his portraits of family members in *Notes of a Son and Brother*, James can do more than use the material about others to develop the story of the identity crisis so masterfully described by Eakin. In ways that are decidedly more specific than the memories recovered in *A Small Boy*, James also continues his seemingly inexhaustible probe into the role his father played in his development and seriously implicates his father in the discomfort, confusion, and shame that form so much of his account of young manhood. The process of questioning and critiquing his past is both corroborated and complicated by the testimony about his father provided in the family letters themselves. It is further complicated by the highly idealized treatment he gives his mother, Mary James, in the midst of describing his father's professional life.

Notes also enables James to go beyond the effort both to understand and to challenge his father's motives, to seek the truth about his father's elusive personality, and to indict his father for his failings. It allows him to construct a story in which, by becoming a professional writer, he counters his father's example and thus further develops the story of emotional survival he tells in *A Small Boy*. Central to this narrative, of course, is the event that gives rise to the most densely packed and suggestive passages in *Notes*—the "obscure hurt" James incurred fighting a stable fire in Newport in 1861. Like the dream of the Galerie d'Apollon in *A Small Boy and Others*, the obscure hurt is a pivotally symbolic passage that gathers together many of the issues in James's development and alerts us not only to the obstacles the young man had to overcome but also to the stakes involved in his triumph. Because it is associated with the emotional and physical wounds of two previous generations of James family men, James's mysterious injury represents not only the pain and the confusion of the identity crisis itself but also the potent and "obscure" family shame that forms the crux of the crisis.

But there is more to *Notes of a Son and Brother* than this complex probe into parental origins and influence. As my discussion of *A Small Boy and Others* has already shown, James's autobiographical act vacillates between the desire to know the truth about his father and the need to turn away from that truth, to keep his family's secrets and protect the reputation of the dead. In *A Small Boy and Others*, James obscured the truth about his father's vacillations by presenting their European travels as one continuous sojourn abroad. Here he touches up the past by correcting their correspondence and attempting to avoid anything unseemly in their expression, an editorial decision that once again creates conflict with Harry. In order to protect them from the humiliation of misfortune and failure, and thus to protect himself, he also portrays family members and friends as if, like his cousin Minny Temple, they existed without a future to tarnish their image. Once again, his memory of his father is central in this attempt. It seems as if every gesture towards uncovering the secrets of his father and probing into his incoherent identity is countered by gestures in the direction of what Feinstein calls remaining "loyal . . . to his childhood part in the family charade."[5] It seems as if every attempt to write, however briefly, about the women in the family likewise shows Henry remaining loyal to his father's belief that women exist in order to serve men.

I

> I should surely be good for nothing, all my
> days, if not for projecting into the concrete,
> by hook or by crook—that is my imagination
> shamelessly aiding—some show of (again)
> mere life.
>   —Henry James (1913)

Notes of a Son and Brother resembles in many ways the history of the imagination that James developed in *A Small Boy and Others*. The wealth of impressions taken in, their contribution to James's youthful imagination, his stance of passive observation—each of these features of the small boy's identity continues to be explored and developed in *Notes of a Son and Brother*. But *Notes* also brings James to a stage in his life in which it is no longer sufficient to be a gaping boy, absorbing impressions through the fence or the window. The young James has reached the period in life in which, as a young American male, he must decide what he is to do with himself. He must choose a vocation or settle for a future of ineffectuality and failure. As he says in chapter 9, "I should surely be good for nothing, all my days, if not for projecting into the concrete, by hook or by crook . . . some show of (again) mere life. This impression was not in the least the flag I publicly brandished; in fact I must have come as near as possible to brandishing none whatever" (411).[6]

This story begins with an account of the turmoil he felt upon being enrolled in a school specializing in scientific studies in Geneva in 1859. "My attempt not therefore to remain abnormal wholly broke down," he explains, "and when I at last withdrew from the scene it was not even as a conspicuous, it was only as an obscure, a deeply hushed failure" (241). Though outwardly a failure, particularly in contrast to his dazzling elder

140

brother, the young James nonetheless possessed a rich inner life; he "moved," as he says, in "a but scantly comparing or distinguishing maze of the sense and the fancy" (245). What distinguishes this period from earlier phases of his life is the fact that his inner life begins to be transformed. Propelled, as it seems, by a power of their own, the impressions so eagerly acquired in years past had begun "to scratch quite audibly at the door of liberation, of extension, of projection; what they were *of* one more or less knew, but what they were *for* was the question that began to stir, though one was still to be a long time at a loss directly to answer it" (253).

It was while William was studying painting in 1860 with William Morris Hunt and Henry, too, was trying to paint that the novelist-to-be began to discover a purpose for his impressions; "Art, art definitely named" was "no longer a tacit implication or a shy subterfuge, but a flagrant unattenuated aim" (285). When he discovered that he lacked William's facility with the brush, the painter John LaFarge taught young Henry that "the arts were after all essentially one and that even with canvas and brush whisked out of my grasp I still needn't feel disinherited" (294). It would be some time before James would determine that writing would replace painting as his life's work, but until then LaFarge had "opened more windows than he closed" by plunging Henry into the study of Mérimée. Such memories, he goes on to say, may seem to the reader "mild" or insignificant, "yet I cherish them as ineffaceable dates, sudden milestones, the first distinctly noted, on the road of so much inward or apprehensive life" (294, 292).

The next milestone in the young James's life came during the outbreak of the Civil War when young American men were called to arms. William had enrolled in the Scientific School at Harvard the previous fall, and Henry had remained in Newport with his family. When the war broke out, he became painfully aware that "just staying at home when everyone was on the move couldn't in any degree show the right mark; to be properly and perfectly vague one had to be vague *about* something." By this time, he knew that what he most " 'wanted to want' to be was, all intimately, just *literary*." But "a decent respect for the standard" had not yet been established, and the young man was unable to advance directly towards his goal and publicly declare himself a writer. Adopting a subterfuge, he followed William to Harvard and determined to study law. Harvard, after all, symbolized "after a queer fashion, the independence, blest vision (to the extent, that is, of its being a closer compact with the life of the imagination), that I should thus both luckily come in for and designingly cultivate: cultivate in other words under the rich cover of obscurity" (412, 413, 414).

What further complicates this crisis in the young man's life is the injury incurred when fighting a stable fire in Newport in 1861. Leon Edel has discovered that the injury was a hurt to his back, most likely a "slipped disk, a sacroiliac or muscular strain,"[7] but James himself describes it in terms that have left generations of readers mystified. "Jammed into the acute angle between two high fences," he explains, "where the rhythmic play of my arms, in tune with that of several other pairs, but at a dire disadvantage of position, induced a rural, a rusty, a quasi-extemporised old engine to work and a saving stream to flow, I had done myself, in the face of a shabby conflagration, a horrid even if an obscure hurt" (415). Looking back, the autobiographical narrator equates his wound with the aches and wounds of the nation; taken together, his "physical mishap" and "the great public convulsion that announced itself in bigger terms each day" had become "a single vast visitation" (414–15).

James deliberately conflates the two crises in order not only to use his injury as a "symbol of the nation's suffering," as some critics rightly contend, but also to use the war to symbolize his personal pain, the pain, that is, of both the physical injury incurred while fighting a fire and the crisis he was experiencing over his vocational identity.[8] The equation between the wounds of soldiers and the "obscure hurt" likewise heightens by association the heroism implicit in James's personal sufferings: "This was at least a negative of combat, an organized, not a loose and empty one, something definitely and firmly parallel to action in the tented field" (417). But this physical wound is only part of James's story, and its ability to represent the confusion and pain of his identity crisis is only part of its symbolic function.

In his fictional autobiography, Henry, Sr., endowed his narrator Stephen Dewhurst with a number of characteristics missing from his own personality. Not only did Dewhurst possess an aptitude for financial affairs but he was also successful in his job at the Treasury Department at Washington. During the Civil War, he threw himself into the war effort by working tirelessly for the government. I suggested in chapter 1 that Dewhurst performs a compensatory function for Henry, Sr., and, as such, alludes to a feature of the father's experience that, to my knowledge, has never been mentioned before. The crippled Henry, Sr., may have been troubled by his failure to serve the Union in an active, identifiable way.

In his autobiography, Henry, Jr., confesses directly to a sense of shame and discomfort from his lack of participation in the war: "the willing youths, all round, were mostly starting to their feet, and to have trumped up a lameness at such a juncture could be made to pass in no light for graceful" (415). As autobiographical narrator James likewise suggests that, fifty years later, he shared with his father a need to compensate in writing for his failure to become directly involved in the war effort. His attempt to minimize his "obscure hurt" as an "infinitely small affair" (414) even as he exaggerates its importance suggests that it was still difficult to make his youthful situation "pass" in some "light for graceful." James even expresses discomfort with the fact that he is passing off his private memories of that time, his record of his inner life, as sufficiently worthwhile and momentous: "If I had not already so often brazened out my confession of the far from 'showy' in the terms on which impressions could become indelibly momentous to me I might blush indeed for the thin tatter dragged in thus as an affair of record" (422).

The associations between this experience and his father's are explicit throughout the text of *Notes of a Son and Brother* and, what is more, they begin to inform James's interpretation of the vocational concerns that were so pressing in the early 1860s. By describing himself as having "trumped up a lameness," James associates his "hurt" with the injury that left his father lamed for life. By calling them a "single vast visitation," he figures the events of 1861 with a phrase that echoes the Swedenborgian term for his father's nervous breakdown—vastation. In an earlier chapter, he equated his father's "scant allowance of 'public recognition' " or professional success with the "grave disability" Henry, Sr., incurred in his youth (414–15, 351), and he did so in a chapter that calls frequent attention to the "thin consolations and broken rewards" of his father's career (333). James even introduces the chapter with a lengthy discussion of his father's singular dedication to an unprofitable career. "He applied himself," writes Henry, Jr., "with a regularity and a piety as little subject to sighing abatements or betrayed fears as if he had been working under pressure for his bread and ours and the question were too urgent for his daring to doubt. This play of his remarkable genius brought him in fact throughout the long years no ghost of a reward in the form of pence, and could proceed to publicity, as it repeatedly did, not only by the copious and resigned sacrifice of such calculations, but by his meeting in every single case all the expenses of the process" (330).

James writes with a great deal of affection for his father and the outward equilibrium with which his father responded to his lack of recognition; he also expresses genuine regret at his own lack of responsiveness to and interest in his father's ideas (331–32; I say more about these passages in part 2). But over and again James suggests that his father was a failure and his lameness was somehow responsible for or implicated in this failure. Through his frequent allusions and turns of rhetoric, James even touches on the possibility that, having also incurred an injury fighting a fire in his youth, he was repeating his father's history. Among the risks his younger self faced was the possibility that, like his father, he would be lamed for life and become professionally negligible and obscure. No wonder he claims that he would have been "good for nothing, all my days" if he failed to make "some show" of life.

Yet the likeness between father and son also enables James to highlight the difference between his father's situation and his own and, in doing so, to make an important statement about the resolution of his identity crisis and the nature of his career. Of particular importance is the fact that James depicts his obscure hurt as the means by which he was launched in that career. The doctor consulted in Boston failed "to do anything but make quite unassistingly light of the bewilderment exposed to him" (416). As in the recovery process depicted in his letters from 1912–1913, James was left alone, unaided, to discover a solution to his malaise. As a result, he came to think of his "relation" to his injury as a "*modus vivendi* workable for the time" (416). Under the cover of studying law at Harvard, he would be able to go about his business of observing life and reading literature, and, because of the injury, he would be able to do nothing more than to "let everything slide—everything but the mere act of rather difficultly living (by reason of my scant physical ease)." Having thus "fallen back again on the hard sofa of certain ancient rooms in the Winthrop Square," he was able to hold "to my nose for long and sustaining sniffs the scented flower of independence" (439). Here he wooed "the muse of prose fiction"; here he "formally addressed" himself to the "profession of literature" and awaited the response of the periodical to which he submitted his first story (439, 448). Later came "the prodigious little assurance . . . that fortune had in store for me some response" to his "deeply reserved" but "unabashed design" to become thoroughly literary. Later came the faith in his ability to "write with sufficient difficulty and sufficient felicity" that he could get himself published and earn a living with his pen. He even calls attention to the "very greenbacks, to the total value of twelve dollars, into which I had changed the cheque representing my first earned wage" from these literary labors (475, 476).

Once his decision to go to law school gave him the appearance of doing something acceptable, his "obscure hurt" gave him a reason to stick to his rooms and embark on his literary career. Thus the autobiographer who was struggling to recover from an illness has written a life story in which physical disability both creates and represents the crisis point of his life and the means by which he finally achieves independence. He has written a story in which his physical injury enables him to depart from the example of his father and become a professional writer with something tangible to show for his efforts—not only his publications but the money he earned from them as well.

144

When Minny Temple dies at the end of *Notes*, the young James is well launched in the world of letters and her death marks the "end of our youth" and the beginning of James's adult life (544). Her illness and death emphasize the message of his personal account—the paradoxical power of his disability to threaten his security and enable him to move beyond it. Minny's death highlights his own capacity to survive and succeed (I say more about this use of Minny in part 2). The concern he expressed earlier in *Notes* about his father's negative vocational model has been resolved by a conclusion that emphasizes the distance he has come from his father's fate (and the fate of relatives like Minny). Perhaps James's description of his shingles episode in 1912 as a "visitation" and his commitment to self-healing and work is meant to recapitulate the terms of personal and professional survival narrated in *Notes*; perhaps the story in *Notes* was informed by the healing process in 1912 and 1913. Summarizing our conversation on this topic several years ago, Eakin concludes that "it is equally possible that James's concern with illness and disability in the autobiography may have been conditioned by his maladies at the time of writing. In all probability text and context operated symbiotically, each determining and determined by the other."[9] In all probability James's deeply rooted awareness of the relationship between his father's "vastation/visitations" and disappointing professional life also informed the shape of both his epistolary and autobiographical accounts.

Obscure hurt! Physical disability! Identity crisis! The mysterious but disabling injury that enables James to achieve his ambition of becoming a writer represents the pain and confusion of a crisis associated with his father's lameness and marked by fears of invalidism. It also represents the obscure but potent shame that lies at the heart of his struggle to discover his vocation and act upon that discovery. We recall that in *A Small Boy and Others* the boy's sense of himself as inept and failed was continually figured as a pervasive sense of humiliation and shame; we saw that this emotional condition was quietly and subtly related to his sense of paternal incoherence and insignificance. In *Notes of a Son and Brother* James's struggle to discover the purpose of consciousness and to become a writer is fraught with feelings of shame as well.

He is aware, for example, that his rich "impressional harvest" in Geneva could never have "passed at the time for the sort of thing one exhibits as a trophy of learning" (241); he was also aware of being "ashamed" of the "dark difficulty" that his impressions had created for him by clamoring for expression: "Impressions were not merely all right but were the dearest things in the world; only one would have gone to the stake rather than in the first place confessed to some of them, or in the second announced that one really lived by them and built on them" (253, 254). In other words, James's shame was predicated on his awareness that, however much he delighted in his impressions, his developing aesthetic consciousness was negligible in the eyes of the world, so "little" it "seemed to fit into any scheme of" the outward or "the conventional" (411). That is one of the reasons why he wishes to pursue his literary interests under the "rich cover of obscurity" at Harvard. Posing as a law student, he need reveal his true interests to no one.

When he says that he would have been "good for nothing" for the rest of his life, James suggests that he ran the risk of being crippled not only by his physical injury and emotional confusion but also by the shame he felt concerning his identity as a vaguely artistic young man. As such the obscure hurt he incurred at the start of the war represents more than a physical injury that itself is "bristling with embarrassments" (414); it represents as well the condition of shame, the shame-woundedness, that pervaded the young James's identity. Psychologists contend that shame is often experienced as a wound or generalized ache; James himself often figured shame in his fiction as an injury or a wound, and we have seen that members of the James family often claimed to be wounded by behavior that in some way cast a shameful light on the family.[10] As the association of the hurt with his father's physical and vocational lameness suggests, the hurt in all its vastness and obscurity represents the vague, wounded feeling of confusion and unworthiness that was his inheritance in the family. Perhaps this is one of the reasons he is vaguely aware that his "hurt" will penetrate more deeply and will be of longer duration than the historical episode might suggest: "what was interesting from the first was my not doubting in the least its duration. . . . The interest of it, I very presently knew, would certainly be of the greatest" (415). Paradoxically, it is not just the embarrassing injury but also the pain of shame-woundedness that propelled James to use the hurt as the means to move beyond it, to fuel his drive to get beyond his father's fate and become a sought-after and published writer.

What complicates our sense of the magnitude of James's shame experience, the depth of his obscure hurt, is the oft-made suggestion in *Notes* not only that through his wound he is reexperiencing his father's history but also that his father directly contributed to the presence of the wound and the pivotal role it played in his life. I refer, in part, to the subtle pressure that Henry, Sr.'s, lack of a distinct vocational identity put on his children, his second son in particular. I refer to the professed indifference to other forms of social identity—membership in a church, for example—that left Henry, Jr., feeling as if he were living in a social void. I refer to his father's habit of making light of his children's need to portray their father as having a verifiable social identity; "It seemed . . .

indeed greatly to amuse" our father "that he should put us off with strange unheard-of [vocational] attributions, such as would have made us ridiculous in our special circles" (278). In fact, James remembers his father as not infrequently exposing his children to humiliation; "[p]eople stared or laughed . . . and I disliked their thinking us so simple" when, for example, it was announced that the family would return to America so that William could study painting (275). Especially crucial to this portrait of Henry, Sr., is his unwillingness to respect his children's individual interests and talents and his inability to provide them with the proper educational and vocational guidance. As such, the father's role in the history of the fostered imagination that James began in *A Small Boy and Others* comes under a stunning indictment in *Notes of a Son and Brother*. We recall that James's account of his father's attention to him as a small boy gradually gave way to a confused and apologetic story of his father's incoherent approach to their European travels and his children's education. But this was an approach from which the small boy could inwardly profit. In *Notes of a Son and Brother*, the boys are growing older and beginning to consider their future. Here, Henry, Sr., is portrayed as thwarting their talents or interfering in their vocational plans. He is thus portrayed as blocking the boys' attempts to nurture themselves and provide for themselves what their father lacked—a direction in life and a socially recognized vocation.

James begins his account of the ways in which his development was thwarted in the very first chapter of *Notes*. He is "wonderstruck" at the fact that his parents entertained such "a flattering misconception of my aptitudes" that they enrolled him in a school in Switzerland with a math and science curriculum. "I puzzle it out to-day," he concludes, "that my parents had simply said to themselves, in serious concern, that I read too many novels, or at least read them too attentively—*that* was the vice" (240–41). But once he emerged from the school "an obscure, a deeply hushed failure," once he emerged from a period he described as "mere darkness, waste and anguish," his parents quickly compensated for their mistake. They "allowed me now the happiest freedom, left me to attend such lectures as I preferred, only desiring that I should attend several a week, and content . . . that these should involve neither examinations nor reports" (241, 240, 244). Clearly the "freedom" merely to attend lectures is a welcome contrast to the rigor of the math and science curriculum, but James suggests that too much direction in the young Henry's education was superseded by no direction at all.

What soon follows is the chapter which addresses the struggle between William and his father over William's determination to become a painter (chapter 3). William's "declared preference for a painter's life over any other" met with his father's resistance on the grounds of his children's "spiritual" development. Not only did Henry, Sr., respond with "indifference" to the initial "manifestation of special and marketable talents and faculties" but he also endorsed proclivities and interests that would, in some unspecified fashion, promote the expansion of their souls: "What we were to do instead was just to *be* something, something unconnected with specific doing, something free and uncommitted, something finer in short than being *that*, whatever it was, might consist of." Thus the "career of art" was denounced by their father as "failing to uplift the spirit," and William's subsequent pursuits, science, psychology and philosophy, were likewise denounced as "comparatively narrowing" (267, 268, 269).

Eakin observes that James uses "his father's response to William at this critical moment" to prefigure the struggles he would undergo when "I myself, later on, began to 'write.' "[11] And when he did begin, the autobiographer recalls, "it was breathed upon me with the finest bewildering eloquence" that the literary life "was narrowing" as well (269). Both his and William's vocational problems were compounded by the fact that, although they were continually encouraged to experiment with the "choice as to the 'career,' " they were discouraged when they made "any very earnest proposition in particular." At the first "visible result" of any talent or interest, however, Henry, Sr., would express "delight" in the "fruits of application" (302, 268), a reversal of position suggesting that Henry, Sr.'s, approach to careers was informed by a fear of taking risks, and that fear was replaced by delight at patent examples of worldly success.

This inconsistent approach to the children's specific interests and vocational leanings became especially troubling to the young Henry James when the boys broached the possibility of attending college. James remembered the "great revulsion of spirit" his father experienced with regard to the years he spent at Union College. He had ceased to believe in the value of Union College, but without "forming on the other hand, with his boys to place, any fonder presumption or preference" (303). Nonetheless, in the autumn of 1861 William left Newport to enroll in the scientific school at Harvard University, and a year later Henry followed. James is troubled by the memory of this sequence of events because of Henry, Sr.'s, characteristic inconsistency. Having originally discouraged Henry from attending Harvard, his father enthusiastically reversed his position: "To have deprecated the 'college course' with such emphasis only so soon afterwards to forswear all emphasis and practically smile, in mild oblivion, on *any* Harvard connection I might find it in me to take up, was to bring it home, I well recall, that the case might originally have been much better managed" (309, 413). The phrase, "mild oblivion," is especially critical of his father's lack of mindfulness about Henry's future.

To make matters worse, because of his fine "bewildering eloquence," Henry, Sr., could force his will on his children without seeming willful: "The only thing was that our father had a wonderful way of being essentially right without being practically, or as it were, vulgarly, determinant" (269, 267). He could insist on his own agenda yet consistently communicate the force of his "passionate tenderness" for his children (269). At times, he could even get his children to identify against their interests by taking his point of view: "They had by the contagion of their good faith got me in a manner to agree with them; since I could almost always enter, to the gain of 'horizon' but too often to the perversion of experience, into any view of my real interests, so-called, that was presented to me with a dazzling assurance" (241).

Henry, Sr., also had a way of discouraging successes in the lives of his boys by professing the belief that failures and mistakes acquired "an interest greater than was obtainable by the too obvious success." The "marked achievement" seemed to Henry, Sr., to be no less beneficial to the "life of the soul" than the "marked shortcoming." In fact, in a passage I quoted in my discussion of Henry, Sr., James claims, "I am not sure indeed that the kind of personal history most appealing to my father would not have been some kind that should fairly proceed by mistakes" (301). While their father was busy "appreciating failure," the children would be left "with our small savings, our little exhibitions and complacencies, rather on our hands" (301). Once again, the father seems to be imposing his need to justify the course of his own life on the aspirations of his children. When he notes that the "repeated cases" of "disparagement" towards the boys' affairs were suggested by the "stirred memories" of his father's own past, James further clarifies the relationship between his father's personal history and his parenting of his sons (302). James was not consciously aware of the nature of the rift between his father and grandfather; yet *in Notes of a Son and Brother* he also suggests that his grandfather's disparagement of his son Henry was passed along through that son to his grandsons.

The organizational scheme of *Notes of a Son and Brother* is particularly relevant to this negative interpretation of Henry, Sr.'s, parenting. James begins *Notes* with two chapters about his education abroad and the gradual emergence of his artistic sensibility. Here his discussion of Bob's lack of preparation for adult life (chapter 2) prefigures the issue of vocational choice, of education and training, and of parental involvement (or lack thereof) in the boys' vocational futures (261). Before going on with his avowedly autobiographical account in chapter 9, James then allocates three chapters to matters related to William's and his own education and three more to their father (3–5, 6–8; respectively). Eakin demonstrates that these chapters "have an unmistakable relevance to the more distinctly autobiographical focus of the chapters that precede and follow them." William's struggle with his father over his choice of a career prefigures Henry's, as noted above, and the chapters on Henry, Sr., not only take up his father's views on religion and vocation but also include "the negative assessment of his father's career that," as Eakin puts it, "keeps rising to the surface of his account."[12]

Henry, Sr.'s, correspondence in chapters 6, 7, and 8 of *Notes* provides additional insight into the father's vocational struggles. Chapter 6 includes Henry, Jr.'s, revised version of his father's 1842 letter to Ralph Waldo Emerson in which, discouraged at the poor turnout for his lectures, Henry, Sr., asks his friend, "What shall I do? Shall I get me a little nook in the country and communicate with my *living* kind. . . . Or shall I follow some commoner method—learn science and bring myself first into man's respect, that I may thus the better speak to him?" (345). In chapter 7, James quotes a letter to Emerson in which, lamenting the lack of "educational advantages . . . in my youth," Henry, Sr., proclaims that with such "advantages" he "should probably have been now far more nearly ripe for this world's business" (369). There is a certain irony to the presence of the father's self-reflections within the son's narrative of vocational struggle. The man who struggled with the question "What shall I do?" and looked to his friend for advice appears in his son's story as a hindrance and an obstacle. Henry, Sr., even comments on his own limitations as a parent when, in one of the letters in *Notes*, he describes the parental sentiment as a burden and, in another, claims that he is rendered unfit for work by his anxieties over his children (269, 407–08). He claims in yet another letter that he is "so little wilful" about the family's travel plans in Europe "that I am ready the young ones should settle them" (374).

Contained within the letters, then, and presented as part of James's narrative about vocational choice, are passages that supplement the son's ambivalent analysis of his father's attitude towards work and his relationships with his sons. Perhaps the letters allow him to say through his father more than he was willing to say about his father himself. (Did his anxieties about his children, for example, render him unfit to be a parent?) Donna Przybylowicz believes that James's alterations of his father's letters (and his brother's) reveal his "suppressed antagonism" towards the older men in his family. In "one of his father's letters, which manifests dejection and despair, he deletes parts that show Henry Sr.'s strong resolutions to cast off such black moods" and, in doing so, offers a view of his father's personality as not particularly stable or reliable. Habegger has also shown that James chose "to retain two separate passages" in Minny Temple's letters that "cast a highly unflattering light on his own father." "The fact that he retained Minny's 'disgusted' response" towards his father's " 'ignoble and shirking doctrines' . . . is a suggestive hint about James's attitude in old age toward his contradictory and evasive father."[13] These alterations also enable James to emphasize the contrast between his father's professional life and the more successful life for which he, as a beginning writer, was preparing himself.

Through all of his attention to the issue of vocational choice in his family—first through the chapters on William, then through the material on his father—James has thus prepared us for the fullness and complexity of the personal crisis that began with the outbreak of the war. Although the war was the momentous event that clarified his vocational confusion and forced him to take action, the war also became a symbol for both the personal struggles the young Henry was experiencing and the conflict in the family that contributed to his struggles. An event that finally released the pent-up hostility between the North and the South, the Civil War in James's narrative signals the presence of the unexpressed but smouldering personal anger implicit in the conflict between the two eldest James boys and their father. And the complex indeterminancy of the obscure hurt which matches the wounds of soldiers touches not only on his personal shame and vocational uncertainty, informed by his multi-generational inheritance, but also on the emotional wound that was inflicted on him by his father's self-interested mismanagement of his sons' affairs.

For all of his honesty about his father, James also brings to his analysis a good deal of vagueness, evasion, and dismissal. Perhaps it is this tendency towards evasiveness that contributes in part to James's understanding of his hurt as "obscure." He knows he was wounded when he was young; he never doubted "in the least its duration." He knows that his was a "private catastrophe . . . bristling with embarrassments" (415, 414). Yet his unwillingness both then and now to look as directly as possible at his father's behavior guaranteed that the nature of the wound must itself remain confused and contradictory, concealed and obscure.

What of the mother of the family, Mary James? "Significantly," says Eakin, "James concludes his most extended analysis of his father [chapter 6] with a tribute to his mother." *A Small Boy and Others* and the rest of *Notes* make but a few brief references to Mary James, and "the typescript revisions" of *Notes* indicate that the material about the mother was inserted in chapter 6 only after the chapter was finished.[14] (It comes between the end of his discussion of his father's work and the beginning of the presentation of his father's letters to Ralph Waldo Emerson.) The memorial to Mary James that emerges in this addendum is strong on euphemism and weak on detail, and it begins with James's consideration of the impossibility of adequately representing his mother and what she meant to them: "To have attempted any projection of our father's aspect without an immediate reference to her sovereign care for him and for all of us . . . to have so proceeded has been but to defer by instinct and by scruple to the kind of truth and of beauty before which the direct report breaks down" (342).

To write about his mother and her selfless investment in her family, in other words, would be to defer to the kind of transcendent reality, the "kind of truth and of beauty," that defies direct expression. When his mother died in 1882, James professed that her death had given him a "belief in certain transcendent things—the immanence of being as nobly created as hers—the immortality of such a virtue as that"; he also believed that the silence or "eternal stillness" following her death was but a "form of her love." Now, many years after her death, his filial impulse demanded that he preserve the "holy joy" of her silence. As he exclaimed to Harry, when the nephew wondered about the absence of attention to Mary James in *Notes*, "Oh! my dear Boy—that memory is too sacred."[15]

In spite of his temptation to begin and end his tribute with an appreciation of her divine inexpressibility, James nonetheless goes on to ask, "yet what account of us all can pretend to have gone the least bit deep without coming to our mother at every penetration?" For his mother, he continues, lived solely for the members of her family. "We simply lived by her, in proportion as we lived spontaneously," he explains. For their father, she "was a support on which" he "rested with the absolute whole of his weight." She could listen to him read from his papers "by the mere force of her complete availability, and could do it with a smoothness of surrender that was like an array of all the perceptions." As for the rest of them, she "lived in ourselves so exclusively, with such a want of use for anything in her consciousness that was not about us and for us." Really, he concludes, "she *was* he," their father, and additionally "*was* each of us, was our pride and our humility, our possibility of *any* relation, and the very canvas itself on which we were floridly embroidered" (342, 343–44).

What we see here, of course, is the nineteenth-century prescription for woman as "angel" of the house. In his notebook from 1882, James claimed that "she is no more of an angel today," after her death, "than she had always been," and the angelic quality of her existence derived from the fact that hers "was a perfect mother's life—the life of a perfect wife." Totally focused on her family, she lived in them and for them; she expended "herself, for years, for their happiness and welfare—then, when they had reached a full maturity and were absorbed in the world and in their own interests—to lay herself down in her ebbing strength and yield up her pure soul to the celestial power that had given her this divine commission."[16] Now, as then, Henry sees his mother through the lens of the nineteenth-century belief in women's self-sacrificing, other-directed, divinely-sanctioned identity; now, as then, he sees his mother through the lens of that belief as it was codified for the family in his father's writings about women. Woman "is above all things else," wrote Henry, Sr., "a form of *personal affection*. . . . Her aim in life is not to gratify her passions, is not to enlarge her intellect, is not to perform great actions, though, of course, all these issues take place incidentally; but simply to love and bless man."[17]

Even as James's conventional idealization of his mother as living for others provides a rationale for portraying his mother, however briefly, in this chapter on his father, it also explains one of the reasons why James virtually absents her from the rest of his account. Not only does her transcendent nature speak most eloquently in silence, he would contend, but her highly spiritualized nature can only be properly honored and appreciated in private. To go into greater detail about his mother, to quote and reflect upon her letters, would be to consign her memory to the public sphere of his autobiographical discourse, a personal account intended for public consumption, and to present her thus would be to defile her nature as woman and desecrate the sacredness of her memory. As Henry, Sr., once wrote, no right thinking individual could "willingly think of woman coming before the public . . . home *is* the true sphere of woman . . . the seal which society sets to the private or individual sacredness of its members."[18]

The problem with the son's treatment of his mother's memory along the lines of his father's thinking about women is that Mary James has been doubly silenced by the James family men, first in life by her husband, and second in her son's memoir. I have already quoted Habegger's observation that "the preponderance of evidence indicates that" Henry, Sr., "enjoyed a commanding relationship over his wife. She gave up her Christian orthodoxy in marrying him, accepted and defended his ideas, read less and less on her own, and remained silent in those family arguments where her husband's voice boomed loudest."[19] Here in *Notes*, Mary James is never allowed to speak in her own voice through the medium of her letters (or through letters that her son would have revised). And the few paragraphs about her self-sacrificing character are inserted in a narrative devoted to the obviously more important subject of the education and training (or the lack thereof) of the James family men. Like his father in life, the second son as autobiographical narrator ensures that the story of his development over-shadows the portrait of the only woman from his immediate family presented in the text, and presented even then in what seems to have been an afterthought.

Some critics contend, however, that James's relative silence about his mother speaks more than he intended and that her absence is felt as a confusing, troubling presence in the story of her second son's life. Edel believes that James's remark to his nephew—"Oh! my dear Boy—that memory is too sacred"—functions both as an explanation and an evasion. Perhaps, says Edel, James experienced difficulty seeing his mother "as she really was. He tries with all his artistic honesty; he asks questions, he wonders, he justifies, but mainly he idealizes. We may speculate that he experienced difficulty simply because he was emotionally confused by his memories of his mother and rather than record the confusion he took refuge in the 'sacredness' of the tomb." But Edel goes on to note that, like his writings about his father, James's confusion about his mother emerges "in spite of himself." Particularly troubling are the implications that his mother has lived entirely for and through her husband and children. "The only thing I might well have questioned," writes James, "was the possibility on the part of a selflessness so consistently and unabatedly active of its having anything ever left *acutely* to offer; to abide so unbrokenly in such inaptness for the personal claim might have seemed to render difficult such a special show of it as any particular pointedness of hospitality would propose to represent" (343). James seems to be saying, Edel concludes, that "without her family Mary James ceased to have a personality and ceased, also, to be an individual."[20]

To have thus lived without an identity suggests that Mary James was an unfit subject for an autobiographer to memorialize. There is next to nothing to say about a woman who had nothing to offer or show for herself or who, to put it another way, must have been colorless, boring or banal. The letters from family members which James uses in *Notes* are distinguished by a characteristic intelligence or liveliness and, in the case of his younger brothers' Civil War letters, by their historical importance and what James calls their "military mastery of statement" (462). It may be that James did not find his selfless mother sufficiently interesting or distinguished to represent through her letters and his reminiscential commentary.

The fact that James questions his mother's ability to offer a self to her family raises further doubts about the emotional adequacy of his parents. What does it say about James's one-legged father, for example, that he "rested with the absolute whole of his weight" on a woman who lived so completely through her family that she had nothing "*acutely* to offer"? What does it say about Henry, Sr., that he enjoyed the "brief illusion of publicity" because his devoted but intellectually useless wife listened "with the whole of her usefulness" to whatever he had to say? "She lived in ourselves so exclusively," James suggests, that "we almost contested her being separate enough to be proud of us—it was too much like our being proud of ourselves" (342, 343). We can only conclude that, with nothing "in her consciousness that was not about us and for us," Henry James, Sr., saw only his own confused and unpopular ideas reflected back to him, unchallenged and unchanged, through the tacit support and approval of his wife (343). James says, in fact, that the children "were delightfully derisive with her even about pride in our father—it was the most domestic of our pastimes" (343).

Not only does the emotional strength and credibility of both parents come under indictment in this portrait of unquestioning mutual dependence—if each of them lived so fully in and through the other, which of them had a self?—so too does their ability to provide adequate support, direction, and guidance for their children. If she was nothing without her children, James seems to suggest, and too fully absorbed in them to have an identity of her own, then Mary James could hardly have been emotionally present for her children. She appears to have vaguely provided a model for the young Henry in developing his own interests or protecting himself from the intensity of his father's personality: "I owed thus supremely to my mother that I could, in whatever obscure levity, muddle out some sense of my own preoccupation under the singular softness of the connection that she kept for me, by the outward graces, with that other and truly more intenser which I was so little framed to share" (344).

But if their father leaned upon Mary with "the absolute whole of his weight" and depended upon her to affirm his ideas, then Mary James would have been unable to challenge directly Henry, Sr.'s, muddled theories about the benefits of foreign travel and education for their children. "In the context of so transitory a family," writes William Veeder, James

might well wonder about a father who risked taking his five young children to Europe three times in a decade. The very ships that plied the Atlantic often went down like stones. . . . Virtually every year from the ages of six to sixteen he was placed in a different school. . . . Young Henry needed self-protectiveness all the more because the expectable bulwark against his father's unconscious lethalness—his mother—proved startlingly ineffectual in the face of Henry, Sr.'s, migratory urges. Instead of putting her foot down, Mary went along with her husband, in every sense.[21]

Elsewhere Veeder writes that James's evasive indictment of his mother's refusal to stand up for the children's interests is rendered all the more potent by the fact that, if anything, nineteenth-century mothers were supposed to put their children first: "Though the Good Wife should heed her husband, the woman's paramount responsibility—orthodoxy was unambiguous on this point—was to her children. Thus in stressing Mary James' conventional selflessness, Henry was implicitly reproving her unconventional failure to assert herself on behalf of him."[22]

But the "danger of maternal passivity" was compounded for Henry by "the other side of Mary's character—the aggressiveness of her smothering attentions" to the son who was most lovable and compliant. The "uncomplaining Harry was her favorite, her 'angel,' " as Jean Strouse observes, and her letters suggest that she frequently soothed her anxieties about his solitary life abroad by wishing to bathe him in her maternal affections. Beneath his mother's maternal intrusiveness, beneath her anxious smothering attention, however, was the emotionally unavailable or narcissistic mother described by Alice Miller in *The Drama of the Gifted Child* (quoted in Chapter 1 of this study) or the eternally present but nonetheless emotionally absent, even frightening mother, the maternal presence-in-absence, posited by James's psychoanalytic critics. Perhaps James's "fictional mothers," Beth Ash argues, "were never endowed with the selflessness he attributed to his own mother *because* he knew all too well that a selfless mother could make selfishly illegitimate demands."[23]

At the core of his obscure and euphemistic idealization of his mother, then, may be James's need to defend himself against a sense of anger, deprivation, and shame that goes much deeper than his conscious, enforced, or voluntary memories of his mother. Seen in this light, Henry, Sr.'s, presence in *Notes* functions as a kind of substitute or cover for Mary. As autobiographical narrator, James can focus more fully on his father, even to the extent of troubling himself with paternal ambiguities, in order to avoid the more archaic and obscure pain associated with his earliest relationship with his mother.[24] As such, James's description of his mother is obscurely, yet intimately woven into the ambivalent critique of the parenting he received in his boyhood and early manhood, and his mother's emotional absence functions as yet another source of the "obscure hurt" or "huge comprehensive ache" that unexpectedly facilitated his literary vocation.

II

They are what I see, and are all I want to
see, as I look back.
—Henry James, 1914

Every autobiography is "in some degree a drama of intention," an unfolding interplay between the rhetorical and psychological motives behind an autobiographer's public recollection of personal history.[25] Much of what I have written about *Notes of a Son and Brother* demonstrates that James's intentional drama is particularly troubling and complex. James is committed to portraying his family yet determined to talk about himself. He is ashamed of the insubstantiality of some of his memories, yet proud that his consciousness retained so many impressions from the past. His subtle but unmistakable efforts to explore the truth about the past and the reality of his upbringing are frequently countered by his expressed desire to gloss over painful realities and idealize the world of his childhood. Indeed, in a narrative in which his anxieties about the past seem particularly intense, James is especially forthright about his wish to render his past in a positive and comforting light.

At one point in *Notes*, for example, James clearly defines as "commemorative" his purpose in bringing to light the figures from his past. He wants to celebrate or honor the memories of family and friends, and just what this memorializing process entails becomes itself the subject of much of his commemorative discourse. His discussion of the painter John La Farge in chapter 4 is the best case in point. James moves from considering the example of the artist that LaFarge represented for him—the "artist's serenity," according to LaFarge, "must never brook defeat"—to recollecting his personal response to LaFarge's confidence at a time when his own artistic interests were still vague and ill-defined. Given the powerful attraction that LaFarge held for him, James claims to have felt a certain "quietus" about his own interests, "so far," he adds, "as that mild ecstasy could be divorced from agitation." The mention of "ecstasy" and "agitation" suddenly becomes for James an occasion to reflect on the way in which certain emotions rise to the surface of his memory more readily than others: "I recall at all events less of the agitation" of those "primary months . . . than of the ecstasy." But what seems to be an involuntary process of recalling the joys of the past becomes in the next sentence the inevitable result of his imaginative re-creation of the past in the present: "one *must have taken for joys of the mind and gains of the imagination*" all of the "fine accomodations, acceptances, submissions, emotions" of the time (my emphasis). James then concludes with a mandate: Regardless of the historical truth of the past, regardless of the agitation he recalls, the "joys" and the "gains" are "what I see, and are all I want to see, as I look back; there hangs about them a charm of thrilled good faith, the flush and throb of crowding apprehensions, that has scarce faded and of which I can only wish to give the whole picture the benefit" (295, 296).

When he goes on to memorialize William, James's desire to bring out the best of his personal past extends to the life of his family: "yet these familiar pages [of William's letters] testify most of all for me perhaps to the forces of amenity and spontaneity, the happy working of all relations, in our family life" (309). No matter that the letter hints at the troubles William causes his mother when he is home from college, the "general purpose" of the entire volume, he writes to Harry, was from the start "to be a reflection of all the amenity and felicity of our young life of that time at the highest pitch that was consistent with perfect truth—to show us all at our best for characteristic expression and colour and variety and everything that would be charming."[26]

In particular, James wants to preserve his youthful perspective on the world that, for all of his young troubles, was once bright with hope and possibility. It is the "charm of thrilled good faith" in the people around him and in their futures, the sweetness and beauty of the past, that he wants to recreate and immortalize: "I bottle this imponderable extract of the loitering summers of youth, when every occasion really seemed to stay to be gathered and tasted, just for the sake of its faint sweetness" (296). Like the opening chapters of *A Small Boy and Others*, much of *Notes* is a poetic, almost elegiac meditation on a past that, through the explicit re-creation of memories and the self-conscious reflection of the artistry inherent in the autobiographical act, makes permanent what is fleeting and transitory and makes perfect and refulgent what is disappointing, tarnished, or ruined. It is this desire to idealize and preserve, says David Kirby, that accounts for the many times James casts his memories in the form of paintings, theatrical scenes, statuary, or, in the above example, bottled wine.[27] Art makes and re-makes life, as it were.

To look at the application of James's commemorative purpose in *Notes* is to come at once to his treatment of his mentors, John LaFarge and William Morris Hunt. "In his treatment of John LaFarge," Jane Tompkins claims, "James's attitude of wondering approbation is at its purest and most sustained."[28] We have already seen that LaFarge is celebrated in *Notes* for the contribution he made to the young Henry's development and for the occasion he provides for James to discourse on his commemorative purposes. Looking at the man himself, James recalls that LaFarge "swam into our ingenuous ken as the figure of figures," as a "man of the world." He was "so 'intellectual' . . . really an artistic, an esthetic nature of wondrous homogeneity." Though the "legend" of LaFarge from the Newport period would be altered by subsequent developments or events, James chooses to see his old friend "at this hour again" only as "that bright apparition" of the consummate, serenely confident, cosmopolitan artist who "opened more windows than he closed" and suggested "prospects and possibilities that made the future flush and swarm" (287, 289, 290, 291, 294).

But James's recent memory of a commemorative show of LaFarge's paintings creates a more difficult task for the commemorative autobiographer. Earlier he had stated that LaFarge's "long later history, full of flights and drops, advances and retreats" was beyond the scope of his narrative and belonged "quite to some other record" (291). Now, remembering the show and experiencing "the felt intensity of my commission, as it were, to speak for my old friend," James refuses to pronounce judgement on LaFarge's completed *oeuvre*. Did the commemorative show in Boston, he asks, fail to justify our predictions for LaFarge's future greatness? "I like ambiguities and detest great glares," he answers ambiguously and then takes refuge in his memory of the local scenery that they all "felt and cherished" (297, 299). What he preserves with greatest clarity, in the end, is not his critical assessment of LaFarge as a painter, but his happy memory of that "mythic time" in which they painted together at the Glen, some six miles from Newport: "I quite remember how ours [their measure], that morning, at the neat hostel in the umbrageous valley, overflowed with coffee and griddle-cakes that were not as other earthly refreshment, and how a spell of romance rested for several hours on our invocation of the genius of the scene" (297). His concluding assessment of LaFarge as a painter must, he determines, consist only of his youthful opinion of LaFarge's "large canvas of the Paradise Rocks over against Newport": "On the high style and grand manner of this thing, . . . I would have staked every grain of my grounded sensibility—in spite of which, on second thoughts, I shall let that faded fact, and no other contention at all, be my last word about it" (299).

In his discussion of William's painting teacher, William Morris Hunt, James is likewise faced with the task of assessing a career that subsequently proved disappointing; James's response to this challenge is to preserve his most distant memories of Hunt and to emphasize the painter's contribution to the young Henry's development. Hunt thus becomes a figure of importance in *Notes* because it was in his Newport studio that the young Henry found himself "at the threshold" of the world of art: "Frankly, intensely—that was the great thing—these were hours of Art, art definitely named, looking me full in the face and accepting my stare in return—no longer a tacit implication or a shy subterfuge, but a flagrant unattenuated aim." While William and his teacher worked elsewhere, Henry had "a chamber of the temple all to myself." He was inspired by the paintings in the room, "two or three of Hunt's own fine things," and he insists on remembering that, at the time, he "believed them great productions." As for Hunt himself, the painter was the very figure of the artist, "the living and communicating Artist," who "might have stood, to the life, for Don Quixote." It is only at the end of this portrait that James refers to the failure of Hunt's paintings to appeal to the public and, in doing so, signals the fact that, as a commemorative autobiographer, he is consciously working from the knowledge of harsher and grimmer realities than what appears in his rose-colored memories of the past: "But what he [Hunt] perhaps most puts before me to-day is the grim truth of the merciless manner in which a living and hurrying public educates itself, making and devouring in a day reputations and values which represent something of the belief in it that it has had in *them*, but at the memory of which we wince, almost to horror, as at the legend of victims who have been buried alive. Oh the cold grey luminaries hung about in odd corners and back passages, and that we have known shining and warm" (285, 284, 285, 286, 287).

But James most clearly defines the stance he has taken towards his mentors in his assessment of Nathaniel Hawthorne's career. Writing of the novels that followed *The Scarlet Letter* and inspired by a "sort of *bêtise* of tenderness" for an old master, James claims that "the best charm of a relation" to these (obviously flawed) novels was "in the impulse, known from the first, somehow to stand in *between* them and harsh inquiry" (479). He will adopt a defensive, protective posture for the individuals from his past; he will act as a shield that deflects the hard questions and wards off searching criticism. As such, says Jane Tompkins, James's relationship to the figures from his past is comparable to the relationship that, as defined in *Notes*, his mother established with her family.

Mary James, we recall, lived so much for the family that she "*was* each of us, was our pride and our humility, our possibility of *any* relation" (343). Tompkins believes that, through this "conception of his mother as a medium for other lives," James adopts the "posture of self-effacement, the life-fostering instinct, the mood of radical appreciation, the 'cultivated art of exhibition,' the protective gesture," and other maternal traits.[29] Here Tompkins is helpful in thinking about the ways in which James may have used his idealization of his mother as a model for his role as autobiographical narrator and family biographer. As Suzie Naiburg explains, idealizations do not always function as defenses, and James's idealization of his mother in *Notes* may serve not only as a defense against feelings too painful and complicated to confront in the pages of his text but also as a description of those positive maternal qualities with which he can identify in his role as family biographer.[30]

But James's appropriation of these idealized traits is as complicated as his idealization of his mother. We see, for example, that Tompkins is correct in assuming that James adopts a "*posture* of self-effacement" in order to exhibit the lives of others (my emphasis). But, like the persona James adopts in some of his letters to Harry, this *posture* can be just that—a posture, a pretense, a pose. In his treatment of Hunt and

LaFarge, it is primarily their contribution to Henry's development, not William's, that is underscored in the text, and we have seen that James's discussion of William and Henry, Sr., is structured to anticipate and interpret the young Henry's identity crisis in chapter 9. As such, James's stance towards others is more self-serving than life-fostering, and his appearance of concern for others resembles the essentially self-serving or narcissistic personality that in his mother was disguised by the family rhetoric of domestic affection and maternal perfection. Thus we can understand the autobiographical narrator of *Notes* in terms of the Henry who is still acting the role of the "angel" in the family, the good, cooperative son who, in heeding the "social conscience" of the family, ostensibly puts others first. But behind his compliant facade there exists another, more demanding self who meets his own needs and protects others for the sake of protecting himself. The elderly James as autobiographical narrator is the one, after all, who has positioned the others in the family memoir to shed light on the story of his own development. The elderly James as autobiographical narrator is the one who wishes to avoid feeling the anxiety and agitation that his negative memories of others evoke.

It is with these points that I turn more fully to the psychology at work in James's commemorative purposes and to James's reiteration in *Notes* of the James family myth, a defensive structure intimately intertwined with the family's legends about their father.

The second son, whose ostensible purpose in *Notes* was to shield his loved ones from "harsh inquiry," embarks in chapter 8 on the re-telling of the "most personal, most remembering and picture-recovering 'story' " of his father's young manhood. The story is one that Henry, Sr.'s, children knew well; James remembers his "own inveterate, childish appeal" to his father "in early New York days, for repetition" of this story "in the winter afternoon firelight" (396). The subject is a trip his father made to relatives in Ireland five years after the death of *his* father, William of Albany.[31] In the version of this visit recounted in *Notes*, however, Henry, Sr., appears as the son of his still living father, the son who had not yet been disinherited, and thus as "the representative of an American connection prodigious surely in its power to dazzle." The son of *that* son accordingly finds himself thinking in his autobiography of the dignity of the negro servant who accompanied his father and of "a glamour still more marked" of the "very air" in which his father as "the young emissary would have moved." He even finds himself envying in retrospect "the friendly youth who could bring his modest Irish kin such a fairytale" of self-made American riches "from over the sea" (396).

James then becomes distracted from this account of his father's story by the "melancholy gaze" he casts on "the cloud of images of what might have been for us all that" the fairy tale of grandfather's fortune "throws off." Briefly recounting the fact that William of Albany began making his fortune from the moment he arrived in Albany in 1789, James then begins to wonder—or recalls the way in which Henry, Sr.'s, children wondered—"what had become even in the hands of twelve heirs . . . of the admirable three millions," of the "mass of property" left after William of Albany's death. James's bewilderment prompts him to consider his father's unwillingness to speak about his inheritance. He says that the question of the inheritance "was to flit before my father's children, as they grew up, with an air of impenetrability that I remember no attempt on his own part to mitigate." He adds that their "dear parent, we were later quite to feel, could have told us very little, in all probability, under whatever pressure, what had become of anything. There had been, by our inference, a general history—not on the whole exhilirating, and pressure for information could never, I think, have been applied." What remains of the story his father passed down, then, is the "image" that most appeals to James's "filial fidelity"—the young Henry, Sr., "in the character of the gilded youth, a youth gilded an inch thick and shining to effulgance" before his relatives as the emissary of his immensely successful father (396, 397).

Feinstein believes that it is impossible to separate the father's version of the story in times past from the son's autobiographical rendition; "one or both made the story into the visit of a much younger man" who had not yet been affected by the death of his father and the knowledge of his disinheritance. But Henry, Jr., writes about the event as if he knew "only vaguely of his grandfather's will and nothing of the harsh judgment imposed by that document. This suggestion raises the distinct possibility that the gilded youth rather than the prodigal son was his father's public version of his younger self." Either way, the version in *Notes of a Son and Brother* is one that appeals greatly to Henry, Jr.'s, desire to regard his father in a positive light. It is a version consistent with the anxieties about his father's ineffectuality and inconsistency that surface when Henry, Sr., becomes the focus of his account. The fact that he passed on the story of the "gilded youth" and continued to keep "the affair shrouded in vagueness" shows his willingness to perpetuate the legend of his father's boyhood. It shows that the "aging novelist" had remained loyal "to his childhood part in the family charade."[32]

In psychological terms, legends like the one passed on by the James father and son are stories that uphold a cherished image of a particular member of a family and of the family as a whole. They "contain important messages about how the family should or should not behave and how it should see itself." Although they are presented as true, family legends are "nevertheless edited and re-edited by each generation," much in the way Henry, Jr., may have revised his father's story about the visit to Ireland. But legends may also be woven into a larger, all-inclusive construction about the family that psychologists call the family myth. This myth traditionally consists of the rules or understandings about a family "embodied in the beliefs and mutual expectations that the family members entertain about themselves and the relationship. From their smooth operation, it is apparent that these beliefs are well integrated in the patterns of every day, and have become a fundamental part of the perceptual context within which the family members draw their life together. Although, at times, these beliefs constitute a blatant distortion of the facts, and a flagrant misinterpretation of life in the family—they are shared and supported by all family members, as if they were a sort of ultimate truth that must remain above challenge and inquiry."[33]

Family myths are found in practically all families, and psychologists contend that a certain amount of family mythology may be necessary for the smooth operation of even the healthiest family relationship. But "pathologic" families are often marked by the presence of a rigid family myth, one in which covert rules of behavior often replace those that are explicit or overt. These unspoken but nonetheless firmly-fixed myths defend the family against painful truths and long-buried family secrets. They are "to the family what the defenses are to the individual."[34]

Much of what I have written about the James family speaks to our understanding of how the family myth functions for the Jameses. The legend of Henry, Sr., as a cherished representative of William of Albany's family fits the sanctioned image of the family he created as a mutually devoted, mutually interdependent, intensely loving group. Henry, Sr., and Mary James's family figured their home environment as a kind of "pure paradise" in which the children grew up under the protection of a saintly, self-sacrificing mother and a brilliant, delightful father who, in addition to his writings, devoted himself to being a loving and liberal parent and who used his writings to espouse a philosophy of universal love and brotherhood.[35] We have already seen versions of the family myth in Henry's idealization of his mother in *Notes* and in his description in *A Small Boy* of James family unity: "We were, to my sense, the blest group of us . . . so fused and united and interlocked" (4). We have seen, too, that in *Notes* James was determined to sustain the myth (consciously, at least) by focusing on the warmth, happiness, and spontaneity in their family relations. As he says in chapter 4, the spiritual atmosphere his father created at home was "doubtless delightful," *doubtless* because, regardless of the truth, *delightful* is the way he has determined to regard it (302).

But Henry is not the only James child who, looking back on their childhood, drew on the myth of family perfection. In her *Diary*, Alice not only reiterates the image of their mother's "extraordinary selfless devotion," but also celebrates the perfect love that the parents showered on their children: "It seems now incredible to me that I should have drunk, as a matter of course, at that ever springing fountain of responsive love and bathed all unconscious in that flood of human tenderness. The letters [Father and Mother's] are made up of the daily events of their pure simple lives, with souls unruffled by the ways of men, like special creatures, spiritualized and remote from coarser clay." Robertson, too, remembers his childhood as "a beautiful and splendid childhood for any child to have had, and I remember it all now as full of indulgence and light and color and hardly a craving unsatisfied."[36]

We know that the James children learned at a young age to keep the secrets about the family, to disavow, for example, the conflict between William and his parents or between William and Henry, or to remain satisfied in their ignorance about the relationship between Henry, Sr., and his father. As Strouse contends, the children grew adept at presenting for public and, at times, personal consumption, the mythology of a close-knit, harmonious, and untroubled family. Mary James was the self-appointed guardian of family secrets and shame, the one who upheld the "social conscience" of the family and insisted that the children follow suit. She is even described in *Notes* as the guardian of the children's attitude towards their father. Had "there been danger of" the children lapsing from their "admiration" for father, mother was there with the "sacred reminder" of father's "almost solely self-nourished equanimity" or of his need for *their* support (333). In turn, her husband insisted on the divine saintliness of his wife; he was known, as Alice put it, for "ringing the changes upon the Mother's perfections" and, as such, he insisted on the absolute dependency and blessedness of their union. All of them participated, finally, in perpetuating the image of Henry, Sr.'s, loving benignity, even casting as dear and delightful some of his most characteristic displays of self-indulgence.[37]

Strouse contends that, themselves trained to be articulate and perceptive, the James children grew as "adept" as their father "at giving eloquently ambiguous voice to the way things were supposed to be. They learned to see and not see, say and not say, reveal and conceal, all at the same time."[38] Henry and William may well have picked up on their mother's anxiety about conflict in the family when she reported on Grace Norton's remarks to Alice about sibling rivalry between William and Henry. But they were not allowed to identify this anxiety directly or to admit to their rivalry. Alice in turn unwittingly reveals her hostility towards her father when, recalling her breakdown in the late 1860s, she claims that "I used to sit immovable reading in the library with waves of violent inclination suddenly invading my muscles taking some one of their myriad forms such as throwing myself out of the window, or knocking off the head of the benignant pater as he sat with his silver locks, writing at his table."[39] But Alice would never openly identify that anger towards the "benignant" and supposedly blameless father. In a letter quoted in *Notes of a Son and Brother,* William writes that at home "I see only" father's "striking defects"; but, without naming the defects, he adds that father "seems all perfection" when viewed from a distance: "Having such a Father with us, how can we be other than in some measure worthy of him?" (265–66). And Henry, Jr., clearly picked up the double messages sent all of the children by a number of the dynamics in the family, the relationship between Henry, Sr., and Mary, the parenting practices of both mother and father, and the contradictions in Henry, Sr.'s, philosophy and attitudes towards vocational success, to name a few.

In protecting friends and loved ones in the past from the critical glare that would be cast by an honest evaluation of their lives, James idealizes everyone in the fashion he learned in the family and works each individual into the James family myth. He has turned his own life into a fable of sorts, a story of personal survival and professional growth that remains unchallenged by the problematic events in his adult life, the financial failure of the New York Edition and his nervous breakdown, to name two. He has turned the rest of his account into a fable or fairy tale of the significant others in his past, their relationships to one another and, in particular, their contribution to his development. But, as we have seen, James's success story signals the presence of vague discomforts and anxieties beneath the surface of the text, just as his rationale for romanticizing the lives of others alerts us to the presence of the painful realities he is holding back. That these realities are indeed painful for him as autobiographical narrator, that his mythologizing functions in part as a defense against the personal pain he inherited from his family, becomes especially apparent in his writings on Wilky and Bob. These writings shed a good deal of light on the ways in which, in his own life story, he wants to stand *between* his younger self and "harsh inquiry," to protect his personal history of the imagination from the charge that his passive, artistic approach to life was negligible and ineffectual.

James hints at the difficulties he will encounter writing about his two youngest brothers when he discusses his cousin, William James Temple, one of the most handsome and gifted young men of their youth. My "personal memory," James says of Will's "striking good looks and his manly charm" is "a mere recapture of admiration, of prostration, before him." He had entered Harvard, only to jump "a couple of years of the undergraduate curriculum" and, given Will's lustre, the James children and their friends entertained visions of their cousin's future that were apparently as "radiant" and "splendid" as Will himself. But Will Temple died at Chancellorsville in 1863, and, "thanks to his early death," James retains only the charm of their youthful dreams for his future. The elderly James particularly likes "to think of our easy" imaginative "overstrainings" for Will; he clings to "the idea that the siftings and sortings of life, had he remained subject to them, would still have left" to Will "the lustre that blinds and subdues." He even believes that "blest beyond others" are not the soldiers who died young but the young Henry's dreams or "admirations, even the fondest . . . that were not to know to their cost the inevitable test or strain; they are almost the only ones, of the true high pitch, that, without broken edges or other tatters to show, fold themselves away entire and secure, even as rare lengths of old precious stuff, in the scented chest of our savings" (306–07).

But James's memories of Wilky and Bob were not without the "inevitable test or strain." Initially both of the brothers appeared to have promising futures. They possessed the charm, the wit, and the eloquence of the James family men and, from an early age, they were exposed to the cultural riches of the old world. But both Wilky and Bob's lives were marked by illness or alcoholism, by vocational disappointment and failure. By James's scheme, all they had to show for their adult lives were "the broken edges or other tatters." James thinks, in fact, of the sad case of a "future reduced to the humility of a past" when he considers the boys' post-war attempt to run a Florida cotton plantation with the labor of newly-emancipated slaves. The plantation was a "scene of blighted hopes," a "vain experiment" that "dragged on . . . finally to our great discomfiture." When he thinks of the artistic "material" or "images" that were "wasted" by this failure, James hints at the money, the resources, perhaps even the youthful hopes that were "wasted" as well (461).

A letter written to Wilky's widow, Carrie, in 1913 reveals that some extremely painful feelings informed James's memories of such wasted material and blighted hopes. "*[So] trying, so upsetting indeed to nerves and spirits*," he writes to Carrie about his autobiographical act, "do I sometimes find it to plunge into this faraway and yet so intimate ghostly past, where everything and everyone lives again but to become lost over again, and *what seems most to come forth are the old pains and sufferings and mistakes. . . .* It's not the war letters that are saddest, but those . . . of the dreary attempt at cotton raising in Florida afterwards (it was so unsuccessful and delusive and dismal as to life, even had better things come of it) where his [Wilky's] extreme youth for such wretched responsibilities—his and Bob's—again *bring tears to my eyes*."[40]

Striking about this letter is the way in which it counters James's apparent delight in recalling not the "agitation" of his youth but the "ecstasy" and the joy. To Carrie he claims that the "old pains and sufferings and mistakes" are what surface most in his memory and, in doing so, he invites us to imagine the effort it took to suppress those painful memories and emphasize the heroic or the charming in his brothers' pasts, if not in the pasts of old friends and other members of his family. He feels oppressed by the memory of the delusions that nourished the boys' attempt to run the Florida plantation and the dismal failure that it became; he is powerfully affected by the memory of his brothers' youth at the time they embarked on the experiment. He even admits to crying over the memory of the vulnerable and inexperienced Wilky taking on such a large responsibility. Even had "better things come of it," he says, the Florida venture was "so unsuccessful and delusive and dismal as to life." But the fact that "better things" failed to come must have made James's memory of the venture all the more depressing.

James's memories are also "trying" and "upsetting" because they are associated with the confusion and discomfort he feels over the lack of direction and guidance he, too, experienced as a young man. The failed dreams or "delusions" of the Florida experiment cannot help but be associated with the delusions that nourished Henry, Sr.'s, disappointing career as a self-styled theologian, and it was these paternal delusions that informed so many of James's anxieties about his own career. James's memories of Wilky and Bob are thus intimately associated with the vast and obscure field of negative affect about performance and invalidism, success and failure, honor and shame in the James family men. Because, as Feinstein believes, the younger boys in particular were forced "to bear the mark and the burden" of Henry James, Sr.'s, negative identity—of his "unregenerate prodigality," his "wild youth," and professional amorphousness—memories about them would be particularly fraught with vast and obscure anxieties. They were sufficiently fraught with negative affect, in fact, that in a letter written after Wilky's death, James reveals his satisfaction in having avoided first-hand knowledge of his brother's demise and in taking refuge in his happy memories of Wilky's boyhood. "I can't help being glad that I was spared all that closing spectacle," he wrote to Robertson, "I thank heaven it is over, and that he has become simply a genial, gentle, sociable memory, carrying me back to all sorts of innocent rose-coloured incidents in the far past."[41]

Given James's desire in 1883 to reside only in the "rose-coloured incidents" of Wilky's "far past," it is no wonder that years later in his autobiography he makes as much of Wilky's combat experience in the Civil War as the young Wilky's letters and his own recreative powers will allow him. James had already relied on family letters to organize his portraits of William and Henry, Sr., and family correspondence would enable him to focus and amplify specific events from his younger brother's past as well. But James also wanted to use family documents to present Wilky in the best light possible, and the Civil War letters allow him to build on his brother's provisional identity as a soldier and, along with his own memories of Wilky's military experience, to arrest him in a series of highly romantic, heroic postures untainted by the unhappy years that followed.

The first of such memories appears at the end of a chapter devoted, among other things, to his father's correspondence to a family friend, Caroline Tappan (chapter 7). The last of these letters takes James back to the summer of 1863 when Wilky "received two grave wounds" in the assault of the Massachusetts 54th on Fort Wagner, South Carolina. Henry, Sr.'s, letter describes Wilky's condition, both physical and emotional, and comments on the fact that he has been "educated" by the war "so suddenly up to serious manhood." (It also refers to a spirited letter from Bob describing the work of "building earthworks and mounting guns" at Morris Island.) Although the letter itself depicts Wilky's heroic suffering and emphasizes his desire to return to his regiment, James elevates the scene described in the letter to a memorial to both his father and his brother—and to the emotions experienced by the entire family, the "feast of *our* relief," when the wounded Wilky was restored to them (381, 382, 383).

James begins with an extended disquisition on what he calls "my 'relation to' the War," past and present. Though it was at the time "a mixed and oppressive thing," as his passage on the "obscure hurt" reveals, James claims that his relation to the war "is at present a thing exquisite to me, a thing of the last refinement of romance." Wilky on the stretcher on which he "was to lie for so many days before he could be moved" and next to him the presence of the worried and devoted father of the letter to Caroline Tappan—this picture appears to James "[c]lear as some object presented in high relief against the evening sky of the west." This immortalized memory is fused in James's vision with the image of Cabot Russell's stricken father, the family friend who, searching out his own son, found Wilky instead and "with an admirable charity brought Wilky back to a waiting home." It is further fused with the image of Cabot Russell himself who, having died in battle, now wears "the arrested expression, the indefinable shining stigma" of those fallen in the war (383, 384).

James begins to wind to a close in this passage by discussing his desire to immortalize the dead; "memory and fancy," he says, want, and never cease "to want to 'do' something" for the fallen, to set each "upright and clear-faced . . . in his sacred niche," as in a church or a museum. He imagines them "looking through us or straight over us at something they partake of together but that we mayn't pretend to know," some truth of the experience of war and suffering and death. The "us" includes men like Henry and William "who didn't at the time more happily share their risk," and James thus imagines that "[w]e walk . . . rather ruefully before" the dead as they look out from their niches. But when he immediately ends the passage with an allusion to William's drawing of his "poor lacerated brother's aspect," James neatly suggests the ways in which the untried and uninitiated were nonetheless contributing what they could during that painful historical period. "It tells for me the double story," he explains, "I mean both of Wilky's then condition and of the draughtsman's admirable hand" (384).

The memory of the heroically suffering Wilky has thus been immortalized by James's attention to the specific image of the wounded Wilky lying, immobile, on his stretcher and to the image of a father caring for his emotionally and physically tortured son. Wilky's memory has been further ennobled by its association with the others who made even greater sacrifices and by James's emphasis on his family's emotional reaction both to Wilky's situation and to that of Cabot Russell's father. The immortalizing process is further amplified by James's self-reflexive commentary on his desire to do something fine and lasting for those who died in the war and by his allusion to William's drawing of the "great and tender truth" of Wilky's suffering (384). James's memorial to Wilky many years later is, of course, the verbal counterpart to William's drawing, and the wounded Wilky, as a result, is twice arrested in his memorable pose.

James continues his romanticization of Wilky when in chapter 9 he tries to recover other firsthand memories of his brother as a soldier. He unfortunately missed the sight of the Massachusetts 54th marching out of Boston with Colonel Robert Shaw "at its head and our exalted Wilky among its officers." But Wilky's "quick spring out of mere juvenality" and into the "brightly-bristling ranks" of the Massachusetts 44th, Wilky's first regiment, was "fairly made romantic" for the young Henry by his visit to the regiment's encampment at Readville (423). When he recalls this visit in chapter 11, James then claims that only in a "fairy-tale" this "soft companion of my childhood should have such romantic chances and should have mastered, by the mere aid of his native gaiety and sociability, such mysteries, such engines, such arts" (456). Wilky had already been remembered for his delightful spontaneity and expressiveness. "He could talk with such charm, such drollery of candour, such unexpectedness of figure," James says of his younger brother during their years abroad (258). In chapter 11, James goes on to use Wilky's passionately detailed war letters to illustrate the "military mastery of statement" that grew out of his brother's innate verbal facility and, in this way, to fashion a tribute to Wilky's brief moments of glory from the most characteristic feature of his brother's personality (462).

James's treatment of his youngest brother Bob was fraught with much greater difficulty. Bob himself admitted in 1898 that, should it be told, his life story "would have to be the biography of broken fortunes."[42] Early in *Notes* his brother Henry acknowledged that "there was much and of the most agitated and agitating" about Bob's "deeply troubled" life; here he is able to idealize this life only by celebrating his youngest brother's youthful visit to Italy and imagining what might have become of Bob if he had encountered Italian culture a little later in his development or "enjoyed" a "different sort of pressure" with regard to his education or "training" (261). Later in *Notes*, his chance of romanticizing his brother's life depends upon his recollections of Bob's military service during the war. But Bob's letters from the front were not available; perhaps, says Jane Maher, they "were destroyed by Henry, Sr., to protect Bob's privacy."[43] To make matters worse for the elder brother trying to commemorate the younger, James claims to have been "deprived of any nearness of view of my still younger brother's military metamorphosis and contemporary initiation" into manhood (457). He had acquired none of the first-hand impressions of Bob that he had of Wilky when he visited the Massachusetts 44th at Readville or observed him convalescing at home.

James's portrait of Bob in chapter 11, then, shows James straining his hardest as autobiographer to make something substantial from the thinnest tatters of memory. He romanticizes one of Bob's only distinctions, his military service, by emphasizing the significance of Bob's age when he enlisted and his parents' patriotism in letting him enlist: "[W]e smiled as over the interest of childhood at its highest bloom, and that my parents, with their consistent tenderness, should have found their surrender of their latest born so workable is doubtless a proof that we were all lifted together as on a wave that might bear us where it would."[44] He remembers, too, that Bob was "so eager and ardent" for military service that he "had strained much at every tether," and later refused a discharge after he "suffered a serious sunstroke" while his "regiment was engaged in Seymour's raid on Florida." But James's most significant image of Bob was derived from his memory of a letter written by Bob from Charleston. He says, "though I have too scant an echo of his letters from that scene one of the passages that I do recover is of the happiest." He goes on to quote from memory Bob's description of the moment in which, upon observing the death of his commanding officer during the seige of Charleston, he spurred on his horse and charged the rebel lines. "For this action," James adds, "he was breveted captain" (457, 458).

The problem with this "happiest" of memories is that it was apparently an invention of the autobiographer. Bob himself testified in an 1896 address at Concord, Massachusetts, that "it was not he but a soldier named Dewhurst whose mare" had been involved in the Charleston incident and that the horse, far from being spurred on by a courageous soldier, "had accidentally balked and surged forward" toward enemy lines. Bob's point in remembering this incident was to emphasize the accidental and arbitrary nature of some military events. "On such slender threads as the balking of a horse," he explained, "is suspended the fate of battles."[45] But surreptitiously displaying his own "military mastery of statement," Bob's elder brother recast the moment to suggest that it was Bob who charged the enemy line and that, inspired by his regiment's perilous situation, it was Bob who acted swiftly, deliberately, and decisively. "It was when the line wavered," Henry remembers Bob writing, "and I saw Gen'l Hartwell's horse on my right rear up with a shell exploding under him that I rammed my spurs into my own beast, who maddened with pain, carried me on through the line, throwing men down, and over the Rebel works some distance ahead of our troops." James's version of the letter implies that Bob opened a hole for his troops in the enemy line and was decisive in determining the outcome of the battle. Accordingly, Bob's regiment, the 55th, "was the first body of troops to enter Charleston and march through its streets" (458). A footnote to this reconstructed memory of Bob notes that he, like the other men in the family, possessed the "easiest aptitude for admirable talk"; it includes a poem that illustrates the "note of the ingenious" and the "play of spirit" that occasionally appeared in Bob's unproductive life (458–59). But it is a heroic event re-created in the narrative proper that in his brother's "rose-coloured" memory becomes the high point of Bob's career.

In addition to using (or inventing) whatever personal memories or documentary evidence he could recover about Wilky and Bob, James incorporated into the stories of his brothers' military adventures a discussion of their contribution to his own imaginative development. The "whole quite indescribably intensified time," he writes, was "a more constituted and sustained act of living, in proportion to my powers and opportunities"—"living inwardly," of course—"than any other homogeneous stretch of experience that my memory now recovers" (382–83). In part, he may have felt the need to weave the drama of his personal consciousness into the story of Wilky's and Bob's actions in order to give greater clarity and continuity to his brothers' stories. He may have felt the need to fill out their stories by filling in whatever gaps were created by lapses in memory or time. But James may have also felt that his brothers' highly romantic adventures offered the color and drama missing from an often overly subtle and abstract "personal history" of the imagination and illustrated more fully and concretely his yearning to feast on the rich and romantic adventures of the war (454): "I longed to live by my eyes, in the midst of such far-spreading chances, in greater measure than I then had help to, and that the measure in which *they* had it gloriously overflowed. This capacity in them to deal with such an affluence of life stood out from every line, and images sprung up about them at every turn of the story" (460).

To understand the ways in which James used his brothers to romanticize his personal history, we need to look more fully not only at James's idealizations of his younger brothers but of his father and eldest brother as well. We need to look at the ways in which, as he compensates for what was lacking in the others in his family, family members are used to compensate for what he feared was lacking in himself.

James's portrait of his father in *Notes* raises many doubts about Henry, Sr.'s, consistencies as a parent, his dependencies as a husband, his intelligibility as a theologian, and his reputation as a writer. His son Henry consistently longs for the kind of concrete detail about his father's past that would make Henry, Sr., more comprehensible to the son and bridge the gap that existed between their very different sensibilities (see 340, 350). But in spite of his filial ambivalence, James idealizes his father and mythologizes his role in the family by refusing to scrutinize his father more closely than he does and consider in detail the implications of his father's career. Take, for example, the passage in which he conflates his father's physical disability with his lack of professional success. No sooner does he compare the limits of his father's "material action" with his "scant allowance of 'public recognition'" than James abruptly puts an end to considerations of his father's limitations. "Too many such reflections, however, beset me here by the way," he says, before turning to an area in which his father shines—his letters to Ralph Waldo Emerson (351).

Tompkins observes that, in speaking of the "failure of his father's books and lectures to elicit the slightest public acclaim, James never allows the actual merits and demerits of his work to become an issue. The account focuses instead on the devotion with which those studies were pursued and the magnanimity and gaiety of spirit with which their failure was borne." As if he were modelling his portraits on his father's observation—"I am getting to the time of life when one values one's friends for what they are more than for what they do"—James is primarily interested in the "qualities of the mind and spirit" that, as exemplified in his letters, informed his father's ideas and created the atmosphere of their home (357).[46]

It is his father's correspondence, in fact, that allows James to say the most positive things about his father that he can and, in doing so, to focus not on his father's performance as a parent or writer but on his personality. His father's epistolary discourse is remarkably vivid and energetic, and James revised the passages he selected for publication to make the writing smoother and seemingly more felicitous (and, as one of his letters to Emerson suggests, to omit passages that make his father seem overly effusive, overly discouraged, or excessively dependent on Emerson).[47] "Almost all my dear father is there," he says of his father's May 1868 letter to James T. Fields, "making the faded page to-day inexpressibly touching to me; his passionate tenderness, his infinite capacity for reaction on reaction, a force in him fruitful in so many more directions than any high smoothness of *parti-pris* could be, and his beautiful fresh individual utterance, always so stamped with the very whole of him" (269–70). James uses his father's letters to celebrate his "spontaneity," his "observational powers," his "extraordinarily animated" soul, a soul that *"so far as he himself at least was concerned"* was "guiding and governing" (360, 268; my emphasis). "Almost all of my father shines for me at any rate in the above passages" of Henry, Sr.'s, letters, James maintains, all of "the original charm, the peculiarly social and living challenge (in that it was so straight and bright a reflection of life) of his talk and temper" (362–63). Instead of commenting on the need to limit his reflections on his father's letters, as he limited reflections on his father's career, James feels compelled to present the most attractive passages from his father's (revised) letters and to continue quoting and amplifying; "his expression leads me on and on so by its force and felicity that I scarce know where to stop," he exclaims (352–53).

One of the motives that inspired James to celebrate his father's personality is his memory of having been particularly unresponsive to or uninterested in his father's ideas. In spite of the fact that his mother encouraged the family joke about "your father's *ideas*," "there came to us from our mother's lips . . . a fairly sacred reminder of that strain of almost solely self-nourished equanimity, or in other words insuperable gaiety, in her life's comrade, which she had never seen give way" (333). It is unclear in this passage whether their mother reminded them directly of their father's emotional heroism, or whether she simply modelled for them the kind of verbal support and praise she felt was his due. Either way, James labors not only under the burden of his muted uncertainties about and resentments towards his father's parenting but also under the memory of a filial neglect deemed inappropriate or ungrateful by his mother. James mentions, of course, that the differences between his father's and his own "schemes of importances" communicated "an implied snub to the significance" of his youthful concerns: "I gaped imaginatively, as it were, to such a different set of relations. I couldn't have framed stories that would have succeeded in involving the least of the relations that seemed most present to *him*" (339). Even so, he feels that it was "graceless" of him as a son not to honor the family code and, by sympathizing more with his father's ideas, do greater justice to his father's seemingly self-sacrificial labors. "Our admirable mother," he says, "sat on the steps at least and caught reverberations of the inward mystic choir" that emanated from "the inhabited temple" of father's theological speculations; "but there were positive contemporary moments when I well-nigh became aware, I think, of something graceless, not to the credit of my aspiring 'intellectual life,' or of whatever small pretensions to seriousness I might have begun to nourish, in the anything but heroic impunity of my inattention" (332–33).

By celebrating the "wondrous" nature of his father's character, Henry, Jr., is now making up not only for his youthful lack of interest in his father's philosophy but also for his failure to appreciate the professional burdens under which his publicly unappreciated father labored. He makes a point of noting that William had labored at the task of compensating for his brother's inattention much earlier: "William, later on [particularly in *The Literary Remains*] made up for this not a little, redeeming so, to a large extent, as he grew older, our filial honour in the matter of a decent sympathy, if not of a noble curiosity" (333). By acknowledging William as the son who redeemed "our filial honour," James is also able to amplify William's character in a way that elevates and ennobles his elder brother. Remembering "certain echoes of passages between our father and his eldest son that I assisted at, more or less indirectly and wondering," James recalls that he then discerned "my brother's independent range of speculation, agitations of thought and announcements of difference, which could but have represented, far beyond anything I should ever have to show, a gained and to a considerable degree an enjoyed, confessedly an interested acquaintance with the paternal philosophic *penetralia*" (333).

To some degree, this difference between himself and his eldest brother, a difference that extends to the capacity for sympathy with their father, forms the core of James's initial narrative about William in *Notes*. When abroad, William is the brother who "moved on the higher plane of light and air and ease" than the other three brothers; he is the superior elder brother who enjoyed such a "wondrous" capacity to react that he continually turned from one interest to another, from painting to science, from science to philosophy (262, 269). In everything he touched, William took on for his younger brother Henry "such authority," such a "perpetually quickened . . . state of intellect and character" that, as in the case of painting, Henry was disabused of any "presumption" that he, too, might aspire to William's genius and ability (307, 293).

In part, this complementary portrait of William grew out of the plan with which James originally began his autobiographies—to commemorate William by publishing portions of his letters and, like William did for their father in *The Literary Remains*, by testifying to his remarkable genius. As he wrote to Harry in November 1913 James wanted to make the greatest "claims" for William that he could, to present him at his best and brightest and most expressive. By making frequent comparisons between his younger self and his splendid elder brother, Henry can consistently emphasize as superior William's intelligence, his abilities, and his capacity for life. But he also tries to improve on William's character by revising the tone and the diction of William's letters. " 'Oh but you're not going to give me away, to hand me over, in my raggedness & my poor accidents, quite unhelped & unfriended,' " James imagines William's spirit imploring him; " 'you're going to do the very best for me you *can*, aren't you, & since you appear to be making such claims for me you're going to let me seem to justify them as much as I possibly may?' "[48]

But like his portrait of his father, James's memorial to William is constantly designed to reflect primarily on Henry's youthful development. When seen in this light, Eakin's observation that chapters 3–5 concern William James's choice of career is somewhat overstated.[49] William's interests in art and science introduce these chapters, to be sure, and they accordingly focus the chapters on the James brothers' preparation for a career. But James is directly concerned with William and his delightful (and retouched) letters only at the end of chapter 5. In the meantime, he uses the fact that William studied art with William Morris Hunt and their friendship with the painter John LaFarge to trace his own efforts to discover his vocation and to discourse on his protective attitude towards his mentors. He also devotes a good deal of space to the effect that his father's ideas on religion, education, and vocation had on his as yet "somewhat undetermined, but none the less interesting sons" (394). As usual, it is his own response to these ideas that receives the most attention.

When he returns to William in chapter 12, Henry continues the story of his artistic development by using William as a reflector of the impressions denied to the incapacitated and less active Henry. Earlier he described himself as picking up "and to the effect not a bit of starving but quite of filling myself, the crumbs of his feast and the echoes of his life." He explains that it "was in the day's work if I might live, by the imagination, in William's so adaptive skin" (246–47). Now the intermittent arrival of William's letters from Brazil in 1864 "comes back to me," he claims, "as perhaps a fuller enrichment of my consciousness than it owed for the time to any other single source." Thanks to the "constant hum of borrowed experience" from all of his brothers, he adds, "my stage of life" during the early 1860s "knew no drop of the curtain" (481).

When at the beginning of chapter 11 he announces that his entire narrative grew out of a long cherished desire to tell "the personal history, as it were, of an imagination," he clearly relates his material on William to his autobiographical purpose and even justifies the imaginative appropriation of William's experience at several key points in *Notes*. In other words, William is not just the "pretext" that Henry needed to relate his "personal history." As a medium through which Henry can live, William is also one of the key contributors to the "cultivation" of the young Henry's "imaginative faculty" and the elderly Henry's capacity to recover and reflect so richly on memories from the past (454–55). Henry is going to keep William from appearing in too realistic a "raggedness" in his life and his letters, and William in turn will help fill out and compensate for an inward life that has little to show for itself beyond the vague nuance and tenuous impression.

But William cannot justify his brother's imaginative life in the 1860s as effectively as can the two brothers mentioned earlier in this discussion. We have seen that James wished to defend himself and his account from his memories of his brothers' troubled lives by romanticizing their most glorious moments from the distant past, their Civil War experiences. But Wilky and Bob help their elder brother negotiate the most problematic passage in his narrative—his justification of his failure to fight in the war. James admits that "to have trumped up a lameness," a "horrid" and "obscure hurt," when other young men were rushing to war "could be made to pass in no light for graceful" (415). He is also highly self-conscious about the fact that as autobiographical narrator he must claim as worthy of public attention the inward vibrations and intimations that make up his experience of the war: "There are memories in truth too fine or too peculiar for notation, too intensely individual and super-subtle—call them what one will. . . . Their kind is nothing ever to a present purpose unless they are in a manner stable, but is at the same time ruefully aware of threatened ridicule if they are overstated" (426). At stake in his presentation of his life during the war, then, is the integrity of his justification for not answering President Lincoln's call to arms and, even more, of his assertion that the imaginative life for an American man is as worthwhile and valuable as the active and engaged life.[50] As he said in comparing himself with Wilky in *A Small Boy and Others*, "one way of taking life was to go in for everything and everyone, which kept you abundantly occupied, and the other way was to be as occupied, quite as occupied, just with the sense and image of it all, and on only a fifth of the actual immersion. . . . Life was taken almost equally both ways" (164).

But it is one thing for James to make grand claims for the imaginative life when portraying himself as a small boy; it is quite another, he realized, to depict as equally worthy one's imaginative life at the outbreak of the war. James attempts to compensate for the insufficiency (or cowardice?) of his response by, among other things, claiming that his wounded condition was the equivalent in pain and suffering of the wounds of the soldiers he visited at Portsmouth Grove: "measuring wounds against wounds, or the compromised, the particular taxed condition, at the least, against all the rest of the debt then so generally and enormously due, one was no less exaltedly than wastefully engaged in the common fact of endurance" (426).[51] But James also attempts to elevate and ennoble his status as non-combatant by claiming to have lent to his brothers "visionary 'assistance' at the drama of the War, from however far off." He says that though he "couldn't 'do things,' " he could wonder and gape. He even claims that his wish to experience the war vicariously was superior to his brother's accounts: "I longed to live by my eyes . . . in greater measure than I then had help to." In defining his relation to the war as "seeing, sharing, envying, applauding, pitying, all from too far-off," James also asserts that "whether or no they would prove to have had the time of their lives, it seemed that the only time I should have had would stand or fall by theirs." And though his own experience was clearly not of epic character, his "vision" of Sherman's army as he encountered it through "privileged" Wilky's letters nonetheless became "a vast epic vision" (456, 460, 461, 470, 471).

To read these passages from chapter 11 is to clarify further James's declaration of autobiographical purpose at the beginning of the chapter. Here James claims that as a "teller of tales" he had always been interested in tracing the history of the "man of imagination" and, what is more, that he had conceived of this story as a kind of supreme fiction: "Fed by every contact and every apprehension, and feeding in turn every motion and every act, wouldn't the light in which it might so cause the whole scene of life to unroll inevitably become as a fine a thing as possible to represent?" (454–55).[52] James then goes on to characterize the man of imagination—James himself, of course—as a hero of a special sort: "the man of imagination, and of an 'awfully good' one, showed, as the creature of that force or the sport of that fate or the wielder of that arm, for the hero of a hundred possible fields" (455). The rest of the passage concerns James's disingenuous account of how he finally discovered the "man of imagination" he wished to portray: "What was *I* thus, within and essentially, what had I ever been and could I ever be but a man of imagination at the active pitch?" It moves to consider his readers' evaluation of the failure or success of the project and his assessment of the success he would nonetheless feel in the face "of certain sorts of failure": "I shall have brought up from the deep many things probably not to have been arrived at for the benefit of these pages without my particular attempt." Thus, by the time he turns to a discussion of his visionary participation in the war, James has prepared us to view his former self as "the hero of a hundred possible fields," including the field of war, and his present self as the intrepid autobiographer who, like a deep-sea diver, brings up memories "from the deep" or, like a seasoned soldier, can find value even in the worst sorts of "defeat" (455). From there, the success or credibility of his story must depend on the quality not of his own vision but of Wilky's and Bob's, and, to the extent that he can present their experience as suffused with heroism, color, and romance, so can he present his own.

The James family, we have seen, was characterized by a troubling sense of psychological dependence. Henry, Sr.'s, observation that "what man finds in woman, the satisfaction of his own want, the supply of his own lack" applies to the tendency of family members to depend on each other to compensate for their deficiencies and ward off their shame. In *Notes of a Son and Brother*, James has created a mutually compensatory relationship between his dead brothers and himself and, as such, he has attempted to justify and ennoble all of their lives.

The use to which James puts the women in his family and the image of them that survives constitutes a self-serving act of appropriation that is likewise masked by the sanctity of James's autobiographical art. We have already considered the ways in which James protects himself from directly confronting his memories of his mother, her role in the family, and her relationship to her husband and children through his brief and highly idealized portrait of her. But even this cursory and evasive portrait of his mother exceeds his treatment of the other women in his immediate household. Aunt Kate is barely mentioned in either autobiographical volume, and his sister Alice gets even less space than his mother. When she does appear, Alice is one of the family members described or addressed in the letters written by her eldest brother and her father in the family's correspondence from the 1850s. As such, she appears only as the little sister, object of William's flirtatious banter or father's playful irony. Says William, "cover with kisses the round fair face of the most kissworthy Alice" (311) and "[l]et the delicious little grey-eyed Alice be locked up alone on the day after the receipt of this with paper and envelopes to write a letter unassisted, uncorrected and unpunctuated to her loving brothers" (265). Her father writes, "Our Alice is still under discipline—preparing to fulfill some high destiny or other in the future by reducing decimal fractions to their lowest possible rate of subsistence" (375).

Neither of these letters takes the young Alice seriously as a person; in both, she is contained by the self-exhibiting and expressive discourse of her father and elder brother, defined by their conventional notions of girls as cute, kissable, and ornamental creatures, not to be taken seriously, and devoted to her brothers. What is more, both of these epistolary responses to Alice capture the family dynamics that contributed to Alice's emotional fragility and invalidism—the quasi-incestuous relationship that William established with Alice, a self-serving relationship for William that was confusing and debilitating for Alice, and her father's need to believe that women were intended for no higher "destiny" than marriage and motherhood. Henry, Jr., once remarked that "in our family group girls seem scarcely to have had a chance," and these few examples of Alice as the subject of William's and Henry, Sr.'s, teasing discourse show us why Henry would have made such an observation.[53]

Henry, Jr., is thought to have developed a different, more respectful relationship with Alice. Strouse maintains that "Alice and Henry shared throughout their lives a deeper intellectual and spiritual kinship than either felt with any other member of the family." He was the only male in the family who treated Alice more "as a person" than "as a girl," and early on they developed a special bond, a mutual understanding, that was strengthened, following the death of their father, by Alice's move to England and her dependency on Henry.[54] Yet for all of his closeness to and admiration for his sister, James was unable to portray her in *Notes* because, as he wrote to Harry, Alice's correspondence, her *usable* correspondence, at least, was unavailable: "what I most deplore my meagre provision of is those [letters] of your Aunt Alice written to our parents mainly during her times, and especially her final time, in Europe. The poverty of this resource cuts from under my feet almost all ground for doing much, as I had rather hoped in a manner to do, with her."[55] James claims, in other words, that Alice is unrepresentable without the documents that would focus his remarks about her and provide the "ground" for his memory and imagination. She is particularly unrepresentable without the letters which, written during her European tour in 1872, would have captured Alice at a happy and healthy time of her life.

It is curious that James wrote his sister-in-law in 1911 that, given the absence of Alice's letters, he might rely on "all my own intimate memories" of his sister, much as he had originally planned to rely on his memories of Minny Temple. How do we account for the fact that, in the end, no such memories appear? Associated as they were with "her disastrous, her tragic health" and her life-long emotional dependence on her parents, Henry, Jr., and Katherine Loring, Henry may have felt that his "own intimate memories" of Alice would have unintentionally violated the personal privacy and family honor cherished by Henry and Alice alike. They would have touched too readily on what James explains was the central difficulty of Alice's life, "that the extraordinary intensity of her will and personality really would have made the equal, the reciprocal life of a 'well' person—in the usual world—almost impossible to her."[56]

By omitting his own references to Alice, however, Henry not only silences and erases Alice as the bright and responsive young woman he knew her to have been, but also, by virtue of her appearance in the early letters of the most dominating men in the family, he defines her entirely within a male context and reduces her permanently to her identity as a cute little girl. In *Notes*, James quotes Henry, Sr., as praising him for the "paternal panoply" that he wore "toward" Alice and Aunt Kate on their European tour (407). Here Henry likewise wears a "paternal panoply" toward his younger sister, and the result is a text that calls attention both to the paternalistic attitudes of William and Henry, Sr., and to Henry, Jr.'s, shining and protective textual display.

James's 1913 letter to Harry concerning the paucity of material on Alice sheds additional light on the way in which, in the so-called Family Book, Alice becomes eclipsed by the men in the family. James begins his discussion on *Notes* by saying, "The Book will have to be a longer one than 'A Small Boy,' but even with this there must be limits involving suppressions and omissions." There is, first of all, "[m]y own text," and the autobiographer in James "can't help attaching enough sense and importance and value" to his own reflections "to not to want to keep *that* too utterly under." The letters of Henry, Sr., and William must also be considered. "I am more and more moved," he explains, "to give all of your Grandfather, on his vivid and original side, so beautiful and individual and amusing a side, that I possibly can. Add to this all the application, of an illustrative kind, that I can't but see myself making of your Dad's letters, and I see little room for anyone else's." Although he then deplores "the meagre provision" of Alice's letters, James has already implied that he is most compelled by and interested in his reflections on the most notable members (all men) of the family—his father, his elder brother, and himself.[57] Intentionally or not, James thus re-inscribes in both the autobiography and the letters the fact that, given the needs and the priorities of the men, girls in their family had "scarcely . . . a chance."

Alice, Aunt Kate, and Mary—silent and infantilized, or silent and invisible, or silent and idealized beyond recognition. The only woman from the James family who speaks through her letters and appears in some detail in *Notes of a Son and Brother* is Minny Temple, a James family cousin who died of tuberculosis in 1869. Minny had already been the subject of a brief and characteristically idealized sketch, written early in James's composition of *Notes* and incorporated into the discussion of William and Henry's Newport experience in chapter 4. There she was remembered by James for her liveliness and charm, for "the originality, vivacity, audacity, generosity, of her spirit," for her "indescribable grace and weight—if one might impute weight to a being so imponderable in common scales" (282).

But when he was "3 quarters done" with *Notes*, James received copies of the twenty-three letters that Minny had written to John Chipman Gray, a family friend and teacher of law at Harvard, in the 1860s.[58] James was unable to resist the desire to incorporate the letters into his already crowded Family Book. He claimed that "no loose clue that I have been able to recover unaided touches into life anything like" the "tract of the time-smothered consciousness" that surfaces in the letters (505). "They enabled him," says Habegger, "to sketch a vivid picture of a bright and lively social circle. They also gave him the 'chance to do what I had always longed in some way to do without seeing quite how—rescue and preserve in some way from oblivion, commemorate and a little *enshrine*, the image of our admirable and exquisite, our noble and unique little Minnie.' "[59]

James's language here signals the fact that, in spite of the considerable space he allots her at the end of *Notes*, James will be no less paternalistic in his treatment of her memory than he was towards his mother or sister. She is "little Minnie," she is "our" Minny, phrases that embody the attitude of condescension, superiority, and entitlement. Alfred Habegger has shown that James also adopted this attitude of entitlement in his revision of Minny's letters and his portrait of her in his text. "James did what any contemporary editor would have done," with Minny's letters, "and standardized her punctuation and syntax. He also trimmed wordy passages and omitted repetitions," as he did with his brothers' and father's letters. But James also "sought to make" Minny's writing "smoother, more regular, and more professional." He made her seem more serious and cultivated than she appears in the original versions of the letters, and less ordinary, colloquial, or vulgar.[60] He further omitted any evidence of her somewhat bold and unconventional attitude towards men, of "her teasing directness," and of her unconventional answers to questions of faith.[61]

In his final chapter, James thus preserves the image of the Minny that we first meet in chapter 4—the Minny who is vibrant, energetic, and alive—but, by re-writing her letters, he makes her into a perfectly acceptable heroine for their "easy and happy" social circle of men (507).

"She had beyond any equally young creature I have known a sense for verity of character and play of life in others"; "it was this instinct that made her care so for life in general." But "never"—and I emphasize this *never*—"was a girl less consciously or consentingly or vulgarly dominant—everything that took place around her took place as if primarily in relation to her and in her interest." By the end of *Notes*, therefore, Minny has become the vibrant and spontaneous woman whose genial spirit forms the emotional and social center of their circle of friends, but she has also become an utterly conventional woman through James's insistence on her gentleness, her other-directness, and her decorousness. He claims that she was "the heroine of the scene," a phrase that implies a good deal of presence and strength. But she was the heroine who met the elderly James's expectations for a woman who, in a book about James family men, could nicely and quietly play a prominent role in his young development and who, through her death, could represent "the end of" Henry's and William's "youth" (509, 544). "All in all, James's rewriting of Minny Temple's correspondence," and his rewriting of her character in his autobiographical text, "affords an unparalleled insight into the processes by which this nervous and resourceful wizard turned life—female life—into art."[62]

James's early correspondence reveals that this attitude of artistic entitlement was firmly established at the time of Minny's death in 1870. The living, breathing and feisty Minny, the woman who challenged and joked, who questioned and doubted, became a much-tamed and cherished possession of the young Henry James's imagination only hours after hearing of her death. To his mother he writes immediately that the news of her death is "more strong and painful than I can find words to express." But as he thinks about Minny, letting all of his "recollections and associations" awaken and "swarm," Henry begins to consider how she will survive in the memories of her friends. "Twenty years hence," he realizes, "what a pure eloquent vision she will be." Within a matter of days, much of his pain has been converted to joy at the thought of her death, and much of his thought to satisfaction at what she has become for him: "The more I think of her the more perfectly satisfied I am to have her translated from this changing realm of fact to the steady realm of thought. There she may bloom into a beauty more radiant than our dull eyes will avail to contemplate."[63]

Habegger observes that a note of indecent, almost sinister delight appears in these early writings about Minny.[64] Anticipating the use to which he will put her memory in *The Portrait of a Lady* and *The Wings of the Dove*, James revels in the way in which his imagination has transformed the real, human Minny, living in illness and pain, into an image of "sweetness and weakness," "greater sereneness and purity," a "sort of measure and standard of brightness and repose." James's relief at what she has become for him at her death leads him to conclude that her death is "the happiest, fact, almost in her whole career. So it seems, at least, on reflection: to the eye of feeling there is something immensely moving"—moving for the budding novelist, that is—"in the sudden and complete extinction of a vitality so exquisite and so apparently infinite as Minny's."[65] Minny's death, then, has served Henry, not Minny herself; it has met not her needs but his needs as the writer who has already learned to transform unmanageable emotions (and people?) into the exquisitely malleable and "moving" images of art.

Young Henry's thinking about the ways in which Minny's example ministered to and inspired him in his development also informs our understanding of the role she plays in *Notes*. In his first letter concerning her death, he writes that she "certainly never seemed to have come into this world for her own happiness—as that of others—or as anything but a sort of divine reminder and quickness." As he thinks of her "softened and sweetened by suffering," he realizes that "her image" all along "has operated in my mind as a gentle incentive to action and enterprise." Writing to William three days later, he claims that he is inspired not just by her suffering but by her death: "It's almost as if she had passed away—as far as I am concerned—from having served her purpose, that of standing well within the world, inviting and inviting me onward by all the bright intensity of her example." As far as the young Henry is concerned, Minny has lived her life in order to heal and to inspire Henry. Now that he is "crawling from weakness and inaction and suffering into strength and health and hope," she has completed her mission and gone to her rest.[66] Serving as a muse of sorts, Minny in dying has passed to Henry her passion for life, her interest in other people, her vision of goodness and beauty. Feasting on her memory, the young Henry can go on to fulfill his destiny as a writer.

Tompkins says of James's treatment of Minny in *Notes of a Son and Brother* that his long-dead cousin "summarizes all the brightness, hope, and promise that surround the people and events in James's memories. With her intelligence and bravery, her honesty, humor, and restless spirituality, she was for James, and remains for the reader, a consummate symbol of youth."[67] She represents all of the vitality and hope of the young men and mentors in the volume, of the Wilkys and Bobs, the William Hunts and John LaFarges, who lived before time wrought on their lives its "strange revenges and contradictions" (520). Most of all, Minny represents the promise of the future for the young Henry whose story is the focus of the book and around whose story the other men have been clustered. She was Henry's inspiring example, his enabling vision, his female muse in his youth, and she is re-cast in that role in his autobiography. "None the less did she in fact cling to consciousness . . . she would have given anything to live," he says at the end of the narrative in which clinging to, standing by, and nurturing one's consciousness has become an absolute value for the young man of letters (544). It is his destiny now to live, to live as he has aspired to live throughout these sore and troubled years, and the death of Minny Temple not only marks the end of those years but the promise of the vital, literary future to come.

Finally, for this reader the portrait of Minny Temple demonstrates that, in spite of the presence of the long, final chapter devoted to her memory, *Notes of a Son and Brother* is a book about the James family men, their cousins and friends. Though contradictory and conflicted, it is a highly idealized account of their hopes and aspirations, their expressiveness and charm, their heroism or genius and, in the case of the diffident youth who is marked as much by his obscure physical wound as by his artistic genius, *Notes* is the story of the young Henry James's triumph over the obstacles of his upbringing, his lack of formal education, and his nearly debilitating uncertainty and shame. When the women appear, they appear in relation to the men, and this patriarchal reality is another shame that unsettles the autobiographical account. James did not want to resemble his father and be dependent on the women whose lives were organized around his father's needs. But he uses the women in *Notes* to much the same effect. It is by suppressing the reality of the James family women, by revising them beyond recognition or effacing the memory of their lives, that he has constructed his complicated story of development and success.

Epilogue

> Glad you will be to know that the thing appears to be quite extraordinarily appreciated, absolutely acclaimed, here.
>
> —Henry James (1914)

A Small Boy and Others was published in the United States by Scribner's in March 1913 and in England by Macmillan in April; *Notes of a Son and Brother* appeared under both imprints in March of the following year. Because "all vestiges of his old depression seemed to have left him" by March 1914, biographers and critics have long believed that by writing his autobiographies James cured himself of the despondency that had afflicted him intermittently since 1909.[1] Some critics have stressed the benefits of "the successful effort to work" and the affirmation of artistic power this effort made possible.[2] Others have emphasized the therapeutic powers of the autobiographical act.[3] But whatever their emphases, Jamesians have invariably propounded a psychology of self-healing similar to that which James adopted in dealing with professional setbacks during the late 1880s and 1890s—turning his back on his public and working off his pain through his art. Critics have invariably quoted as evidence of James's success at self-healing his March 21, 1914, letter to Henry Adams, written shortly after the publication of *Notes of a Son and Brother*:

You see I still, in presence of life . . . have reactions—as many as possible—and the book I sent you is a proof of them. It's, I suppose, because I am that queer monster the artist, an obstinate finality, an inexhaustible sensibility. Hence the reactions—appearances, memories, many things go on playing upon it with consequences that I note and 'enjoy' (grim word!) noting. It all takes doing—and I *do*. I believe I shall do yet again—it is still an act of life.[4]

We know from both the letters of 1912–1913 and the autobiographies that James believed in his ability to heal himself by casting off his medical advisors, trusting in his ability to diagnose himself, making an

185

effort to get well on his own, and, most important of all, recovering (or rediscovering) his powers to work. We will see that James's correspondence from the spring of 1914 proclaims a renewed appreciation for life and a sense of enthusiasm about his career. But it also suggests that the emotional well-being and confidence in artistic power James experienced at that time was due to a complicated set of factors, not only to the salutary effects of his writing. It shows, for one, that James's optimism was inspired by the favorable reception that *Notes of a Son and Brother* received from the British press. Just as public indifference to his work was the cause of his depression in 1909, in other words, so was reader approval a significant factor in his recovery several years later. By applauding James's account of his past as well as the author who provides it, these positive, enthusiastic reviews both appeased James's anxieties about how the books would be received by his audience and allowed him to show an increasingly proud and triumphant face to his family and friends, especially to the nephew who had questioned his intentions in *Notes.*

The completion of a project that stirred up troubling memories and embroiled James in yet another dispute with Harry must also have been a factor in his recovery of good spirits in 1914. As his correspondence reveals, rewriting family documents in order to present an idealized portrait of his original family disrupted in the present the familial harmony and happiness he had wished to celebrate in the past. The autobiographical act, then, was often more troubling than therapeutic for James, and the completion of *Notes of a Son and Brother* and the end of family conflict were themselves a source of joy and relief.

The context for the last phase of family drama relating to James's autobiographical act, James's final quarrel with Harry, is Henry's revision of the family letters in *Notes.* Harry had become aware of the fact that his uncle had reworked all of William's correspondence intended for the Family Book, just as he had reworked the letters of Henry, Sr., Wilky, and Minny Temple. On November 4, 1913, he wrote a letter of objection to James, and soon after his uncle responded with the note of anxiety and urgency that sounded in letters from 1912. "I seize many of your points," wrote the nervous and apologetic Henry on November 15, "all the others in fact, I think, perfectly, & shall be able to meet them in a manner if you will have patience with me." He agrees with Harry that his "procedure" was "a mistake from the point of view of the independent giving to the world of your Father's correspondence as a whole . . . in the light of what you tell me of the effect on you of the *cumulative* impression you get from individual retouchings often repeated." He agrees that the revised letters were a mistake if they were to appear outside of the context of

Henry's artful and autobiographical reflections, particularly if they were to appear in the serial form in Scribner's Magazine that was to have preceeded their publication in *Notes*. But in a lengthy attempt to explain the interrelated " 'ethic' & aesthetic" behind his handling of the letters, James writes that the "ideal" with which he approached the inclusion of letters had never been one "of documentary exactitude, verbatim, literatim et punctuatim" anyway. My "superstitions," he asserts, "were wholly other, & playing, such as they were, at every point" with regard not only to William's but also to "my father's" letters, to "your Uncle Wilky's, and even with some of my brother Bob's and sister Alice's, as I fallaciously hoped (for these last)." It was "the essence of the artistic ideal that hovered before me," James claims; it was his "conception of an *atmosphere* which I invoked as, artistically speaking, my guiding star."[5]

James goes on to explain that his artistic ideal is inseparable from his desire to recreate his family according to a particular vision of the past. As an artist, James claims, "I have to the last point the instinct & the sense of fusions & interrelations, for framing & encircling (as I think I have already called it,) every part of my stuff in every other." When he came to working letters into his text, therefore, he was considering the interrelations within or the "whole harmony of my text—the general purpose of which," we saw in the previous chapter, "was to be a reflection of all the amenity & felicity of our young life of that time at the highest pitch that was consistent with perfect truth—to show us all at our best for characteristic expression & colour & variety & everything that would be charming." The idealized version of what he was claiming for his family in *Notes* had to be consistent with the style and the tone of the family letters he wished to weave smoothly and harmoniously into his narrative. That is why, to take one example, he changed his father's reference to Abraham Lincoln from " 'poor old Abe' " to " 'poor old Abraham.' " "Never, *never*," he insists, "under our Father's roof did we talk of Abe, either *tout court* or as 'Abe Lincoln'—it wasn't *conceivable*: Abraham Lincoln he was for us, when he wasn't either Lincoln or Mr. Lincoln (the Western note & the popularization of 'Abe' were quite away from us *then*.)"[6]

James provides in this letter more than artistic reasons for his revision of family documents and hints at the connection between quelling anxieties and mythologizing the family as he sees fit. In the fall of the previous year, he explains, he began using his revisionist impulse to maintain a sense of well-being and serenity in the present. Among "the horrid premonitions of my illness of last autumn—I mean my so long *acute* one," James explains, he had revised a series of letters he was ultimately unable to work into *Notes*—William's letters from his scientific expedition to Brazil. James was too nervous and unwell to "get into any closer quarters with composition" of *Notes*, and his "quasi-mechanical Brazil dealing helped to *tromper* a little my dismal consciousness of not making head." What is more, his "desparation of *nervousness* in the whole connection" of his illness and the Family Book was "a positive anguish" which he tried "with that practical futility," the process of revising, "to work off." In other words, at the time when family conflicts gave rise to his illness, James had turned to rewriting William's letters, a process intertwined with his idealization of family, in order to restore a sense of serenity within. He defines as "quasi-mechanical" the process meant to "work off" his anguish, and, in doing so, he may allude merely to the mechanical process of dictation. But this process was greatly informed by an emotional need to have both his working life and his relationships with his family conform to his expectations for productivity, harmony, comfort, and ease. Apparently, the elderly James felt he could meet this emotional need in art, if not in life, by revising his brother's correspondence from Brazil.

Even as he writes about his use of revision to ease his anxieties, James is confronted by the need to smooth over this most recent rift with William's eldest son and to calm his recently agitated nerves. The process of justifying himself to Harry, he says, is a difficult one. "I am not pretending to pick up any challenge to my appearance of wantonness," but "I should be able to justify myself (*when* able) only out of such abysses of association" of the past—abysses that he described to Wilky's widow as "so trying, so upsetting" to "nerves and spirits"—and "the stirring up of these, for vindication, is simply a strain that stirs up tears." Other letters to Harry have familiarized us with the manipulative strategy James employs in this letter. He could fully justify himself to his nephew if he could plunge comfortably into his memories of the past. But he cannot. The old associations are too straining to his nerves; they tug too much on his feelings and threaten his sense of well-being. And his nephew, we know, does not wish further to upset his fragile uncle.

But James does "positively yearn in fact to do something that may redeem my reputation with you." "It is very difficult," he begins, "& even pretty painful, to try to put forward after the fact the considerations & emotions that have been intense for one in the long ferment of an artistic process; but I must nevertheless do something toward making you see a little perhaps how what strikes you as so deplorable an aberration—I mean the editing of those earliest things other than 'rigidly'—had for me a sort of exquisite inevitability." He then tries to justify himself *indirectly* to Harry by appealing to his relationship with Harry's mother Alice and describing the contribution that Alice made to his "intense artistic process."

The story begins with a conversation between Alice and Henry in the fall of 1911, not long after William died. At some point, their talk turned to "your Dad's & my old life of the time previous, far previous, to her knowing us." Having emphasized his sense of entitlement to these distant memories, James then quotes Alice as having said "with the most generous appreciation & response, 'Oh Henry, why don't you *write* these things?'—and with such an effect that after a bit I found myself wondering vaguely whether I *mightn't* do something of the sort." Indeed, "that turn of talk," he claims, "was the germ, it dropped the seed." Not only did the impulse to write the Family Book date from this utterance but also "the spirit of my vision—a spirit & a vision as far removed as possible from my mere isolated documentation of your Father's record."

We know from chapter 11 of *Notes* that James had been searching for a pretext to write the story of the "man of imagination"; we know that his inspiration for this story went back at least as far as his preface to *The Portrait of a Lady*. In his letter to Harry, however, it was more convenient to omit any reference to these earlier inspirations and to identify his mother's idea as "the germ" or "the seed" for the book to which Harry has objected. It was also convenient to portray Alice's suggestion as the origin of an imaginative (rather than documentary) vision for the inclusion of family letters. "We talked again, & still again, of the 'Family Book,'" he goes on, "—& by the time I came away I felt I had somehow found my inspiration" and, apparently, his vision. Alice played a central role in the inception and the development of the project, and her eldest son (or so James implies) could scarcely object to an approach which his mother both encouraged and approved.

James's next move is to invoke his special, almost sacred relationship to Harry's father William. Immediately he falls back on his sense of entitlement. As if to challenge Harry's right to question his decisions, he claims that "[e]verything" William's letters "meant affected me so, in all the business, as of *our* old world only, mine & his alone together, with every item of it intimately known & remembered by me." He "instinctively" regarded the truth or accuracy of the Family Book "as all *my* truth, to do what I would with." Besides, to lay his "hands upon the weak little relics of our common youth" was to find himself "again in such close relation with your Father, such a revival of relation as I hadn't known since his death." James felt a "passion of tenderness for doing the best thing by him that the material allowed," and William himself seemed to appear at Henry's side supporting him in his vision: "It was as if he had said to me . . . 'Oh but you're not going to give me away, to hand me over, in my raggedness & my poor accidents, quite unhelped & unfriended, you're going to do the very best for me you *can*, aren't you, & since you appear to be making such claims for me you're going to let me seem to justify them as much as I possibly may?'"

It was through this thoroughly intimate relationship with William, a relationship that began in their infancy and continued on after William's death, that James justifies a series of revisions that William himself may have very much disliked. Henry does not want to "give" William "away" to the shame of real life any more than he wanted to "give away" his father, his mother, his brothers—or himself. So he fabricated a scene in which the spirit of his brother approves of his vision and urges him on. He even justifies himself by claiming that, in his worry about being given away, William begs his brother "to let me seem to justify" the claims on his behalf that Henry will be making. Assumptions about the family's need for and the right to justification are thus intimately woven into the psychological fabric of this letter, itself a massive display of evasion, manipulation and justification.

Several months later an unexpected source further justified James in his handling of the Family Book—the British press. The previous April, James had been able to write home that *A Small Boy and Others* had already been positively received: "The Book appears to be really most handsomely received hereabouts. It is being treated in fact with the very highest consideration."[7] A week later an unpublished letter to Harry carried similar news. Naturally, James was disappointed to hear that he was "well-nigh as 'difficult' as ever to read, though 'all right when you know' (that is understand) me. I groan at this, because I want to sell, and such remarks discourage sale." But, he continues, ". . . the thing seems, all the same, to flourish a good bit *less* mildly than my stuff in general, and such Notices as I have been aware of, both public and private, have been in the last degree pleasant—and some of them even perceptive!"[8] On August 13, 1913, he makes a similar observation in a letter to his childhood friend, T. S. Perry: "I thank you most kindly for your good expression about *my* rum boyhood's chronicle; it came as it could & would & had to; & has been received here with a benevolence & sympathy that has surprised me."[9]

At this point in the correspondence, James's response to the "Notices" is sanguine, but subdued, somewhat like the notices themselves. Reviewers invariably alerted readers to the difficulty of James's labyrinthian late style, as James himself observed. But they were otherwise receptive to and intrigued by both the story of the young artist *A Small Boy and Others* presents and the experimental form in which this story is rendered. With the publication of *Notes of a Son and Brother* in March 1914, however, the response of reviewers went from the "pleasant" to the enthusiastic. Present in these notices was much of the interest in James's life and insight into his methods that characterized the commentary on *A Small Boy*. Some readers valued *Notes* precisely for the story of

James's artistic development that, continued from volume one, is woven into and around the portraits of others, and one reader found this story sufficiently compelling to claim that both *A Small Boy* and *Notes* are "already crying for their sequels." But prominent in the reviews as well is a marked appreciation for, even a delight in, the emotional warmth made possible by the portraits of such figures as Henry, Sr., William, and Minny Temple. Says the appreciative reviewer for the *Times Literary Supplement*, "if there are any who have accused Mr. James as an artist of wanting the warmer emotions, they may correct themselves before" the moving portraits in *Notes of a Son and Brother*. Says the reviewer for the *Nation*, "if one were invited to name the literary masterpiece of the twentieth century, one would do well to hesitate before passing further than Mr. James's autobiography."[10]

Beginning with a March 18 report to his sister-in-law, James's letters energetically reflect the enthusiasm for *Notes* that was conveyed in the first reviews to appear in the British press:

Within a few days my Book has come out here, & there are signs already of a really great acclamation of it—greater than of its predecessor, though that was marked, & far greater than anything of mine has ever had. I imagine the thing will do as much better here than in America as was the case with its predecessor; but what I hear from you will help me to see . . . The whole working in of Minnie was difficult & delicate—highly so; but I seem already to gather here that my evocation of her appears by her touchingness & beauty, *the* stroke, or success, of the book. I am extremely struck (as I was for the other one,) with the breadth & handsomeness of appreciation of my English readers, and the *tone* of such reviews as I have seen, though I most keep clear of these.[11]

When he wrote again to Alice on March 29 his sense of the critics' judgment remained unchanged: "Glad you will be to know that the thing appears to be quite extraordinarily appreciated, absolutely acclaimed, here—scarcely any difficulties being felt as to 'parts that are best' unless it be that the early passage & the final chapter about dear Minnie seem the great, the beautiful 'success' of the whole."[12]

To read together these reports to Alice is to see that James was excited enough about the reception of the book to make it a repeated topic in the letters he wrote her that March. It is also to see him make some striking claims for the book's success. First, the success is immediate. There are "signs" of acclaim only days after the book has "come out." Secondly, the success is substantial: In language that is decidedly embellished over that of his letters on volume one, James writes that volume two is receiving a "really great acclamation," that it is "quite extraordinarily appreciated, absolutely acclaimed." This is significant language for a writer who once entertained visions of achieving a great success in the theater only to be booed off the stage after the performance of *Guy Domville*. It is significant language for a writer who in the preface to *The Golden Bowl* imagined his New York Edition as an "invitation to the reader to dream again in my company and in the interest of his own larger absorption of my sense."[13] It is significant language, too, for an autobiographer who incorporated into his autobiographical discourse his anxieties about his readers' response, and who, throughout his story of childhood, emphasized his fears of exposure and his youthful sense of failure and shame. To be acclaimed, after all, is to receive a grand and vociferous response, as after a musical or theatrical performance. It is to receive to your face the unqualified celebration of one's work and affirmation of one's artistic identity that James had always wanted from his readers, but all too often failed to get. So struck is James by this unexpected affirmation, and obviously so uplifted, that he indulges in the exaggerated pronouncement that the acclaim *Notes* received was "greater than of its predeccessor, though that was marked, & *far greater than anything of mine has ever had* (my emphasis)."[14]

When James first reported on the book's reception to his sister-in-law on March 18, only two of the reviews I consulted for this chapter had appeared in the British press; by the time he wrote to Harry on April 7, however, *Notes* had received eight reviews in all, and of the eight, seven paid almost unqualified tribute to James. What we see in his subsequent reports on the autobiography's reception, then, is an emboldened response to a growing number of highly favorable reviews. He writes to Harry:

I fear to appear vulgarly to swagger, in the manner of performers who flaunt advertisements & press notices about, in telling you of what an extraordinary 'Press,' or unanimity of welcome, of intelligent appreciation & acclamation, the thing has had in this country. I have only 'seen' a small number of the direct evidences of this, but the very general fact & sense of them is wafted in upon me, & I am very much touched by it, as I was in the case of the Small Boy. The two books together appear to have made me (vulgarly speaking,) famous, & to be greeted as a new departure, a new form and manner struck out in my 70*th* year. I am much moved, as I say, by the geniality and sympathy of it all.[15]

An April 13, 1914, letter to T. S. Perry reiterates many of the claims of the letter to Harry, though in comparison to the earlier report its tone is somewhat subdued. Once again, it is important to recognize not only the unanimity of James's reports on the book's reception but also the frequency with which he makes these reports:

. . . the volume has, like its predecessor, or even more, enjoyed an acclamation of welcome here, an unanimity of really intelligent appreciation, by what comes home to me, which I can't speak of emphatically without seeming to vaunt and

flaunt my wares after a fashion incompatible with true refinement. I never 'see
many Notices,' but the general sense of the Press, such a 'bonne Presse,' is blown
in upon me by wandering airs, & appears to be really a very handsome exhibition
of competent appreciation. I wish I could say as much of any wandering airs that
come to me from your side of the sea; but the less said about these, as usual, the
better—especially as none of them, practically, come. 'Press agencies,' whose
demand that I shall take up with them I have for 50 decent years absolutely
ignored, thrust in upon me from time to time some effusive little ineptitude or
illiteracy (as a bribe to subscribing to them!).[16]

We see in these letters that James is no less concerned with appearances
than he was in the autobiographies or the letters concerning their
composition, but the fact of this ever increasing acclaim creates for him
new problems in self-presentation. Lest he appear too eager for praise, he
must take care to appear uninterested in the notices themselves, even to
assure his readers that he has not sought them out on his own. Lest he
appear too egotistical, he must declare as vulgar both the fame that the
two books have brought him and the pride he takes in boasting of his
success. (Chasing after reviews and boasting about them, after all, would
be "incompatible with true refinement.") But the fact that in his letter to
Harry he communicates his success by adopting the pose of swaggering
"performers" measures the extreme pleasure and pride he takes in being
able to speak of success at all—particularly to the nephew who, by
criticizing his handling of family letters, challenged his uncle's artistic
vision for the Family Book. Beginning with the image of the actor, James
has turned the spotlight of the press away from his productions and onto
himself. Not the books but the artist who wrote them is now being
acclaimed, and James is "very much touched" and "much moved" by this
affirmation of his identity.

The specific nature of this affirmation is also significant. As a young
man just starting his career, James wrote to his brother that "being 'very
artistic,' I have a constant impulse to try experiments of form."[17] Now
that he is old and at the end of his career, James has found this "very
artistic" tendency to experiment with literary form to be responsible in
part for the fame the autobiographies have brought him. "The two books
together," as he says, have been "greeted as a new departure, a new form
and manner struck out in the 70*th* year." Anguished by his conflict with
Harry the previous November, James had pledged "[n]ever again" to
"stray from my proper work," the writing of fiction. Now the prospect of
continuing his work in the autobiographical mode has become more
appealing. As he writes to Harry on April 7:

If I am myself able to live on & work a while longer I probably *shall* perpetrate
a certain number more passages of retrospect & reminiscence—though quite

disconnectedly from these 2 recent volumes, which are complete in themselves & of which the original intention is now a performed & discharged thing; that of producing some picture of the medium & atmosphere in which your Dad & I drew breath & grew up together during the far-off juvenile years previous to the time at which his earlier Letters begins. I wanted to give above all *his* young background, & now there it *is*, given. Anything more I do in the memorizing line will be an evocation of Choses Vues (Victor Hugo's formula is so good!) in my own later connection altogether—though I confess that something of the appeal of the period from 1869 to the beginning of my life in London (the rest of *that* making a history by itself altogether,) *does* a good deal hang about me.[18]

In characteristic fashion, James's intentions to write about things outside himself gradually give way to his desire to focus the attention on himself. Indeed, the project he undertook when he returned to autobiography later in 1914, the unfinished *The Middle Years*, continued into his early London years the story of his literary development that, interwoven with his memories of others, was the major motif of the much-celebrated *Notes*. But there were no family documents to incorporate into his text, no family members to recreate, to fill out and touch up, to justify. Tamara Follini believes that the comfort and fluidity of James's narrative in *The Middle Years* may well reflect his relief at being free to write about himself without the difficulty of writing about family.[19] By "perpetrat-[ing]" another volume of autobiography, moreover, James may have hoped to cultivate not only the "new form and manner struck out in my 70*th* year" but also the audience who enjoyed and applauded it so.

On May 9, 1909, James wrote to Edith Wharton that her "reassurance and comfort" with regard to his writing "makes me *de nouveau* believe a little in myself, which is what I infinitely need and yearn for."[20] On March 21, 1914, James wrote to Henry Adams the letter that has been understood as a statement of faith in the artistic powers renewed through the act of writing *A Small Boy and Others* and *Notes of a Son and Brother*. The "doing" he celebrates in that letter, and the perpetuation of consciousness that "doing" entailed, undoubtedly ministered to James's renewed self-confidence. So, too, did the autobiographical act of returning to his past, discovering the sources of his creativity, and, as Eakin maintains, recovering "the resources of his ego in meeting a life crisis during the Civil War so long ago."[21] But the emotional vulnerability that pervades James's story of his early years reflects the fragility of the elderly James who, having recently experienced professional failure, illness and depression, is haunted by the deep-seated fears of invalidism and failure, of insignificance and loss, that form the shame-bound emotional matrix of the James family. James's autobiographies, accordingly, were not therapeutic in the sense that we understand the term today. They were not a means by which James could re-experience and come to terms with the obscure but painful feelings that shaped his life. Quite the opposite, in fact.

Henry James was skilled in the practice of defending himself against the anguish of family shame, and, to a large extent, the autobiographies only created new reasons and fresh opportunities for him to re-fortify his emotional defenses. Within both his recreated family in the books and the real family that survived, the autobiographies created new opportunities for playing out the narcissistic and self-serving role he had learned within his original family and hid under the mask of the devoted "angel" and privileged artist. This is not to say that James did not seek to explore the sources of the James family shame in his life and its matrix of negative affect. But because this exploration was blocked by his need to defend himself against anxiety and pain, his sense of the emotional truth about the family must remain as hurtful and obscure as the wound he incurred in his youth and re-created in *Notes*. The final stage in the emotional drama of *A Small Boy and Others* and *Notes of a Son and Brother* ends with the only balm for James's pain—the acclaim of the public and the ability to communicate that acclaim to the family whose deep-seated emotional history created the autobiographer's need for a patent and resounding success.

Abbreviations

Notes

Index

Abbreviations

The unpublished letters cited throughout this study can be found in archival collections at the Houghton Library, Harvard University, and the Beinecke Rare Book and Manuscript Library, Yale University. Letters from Henry James to his agent, J. B. Pinker, are taken from the Collection of American Literature, Papers of J. B. Pinker, at the Beinecke and published by permission of Alexander R. James and the Beinecke Library. Likewise, the October 1913 letter from Charles Scribner to J. B. Pinker, also in the Collection of American literature, is published by permission of the Beinecke Library. All other unpublished correspondence is taken from the James Family Papers housed at the Houghton and is published by permission of Alexander R. James and the Houghton Library. Following is a key to the abbreviations used in citations to unpublished letters written by or to individuals who figure prominently in this study. The names of correspondents whose letters are less frequently cited will be listed in full.

AGJ   Alice Howe Gibbens James (1849–1922), wife of Henry James's eldest brother William.

HJ1   Henry James, Sr., (1811–1882), father of Henry and William James.

HJ2   Henry James, Jr., (1843–1916), novelist and autobiographer, the subject of this study.

HJ3   Henry James (1879–1947), the eldest son of William and Alice Gibbens James, nephew of Henry James, Jr., and executor of his father's estate.

MJ   Mary Walsh James (1810–1882), the wife of Henry James, Sr., and the mother of Henry James, Jr.

WJ   William James (1842–1910), psychologist and philosopher, eldest brother of Henry James, Jr.

JBP   J. B. Pinker (1863–1922), Henry James, Jr.'s, literary agent after 1899.

Abbreviations

FREQUENTLY CITED PUBLISHED MATERIALS

The most frequently cited sources in this study are Henry James's two completed volumes of autobiography, *A Small Boy and Others* (1913) and *Notes of a Son and Brother* (1914). All references to these volumes will be taken from F. W. Dupee's edition, *Autobiography: A Small Boy and Others, Notes of a Son and Brother, The Middle Years* (New York: Criterion, 1956) and will be included in parentheses in the text. Other frequently cited primary and secondary sources will appear in the endnotes under the following abbreviations or short titles:

PRIMARY SOURCES

Novel   R. P. Blackmur, ed. *The Art of the Novel: Critical Prefaces by Henry James.* New York: Scribner's, 1934.

Notebooks Leon Edel and Lyall Powers, eds. *The Complete Notebooks of Henry James.* New York: Oxford University Press, 1987.

HJL   Leon Edel, ed. *Henry James Letters.* 4 vols. Cambridge: Harvard University Press, 1984.

LHJ   Percy Lubbock, ed. *The Letters of Henry James.* 2 vols. New York: Scribner's, 1920.

LWJ   Henry James, ed. *The Letters of William James.* 2 vols. Boston: Little Brown, 1926.

Remains William James, ed. *The Literary Remains of Henry James: With an Introduction by William James.* Boston: Houghton Mifflin, 1884.

SECONDARY SOURCES

Fictions Paul John Eakin. *Fictions in Autobiography: Studies in the Art of Self-Invention.* Princeton: Princeton University Press, 1985.

Untried Years Leon Edel. *Henry James: The Untried Years, 1843–1870.* Philadelphia: Lippincott, 1953.

Conquest Leon Edel. *Henry James: The Conquest of London, 1870–1881.* Philadelphia: Lippincott, 1962.

Middle Years Leon Edel. *Henry James: The Middle Years, 1882–1895.* Philadelphia: Lippincott, 1962.

Treacherous Years Leon Edel. *Henry James: The Treacherous Years, 1895–1901.* Philadelphia: Lippincott, 1969.

Master Leon Edel. *Henry James: The Master, 1901–1916.* Philadelphia: Lippincott, 1972.

Becoming Howard Feinstein. *Becoming William James.* Ithaca, NY: Cornell University Press, 1984.

Abbreviations

Woman Business Alfred Habegger. *Henry James and the "Woman Business."* Cambridge: Cambridge University Press, 1989.

Biography Jane Maher. *Biography of Broken Fortunes: Wilkie and Bob, Brothers of William, Henry, and Alice James.* Hamden, CT: Archon Books, 1986.

Thought and Character Ralph Barton Perry. *The Thought and Character of William James.* Vol. 1. Boston: Little, Brown, 1935.

Notes

Introduction

1. *HJL*, 4:796.

2. *Novel* 47.

3. HJ2 to HJ3, September 23–24, 1912.

4. Ibid. In his hand-written letters, James designates the word "and" with the ampersand (&); his dictated, typewritten letters spell the word out. Throughout this study, I quote from James's letters accordingly.

5. R. D. Laing, *Politics of the Family* (New York: Pantheon, 1971), 3–6.

6. *HJL*, 4:801.

7. William Goetz, *Henry James and the Darkest Abyss of Romance* (Baton Rouge: Louisiana State University Press, 1986), 6. For an extended discussion of the history of criticism on James's autobiographies, see Carol Holly, "The Autobiographies: A History of Readings," *A Companion to Henry James Studies*, ed. Daniel Mark Fogel (Westport, CT: Greenwood Press, 1993), 427–446. Not included in this essay is Ross Posnock's discussion of the autobiographies in his recent "historicized intellectual history" of William and Henry James, *The Trial of Curiosity: Henry James, William James, and the Challenge of Modernity* (New York: Oxford University Press, 1991). Posnock's decision "to recover and foreground" in the autobiographies "the heterodox audacity" of James's self-representation in relation to American culture differs from my desire to read *A Small Boy* and *Notes* as the expression of James's complex psychological concerns (viii, 168).

8. Paul John Eakin, "Henry James's 'Obscure Hurt': Can Autobiography Serve Biography?" *New Literary History* 19 (1987–1988): 679. This article can also be found in Eakin's recent study, *Touching the World: Reference in Autobiography* (Princeton: Princeton University Press, 1992), 54–70. Eakin's earlier study of the autobiographies is "Henry James and the Autobiographical Act," *Fictions* 56–125.

9. *Master* 500.

10. Leon Edel, "The Portrait of the Artist as an Old Man," *American Scholar* 47 (1977–1978): 54.

11. *LHJ*, 1:xv, xvi.

12. Since I began this study, two new biographies of Henry James and the James family have appeared, Fred Kaplan's *Henry James: The Imagination of Genius* (New York: William Morrow, 1992) and R. W. B. Lewis's *The Jameses: A*

Family Narrative (New York: Farrar, Straus and Giroux, 1991). Neither Lewis nor Kaplan reiterate Lubbock's and Edel's idealizations of James as an old man. But for his closing paragraphs about the autobiographies, in fact, Lewis' family biography barely touches on James's life after 1910. Kaplan provides a fairly detailed discussion of James's nervous breakdown in 1910, but his treatment of James's subsequent illnesses, his work on the autobiographies, and his relationship with his family is considerably less ambitious and detailed.

13. For studies that discuss James's ambivalent depiction of family relationships in the autobiographies, see Thomas Cooley, *Educated Lives: The Rise of Modern Autobiography in America* (Columbus: Ohio State University Press, 1976); Eakin, *Fictions*; Donna Przybylowicz, *Desire and Repression: The Dialect of Self and Other in the Late Works of Henry James* (University, AL: University of Alabama Press, 1986); William Veeder, "The Feminine Orphan and the Emergent Master," *Henry James Review* 12 (1991): 20–54. In his 1943 essay, "The Ghost of Henry James: A Study in Thematic Apperception," Saul Rosenzweig was the first to argue that James's behavior in later life (and his discussion of family relationships in his autobiographies) often replayed the psychological troubles of his youth [*Character and Personality* 12 (1943–1944): 79–100].

14. Clifford Geertz, *Interpretation of Cultures* (New York: Basic Book, 1973), 7.

15. Ibid.

16. Michael Kerr, "Chronic Anxiety and Defining a Self," *Atlantic Monthly* (September 1988): 35.

17. Murray Bowen, *Family Therapy in Clinical Practice* (New York: Jason Aronson, 1978), 159.

18. Merle Fossum and Marilyn Mason, *Facing Shame: Families in Recovery* (New York: Norton, 1986), 3, 8.

19. Kerr, "Chronic Anxiety," 41.

20. Howard Feinstein, "Family Therapy for the Historian?—The Case of William James," *Family Process* 20 (1981): 97–98.

21. See, for example, Carl Degler, *At Odds: Women and the Family in America from the Revolution to the Present* (New York: Oxford University Press, 1980) and Steven Mintz, *A Prison of Expectations: The Family in Victorian Culture* (New York: New York University Press, 1983).

22. By narcissistic parenting I mean a style of parenting in which children are unconsciously schooled in putting their parents' needs before their own. See Alice Miller, *The Drama of the Gifted Child* (New York: Basic Books, 1981), 3–29.

Chapter 1. The Heritage of Failure and Shame in the Life of Henry James, Sr.

1. Katherine Hastings, "William James (1771–1832) of Albany, N.Y., and His Descendants," *New York Genealogical and Biographical Record* 55 (April, July, October, 1924): 107; *Becoming* 289–92. I am grateful to Alfred Habegger for sharing with me information concerning the death of John James. For more on John James, see Habegger, "Dupine Tracks J. J.," *The Southern Review* 27 (1991): 803–25.

2. Quoted in *Becoming* 54. Feinstein summarizes as follows the evidence to support Henry, Sr.'s, claim that he was "hopelessly addicted" to alcohol by the time he entered Union College:

The elderly shoemaker whom he had euphemistically referred to in his autobiographical sketch as "sacrificing to Bacchus" had in fact been feeding the boy and his friends "raw gin and brandy" morning and afternoon when they stopped by on the way to and from school from the time Henry was ten years old. To compound matters, following his accident, Henry had been encouraged to use "all manner of stimulants" by his "parents, physicians and nurses," with the net result that (as he later confessed to his son Robertson, who was then struggling against alcohol addiction), "I emerged from my sick-room, and went to college . . . hopelessly addicted to the vice."

Feinstein also quotes an unpublished letter from Henry, Sr., to Bob to argue that James " 'fell in with professional gamblers' " during the period when he studied law after his graduation from Union in 1830 (*Becoming* 47).

In his biography of Henry, Sr., Alfred Habegger presents evidence to suggest that Henry, Sr.'s, brother Howard was an alcoholic and that Henry himself was known by friends to have a drinking problem as late as 1849 (Typescript, chapter 3). I am grateful to Professor Habegger for giving me the opportunity to cite material from his manuscript.

3. Archibald McIntyre to HJ1, November 12, 1829.

4. WJ to Archibald McIntyre, December 2, 1829. A letter written by Eliphalet Nott, president of Union College, likewise predicts a ruinous outcome for the rebellious Henry: "I hope he will get into business immediately; or else break down immediately—the sooner his business comes to a crisis; the better for him and for his friends." (Quoted in Harold Larrabee, "The Flight of Henry James the First," *New England Quarterly* (1937): 774–75). For a discussion of this letter and subsequent letters written by Nott about Henry, Sr., see *Becoming* 52–53.

5. Joseph Kett, *Rites of Passage: Adolescence in America 1790 to the Present* (New York: Basic Books, 1977), 45; Archibald McIntyre to HJ1, November 12, 1829. In *Becoming*, Feinstein suggests that William James's attempts to squelch his son's rebellious tendencies also stemmed from his desire to use his son for business purposes: "It must have occurred to William James many times in his long business career that it would be expedient for his financial empire if he had a son who was a lawyer. A son with legal training could oversee his extensive real estate transactions and keep the fees within the family" (51).

6. Henry James, Sr., "Immortal Life: Illustrated in a Brief Autobiographic Sketch of the Late Stephen Dewhurst," *Remains* 154, 160. Henry James, Sr., refers to the family's religious faith as "Orthodox Protestant," and, throughout this chapter, I refer to the family's religious orientation and their attitude towards sinful human nature as Protestant or Calvinist. In his biography of Henry, Sr., Alfred Habegger explains that the family attended Albany's First Presbyterian Church with its "rigid worship service featuring a long and learned sermon by its minister." The church's theology emphasized the Calvinist approach to sin and salvation: "The gospel as heard by Henry may well have become familiar, but it

was still painful and terrifying. All men have sinned against God. All have been condemned to eternal damnation. No one can escape unless he is humbled to the dust, putting all his hope in Jesus Christ, who died on the cross and rose again. To believe anything else, to trust in one's own decency, is to go to Hell" (Typescript, chapter 3).

7. Joseph Kett argues that the Puritan belief in the "value of humiliation" as a broad means of social control continued in the nineteenth century in the form not of "public shaming" but of disciplinary techniques in the schools (*Rites of Passage* 47). But the threat of humiliation as a form of control also extended to the injunctions against dissipation, disobedience, and failure made by authority figures in the family, the community, the church, and the media (see Paul Boyer, *Urban Masses and Moral Order in America, 1820–1920* [Cambridge: Harvard University Press, 1978], 29–30, and Irvin Wyllie, *The Self-Made Man in America: The Myth of Rags to Riches* [New York: Free Press, 1966], 54.) What is more, as David Leverenz has shown, the threat of humiliation for young men was exacerbated in the nineteenth century by the increasing tendency in American culture to associate masculinity with vocational success (*Manhood and the American Renaissance* [Ithaca: Cornell University Press, 1989], 72–90).

8. In *The Self-Made Man in America*, Irvin Wyllie notes that if "a man's fortune could only be justified in terms of his service to mankind, then it followed logically that it was not right for him to transmit it to his children. That any man should acquire wealth through the accident of birth was, from a social point of view, indefensible. In addition, success philosophers believed that heirs lacked those qualities of character necessary for a responsible stewardship. The children of the rich were generally pictured as soft, lazy, incompetent, and immoral. Russell Connwell spoke for the entire cult of self-help when he asserted that 'It is no help to a young man or woman to inherit money' " (89).

9. "The Last Will and Testament of William James, Esquire, of the City of Albany"; William James to Archibald McIntyre, undated. Having helped to establish several of his nephews in business in the years before Henry's flight from Union, James may have found it especially galling and shameful that the sons of his brothers were willing to submit to his control and ascribe to the work ethic while his own son was not.

10. "William James (1771–1832) of Albany" 103. The rumor that William James's family tried to force him into the ministry is echoed in his great grandson's introduction to *The Letters of William James*: "He may have left home because his family tried to force him into the ministry,—for there is a story to that effect,—or he may have had more adventurous reasons" (1:2).

11. Archibald McIntyre to HJ1, November 12, 1829; William James to Archibald McIntyre, undated.

12. Katherine Weissbourd, *Growing Up in the James Family: Henry James, Sr., as Son and Father* (Ann Arbor: UMI Research Press, 1985), 15.

13. Weissbourd, *Growing Up in the James Family*, 15. Weissbourd also suggests that William James's "solid business identity was an alternative to the confusion and loss he felt about his marriages" (15).

14. John James to his mother, February 4, 1824. On attitudes of Christian resignation towards death in antebellum America, see Lewis Saum, *The Popular Mood of Pre-Civil War America* (Westport, CT: Greenwood Press, 1980), 78–104.

15. Neal Tolchin, *Mourning, Gender, and Creativity in the Art of Herman Melville* (New Haven: Yale University Press, 1988), 5, 7; John Bowlby, *Attachment and Loss: Loss, Sadness, and Depression*, Vol. 3 (New York: Basic Books, 1980), 153.

16. See Katherine Hastings, "William James (1771–1832) of Albany, N.Y., and His Descendants," 103–106. In his February 1824 letter to his mother, William James's nephew, John, wrote that the death of his father (William's brother) "will be felt with all its weight, my Uncle William has had many troubles, and some of those but a short time since, this new one will be of no little addition."

17. Henry, Sr., describes his father's response to his amputations as follows: "My wound had been very severe, being followed by a morbid process in the bone which ever and anon called for some sharp surgery; and on these occasions I remember—for the use of anaesthetics was still wholly undreamt of—his sympathy for my sufferings was so excessive that my mother had the greatest possible difficulty in imposing due prudence upon his expression of it" (*Remains* 147); Weissbourd, *Growing Up in the James Family*, 20.

18. Bowlby, *Attachment and Loss*, 3:156–57.

19. Bowlby, *Attachment and Loss*, 3:15; Fossum and Mason, *Facing Shame*, 44.

20. *Remains* 147; *Untried Years* 26.

21. *Remains* 185; *Untried Years* 25; *Becoming* 41.

22. *Remains* 161; *Becoming* 47; *Remains* 185.

23. *Untried Years* 27.

24. Ronnie Janoff-Bulman, "The Aftermath of Victimization: Rebuilding Shattered Assumptions," *Trauma and Its Wake: The Study and Treatment of Post-Traumatic Stress Disorder*, ed. Charles Figley (New York: Brunner/Mazel, 1985): 17, 21–22.

25. *Becoming* 62.

26. *Thought and Character* 42.

27. According to Alfred Habegger, Henry, Sr., made not one trip to England in the 1830s, as has traditionally been thought, but two. See Habegger, "Henry James, Sr., in the Late 1830s," *New England Quarterly* 64 (1991): 46–81. A letter quoted in *Thought and Character* suggests that Henry, Sr., envisioned subsequent trips abroad in relation to his lack of vocation: "When my paper to the Town and Country Club shall be read I shall be functionless, and may study as well, and, better perhaps, abroad as here" (59).

28. *Thought and Character* 50; *Remains* 59.

29. *Remains* 65.

30. See John Owen King, *Iron of Melancholy: Structures of Spiritual Conversion in America from the Puritan Conscience to Victorian Neurosis* (Middletown: Wesleyan University Press, 1983), 90–110. See also *Becoming* (68ff) for a comparison of Bunyan's *Pilgrim's Progress* and Henry, Sr.'s, account of his conversion.

31. *Remains* 43, 71; Henry James, Sr., *Substance and Shadow: or Morality and Religion in Their Relation to Life: An Essay Upon the Physics of Creation* (Boston: Ticknor and Fields, 1863), 126.

32. Gershen Kaufman, *Shame: The Power of Caring* (Cambridge: Schenkman, 1985), 105.

33. Lewis, *The Jameses*, 52.

34. King, *Iron of Melancholy*, 101.

35. Quoted in *Biography* 120, 130; MJ to HJ2, March 21, 1873; *Becoming* 141. See also Habegger, "Lessons of the Father," *Henry James Review* 8 (1986): 10–11.

36. King, *Iron of Melancholy*, 5; Kaufman, *Shame*, 106.

37. *Becoming* 77; see also 87–88. In "Henry James, Sr., in the 1830s," Alfred Habegger traces the process by which Henry, Sr.'s, radical religious thought led him to the conclusion that "one cannot do anything to attract divine mercy, one cannot even believe—since believing is as much an act, a work, as praying, confessing, repenting." Habegger also argues that, on the basis of this position, Henry, Sr., acquired "the fixed belief that individual human agency is an illusion" and, in doing so, furnished himself with yet another justification for professional failure (67, 68).

38. Quoted in *Thought and Character* 43, 36.

39. *Remains* 25, 216, 55. In his discussion of the influence of religious thinkers, Robert Sandeman and John Walker, Alfred Habegger concludes that Henry, Sr.'s, "fervently held doctrine that one's selfhood must be utterly 'vastated'—that is, that we must 'defecate ourselves of private or subjective ambition'—was basically a reformulation of Sandemanian and Walkerite depravity" ("Henry James, Sr., in the 1830s," 78).

40. King, *Iron of Melancholy*, 89. See Feinstein, *Becoming*, for a discussion of the view that "James's theology was intimately connected with his personal history" (78).

41. Habegger, "Lessons of the Father," 11; King, *Iron of Melancholy*, 101. One of the attractions of Swedenborgianism for James may have been the theologian's figuration of personal torments as forces outside the self: "Spirits, genii, and demons . . . that rendered the stricken person 'first unquiet, then anxious' " (King, *Iron of Melancholy*, 103). See Habegger's book on Henry, Sr., chapter 5, for more on Swedenborg's belief that "evil spirits" are present within individuals and responsible for both emotional and physical discomfort.

42. *Remains* 139.

43. *Becoming* 43. The fact that Dewhurst is able to throw himself into the war effort because he lost his wife and son is perhaps Henry, Sr.'s, way of unconsciously excusing his own lack of active involvement in the war. What is more, Henry, Sr.'s, attempt to cover for and justify himself anticipates the self-justificatory Civil War chapters of Henry, Jr.'s, second volume of autobiography, *Notes of a Son and Brother*. My research for chapter 5 of this study has shown that the autobiographical response of both Henry, Sr., and Henry, Jr., towards the Civil War is further complicated by Robertson James's war experience. It appears, for example, that Henry, Jr.'s, account in *Notes of a Son and Brother* of a feat of heroism performed by his brother Bob was actually performed (and somewhat accidentally) by a soldier named Dewhurst. Given the

fact that Bob had written a letter to his family describing Dewhurst's actions, it is possible that in composing his fictional autobiography Henry, Sr., appropriated the name of this Civil War hero for his persona, Stephen Dewhurst. (See *Notes of a Son and Brother* in *Autobiography* 457–58 and *Biography* 69).

44. *Remains* 147; *Becoming* 60, 65.

45. Quoted in Habegger's biography of Henry, Sr., Typescript, chapter 5; *Remains* 147.

46. Fossum and Mason, *Facing Shame,* 8.

47. See Habegger, "Henry James, Sr., in the Late 1830s" and "Lessons of the Father"; Jean Strouse, *Alice James: A Biography* (Boston: Houghton Mifflin, 1980), 209.

48. See Miller, *The Drama of the Gifted Child,* 3–29.

49. *Becoming* 65; *The Diary of Alice James,* ed. Leon Edel (New York: Penguin Books, 1964), 57–58.

50. Quoted in *Biography* 111, 128.

51. MJ to HJ2, December 15, 1872; Miriam Elsen, *Self Psychology in Clinical Social Work* (New York: Norton, 1986), 210. The passage from *Notes of a Son and Brother* reads as follows: " 'What shall we tell them you *are*, don't you see?' could but become on our lips at home a more constant appeal. It seemed wantonly to be prompted for our father, and indeed greatly to amuse him, that he should put us off with strange unheard-of attributions, such as would have made us ridiculous in our special circles" (*Autobiography* 278).

52. James Anderson, "In Search of Mary James," *The Psychohistory Review* 8 (1979): 68.

53. A slip made by Mary James in a letter to her son Henry likewise hints at unconscious negative feelings about her husband. Henry will "soon fall into the arms of Mrs. Lombard and Fanny" during his travels abroad, she writes; both are "great invalids, so avoid committing yourself *father* [sic] than you can help with them" (MJ to HJ2, July 1, 1873; my emphasis). A 1869 letter from Henry James to his parents corroborates James's later memory of the family practice of jeering at father: "In old times when we were all over in this blasted Europe together & poor father used to start on a reconnaissance & turn up the next day and with noble frankness own up to the terrible cause, we all used brutally to jeer at him; & I doubtless, as hard as the rest" (March 2, 1869).

54. *Woman Business* 222.

55. Henry James, Sr., "Woman and the 'Woman's Movement,' " *Putnam's Monthly Magazine* 1 (March 1853): 285, 286, 288; "Is Marriage Holy?" *Atlantic Monthly* 25 (March 1870): 364. A line from one of Mary James's letters to her son, Henry, hints at the extent to which her identity was subsumed by her husband. "[T]he very serious question arose," she writes of a vacation in Canada, "as to what we were to do with ourselves, ourselves meaning father" (August 4, 1873).

56. Quoted in Anderson, "Mary James," 67; quoted in *Becoming* 207.

57. Henry James, Sr., "Is Marriage Holy," 364; MJ to HJ2, December 8, 1873.

58. Henry, Jr., summarized his father's image of woman as the ideal wife and mother when, after her death in 1882, he extolled as follows the virtues of Mary James: "It was a perfect mother's life—the life of a perfect wife. To bring her children into the world—to expend herself, for years, for their happiness and

welfare—then, when they had reached a full maturity and were absorbed in the world and their own interests—to lay herself down in her ebbing strength and yield up her pure soul to the celestial power that had given her this divine commission" (*Notebooks* 230).

59. Note, for example, this passage from one of William's letters to his parents: "We wondered what our beloved parents were doing at that moment . . . and thought that you must all have been in the parlor, Alice, the widow, with her eyes fixed on her novel, eating some rich fruit which Father has just brought in for her from the Palais Royal; and lovely Mother and Aunt Kate in arm-chairs with their hands crossed in front of them, listening to Father, who is walking up and down speaking of the superiority of America to these countries, and how much better that we should go home" (quoted in F. O. Matthiessen, ed., *The James Family* [New York: Knopf, 1948], 91).

60. Elsen, *Self Psychology*, 228; Cushing Strout, "William James and the Twice-Born Sick Soul," *Daedalus* 97 (1968): 1069. See also *Becoming* 107–145.

61. William James, *Varieties of Religious Experience* (New York: Collier Books, 1961), 138.

62. *Becoming* 242, 311 (see also 304–05); James, *Varieties*, 138, 139.

63. *LWJ*, 1:241.

64. *Remains* 8–9; subsequent references to the *Literary Remains* in this chapter will be included in parentheses in the text.

65. *HJL*, 3:62. In his final letter to his father William wrote, "You need be in no anxiety about your literary remains. I will see them well taken care of, and that your words shall not suffer for being concealed" (*LWJ*, 1:219–20).

66. *LWJ*, 1:240.

67. *HJL*, 3:72–73.

68. Helen Lynd, *On Shame and the Search for Identity* (New York: Science Editions, 1961), 27. Kaufman believes that the "affect of shame itself often unconsciously transfers from one person to another without any action being necessary to effect that transfer. . . . Such observers as Sullivan, Kell, and Tompkins have said as much when they described how affects can transfer via affect contagion, empathy, or identification" (Kaufman, *Shame*, 73–74).

Of importance to this discussion of the capacity of the James children to inherit their father's emotional woundedness is the following passage from Robertson James's autobiographical fragment: "at a very early age the problems of life began to press upon me in such an unnatural way and I developed such an ability for feeling hurt and wounded that I became quite convinced by the time I was twelve years old that I was a foundling" (quoted in *Biography* 3).

69. Habegger, "Lessons," 21–23.

70. Habegger, "Lessons," 23.

71. Gay Wilson Allen, *William James* (New York: Viking, 1967), 260; passages from William's letters to Henry are taken from Allen, 261, 262; Henry's letter to William is quoted in *Thought and Character* 388. The entire exchange has recently been published in *The Correspondence of William James*, eds. Ignas Skrupskelis and Elizabeth Berkeley, (Charlottesville, VA: University Press of Virginia, 1992) 1:342–64.

72. WJ to AGJ, January 6, 1883. William goes on to reveal that the ostensible

reason he went abroad (to meet with other psychologists) was "humbug." The real reason was that he and Alice needed a break from one another.

73. Quoted in *Untried Years* 138.

74. *Woman Business* 9.

75. Karen Horney, *The Neurotic Personality of Our Time* (New York: Norton, 1937), 152. In his biography of Henry, Sr., Alfred Habegger notes another way in which Henry, Jr., communicated his sensitivity to his father's shame. Upon reading the memoir of Ezra Stiles Gannett, "another well-known man without a leg," James claimed that the son (William Gannett) who wrote the memoir had "violated the 'filial standpoint.' " William Gannett not only described his father " 'clicking along the sidewalks,' " but also claimed that "he pitied 'the venerable subject in his extreme bereavement of privacy' " (Typescript, chapter 5).

Chapter 2. The Heritage of Failure and Shame in the Life of Henry James, Jr.

1. William James, *Principles of Psychology*, Vol. 1 (New York: Dover, 1950), 306–7.

2. Burton Bledstein, *The Culture of Professionalism: The Middle Class and the Development of Higher Education in America* (New York: Norton, 1976), 14–15.

3. *Becoming* 331.

4. James, *Principles*, 1:310.

5. Manfred Mackenzie, "Obscure Hurt in Henry James," *The Southern Review* 3 (1968): 107.

6. Eakin, "Henry James's 'Obscure Hurt,' " 688.

7. *Untried Years* 63–64. In an observation corroborating James's self-portrait in the autobiographies, Wilky James wrote of his brother's early "poetical" endeavors: "the only difference there is between Willy and Harry's labours is that the former always shows his productions while the modest little Henry wouldn't let a soul or even a spirit see his" (*Untried Years* 150–51). "I shall take the liberty of asking the *Atlantic* people to send their letter of reject. or accept. to you," the young James himself wrote to T. S. Perry a few years later; "I cannot again stand the pressure of avowed authorship (for the present.) and their answer could not come here unobserved. Do not speak to Willie of this" (*HJL*, 1:50). For additional material on James's posture of remoteness and self-protectiveness in his family, see *Untried Years* 43, 64; for a discussion of the relationship between this posture and James's attitudes towards autobiographical writing, see my chapter 3, part 2. For Edel's discussion of the relationship between William and Henry, see *Untried Years* 56–80.

8. *LWJ*, 1:288.

9. Austin Warren, *The Elder Henry James* (New York: Macmillan, 1934), 171.

10. Minny concluded, says Habegger, that Henry, Sr.'s, attitude was "ignoble & shirking" because she "detected the morbidity and self-hatred that shaped

Uncle Henry's system of salvation" (*Woman Business* 135–36); quoted in Alfred Habegger, "In Darkest Henry James, Sr.," *The Henry James Review* 10 (1989): 83.

11. See *Woman Business* 140.
12. *LHJ*, 2: 54.
13. Quoted in *Conquest* 160.
14. Kaufman, *Shame*, 73.
15. *Becoming* 223. A letter written in 1883 by William to his wife describes not only his scorn for Henry's personality but also his emotional investment in it: "Yes, William wrote Alice in substance, Harry is a queer old boy, so good and yet so limited, as if he had taken an oath not to let himself out to more than half his humanhood in order to keep the other half from suffering, and he is unable to credit anyone else with the half which he has suppressed in himself" (summarized by Gay Wilson Allen in *William James* [New York: Viking Press, 1967], 262). This letter suggests that William feels piqued at not being credited with the half that Henry has suppressed, as if Henry's ability to "credit anyone else" reflects somehow on William himself. See *Becoming* 227 for a discussion of the "rivalrous fusion" that Feinstein believes characterizes the relationship between William and Henry, Jr.

16. Quoted in *Untried Years* 43.
17. MJ to HJ2, September 12, 1873; MJ to WJ, January 23, 1874.
18. Anderson, "Mary James," 63.
19. Anderson, "Mary James," 67; Miller, *The Drama of the Gifted Child*, 12; Susan Miller, *The Shame Experience* (n.p.: Analytic Press, 1985), 170–71.

Although Mary James appeared to be the healthy, competent caretaker of the family, her personal history suggests that this caretaking role was both a coping strategy and compensation for the unresolved grief and distress that was generated by the early death of her father and the subsequent emotional breakdown of her mother. (See Rev. William Walsh, *A Record and Sketch of Hugh Walsh's Family* [Newburgh, New York, 1903].) Indeed, it was in this family situation that Mary James learned the caretaking role she assumed in her own family when she married the lame Henry, Sr. As Anderson notes, Mary James "was quick to respond emotionally to illness and handicaps. It is likely that her attraction to her husband before their marriage had something to do with his lameness" ("Mary James," 69).

20. Many critics and biographers have long regarded Henry James's "psychological core" as "ambivalently feminine," as Feinstein says, and some also regard this feminine identity as a protection against threats to his integrity both within and outside the family (*Becoming* 233). Given the rhetoric of manhood in nineteenth-century America, and the equation of manhood with activity, assertiveness and vocational rigor, it would have been impossible for Henry, Jr., to escape the shameful associations implicit in his identification either with women or with women's ways of being in the world. Edel notes, in fact, that to Henry "William implied that writing wasn't quite an active manly, healthy way of existence" (*Conquest* 157). In an 1869 letter to William, Henry describes his complaints about his health as an "old woman's *doléances*" (*The Correspondence of William James*, eds. Ignas Skrupskelis and Elizabeth Berkeley (Charlottesville,

VA: University Press of Virginia, 1992), 1:111). For discussions of Henry James's so-called "feminine identity," see Lisa Appignanesi, *Femininity and the Creative Imagination* (New York: Barnes & Noble, 1973), 21; *Treacherous Years* 209–10; Virginia C. Fowler, *Henry James's American Girl: The Embroidery on the Canvas* (Madison: University of Wisconsin Press, 1984), 4–5; William Veeder, "The Feminine Orphan and the Emergent Master," 20–54.

21. Kaufman, *Shame*, 106.

22. *HJL*, 4:606. In *The Shame Experience*, Susan Miller distinguishes between various types of "felt experience" traditionally defined as shame (4). "Feeling inferior"—feeling small or defective—she defines as the "distress" experienced when a person "defines the self as no good or as not good enough." Labelled by Miller as a shame experience, this "type of misery-about-the-self" does not depend upon the presence of an audience. Yet it "does seem to depend on some sense, however vague, of the self standing before another or potentially visible to another." In other words, "one's defect stands in the context of others as superior and others as [potential] witnesses" (31, 32, 33). Here Miller defines shame along the same lines as Kaufman, Fossum and Mason.

Related to this shame experience is the feeling of being "undone" or "uncomfortably visible," the feeling Miller calls embarrassment. "If the rhythm of shame is a pulling inward and groundward, a hiding and concealing, the rhythm of what I call embarrassment" is that of "the self trying to pull inward or to diffuse itself into non-existence in response to a sudden feeling that an aspect of the self has been opened up to view without one's consent or participation" (38). There is a profound relationship between these two feeling states, embarrassment and shame. The individual who feels shame at the core of the self, who feels intrinsically defective and small, inevitably risks the pain of unexpected exposure or embarrassment more surely than the individual who does not possess a shame-based personality. The shame-based personality has more to feel embarrassed about, more to cover for or protect. Hence the potential for an incident of exposure to release what James calls the pent-up "flood of shame" within.

23. *Memories of Lady Ottoline Morrell: A Study in Friendship*, ed. Robert Gathorne-Hardy (New York: Knopf, 1964), 139–140.

24. *Untried Years* 74–80.

25. *HJL*, 1:185, 148, 158, 177–78.

26. *Becoming* 183–84, 194.

27. HJ2 to HJ1 and MJ, July, 17, 1869; *HJL*, 1:432, 224, 157; HJ2 to WJ, November 30, 1869 (also quoted in *Correspondence of William James*, 1:125).

28. *HJL*, 2:425. I am using Edel's reading of this letter, in which, although the manuscript says "future," Edel claims James "fairly obviously meant 'failure.'" Edel's reading is supported by the next line of the letter in which James says that Norton is marked for success not failure.

29. *HJL*, 1:115–16.

30. Mel Roman and Sara Blackburn, *Family Secrets: The Experience of Emotional Crisis* (New York: Times Books, 1979), 22.

31. *Becoming* 229.

32. HJ2 to Horace Fletcher, September 21, 1905.

33. *HJL*, 1:197.

34. HJ2 to HJ1 and MJ, August 4, 1873.

35. WJ to HJ2, October 2, 1869 (also quoted in Skrupskelis and Berkeley, *Correspondence*, 1:102).

36. *Becoming* 289, 292.

37. Quoted in *Biography* 114; HJ1 to HJ2, November 29, 1872; MJ to HJ2, January 21, 1873.

38. *HJL*, 1:157–58.

39. *Untried Years* 312.

40. *HJL*, 1:298, 432, 429–30, 406, 423–424.

41. Michael Anesko, *"Friction with the Market": Henry James and the Profession of Authorship* (New York: Oxford University Press, 1986), 33, 31–32. Ferguson's article is "The Triple Quest of Henry James: Fame, Art, and Fortune," *American Literature* 27 (1956): 475–498.

42. *HJL*, 2:260; quoted in *Conquest* 142.

43. *LHJ*, 2:150. We see a similar contrast in a letter written to his father three months later: "I can believe that William 'was a great *succes*,' as the Americans in Paris say, in Baltimore. . . . What is Bob doing—and Wilky, who wrote me that at this time he meant to leave his business? I am afraid that '*succès*' is not got there" (*LHJ*, 2:162).

44. HJ2 to WJ, November 30, 1869. The relevant passage reads as follows: "But I can't write to you about your back. The subject is to me too heavy—too sickening. All I can do is to remind you of my own career" (also quoted in *Correspondence*, 1:126).

45. *Correspondence*, 1:315; *HJL*, 2:305.

46. Quoted in *Conquest* 343.

47. Fossum and Mason, *Facing Shame*, 134.

48. *HJL*, 2:293, 295–96.

49. HJ2 to HJ1 and MJ, March 15, 1878.

50. *Notebooks* 225, 226, 232–33.

51. Ferguson, "Triple Quest," 477; Horney, *The Neurotic Personality of Our Time*, 141–42.

52. *HJL*, 2:156.

53. *HJL*, 4:372.

54. *Middle Years* 137.

55. *HJL*, 3:102.

56. Ibid; Roger Gard, *Henry James: The Critical Heritage* (London: Routledge, 1968), 12; *Middle Years* 185; *HJL*, 3:209.

57. *HJL*, 3:209.

58. *HJL*, 3:73, 102.

59. *HJL*, 2:151; 3:329, 326.

60. Gard, *Critical Heritage*, 13.

61. *HJL*, 3:275, 428.

62. *Notebooks* 83; Henry James, *Theatricals: Two Comedies* (New York: Harper, 1894), v.

63. *HJL*, 3:508, 509, 514.

64. *Treacherous Years* 15, 16.

65. *HJL*, 4:167.

66. *HJL*, 4:372, 494.

67. *Notebooks* 109.

68. Habegger, "Lessons of the Father," 23.

69. *HJL*, 4:167, 169.

70. Anesko, *"Friction With the Market,"* 144.

71. *HJL*, 4:366–67.

72. *Novel* 344–45.

73. *Novel* 221, 274.

74. *Master* 434.

75. *Novel* 345.

76. Quoted in *Master* 433–34; *HJL*, 4:497–98; *LHJ*, 2:119.

77. HJ2 to WJ, February 3, 1909; *Master* 435–36.

78. *HJL*, 4:516.

79. Harvey Green, *Fit for America* (New York: Pantheon, 1986), 294, 295; Horace Fletcher, *The A. B.-Z. of Our Own Nutrition* (New York: Frederick Stokes, 1903), xxi; James Whorton, *Crusaders for Fitness: The History of American Health Reformers* (Princeton: Princeton University Press, 1982), 180; promotional brochure for Horace Fletcher filed with William James's letters to Horace Fletcher.

80. *HJL*, 4:415; HJ2 to Horace Fletcher, January 5, 1906 and August 4, 1905; *HJL*, 4:416.

81. HJ2 to Horace Fletcher, September 21, 1905.

82. For discussions of eating disorders and addictive behaviors, see Fosum and Mason, *Facing Shame*, 131–35 and R. L. Palmer, *Anorexia Nervosa: A Guide for Sufferers and Their Families* (New York: Penguin, 1980), 31. Palmer explains that the "exercise of rigid self-control" over one's intake of food "can be viewed as a way of coping with the avoiding emotional turmoil which might otherwise be or seem to be unmanageable."

83. *HJL*, 4:516.

84. HJ2 to WJ, February 3, 1909, and July 18, 1909.

85. HJ2 to Horace Fletcher, September 21, 1905; HJ2 to WJ, July 18, 1909, and October 31, 1909.

86. *Master* 436; *HJL*, 4:521; HJ2 to JBP, July 21, 1909, and August 17, 1909.

87. Theodora Bosanquet to WJ, January 23, 1910; *Notebooks* 260.

88. Quoted in *Master* 438; *LHJ*, 2:155; *HJL*, 4:547.

89. *Master* 439–40.

90. *Master* 441; HJ to WJ, March 15, 1910. For a more detailed discussion of the relationship between James's Fletcherizing and his nervous breakdown, see my essay, "The Emotional Aftermath of the New York Edition," in *Henry James and the Construction of Authorship: Essays on the New York Edition*, ed. David McWhirter (Stanford: Stanford University Press, forthcoming).

91. *LHJ*, 2:158–60; *HJL*, 4:551; *LHJ*, 2:160–61, 162.

92. William James, *The Varieties of Religious Experience* (New York: Collier Books, 1961), 138.

93. *HJL*, 4:706.

Chapter 3. Strategies of Self-Protection and Vocational Success in *A Small Boy and Others*

1. *Novel* 47; "The Turning Point of My Life," first published in my essay, "Henry James's Autobiographical Fragment: 'The Turning Point of My Life,' " *Harvard Library Bulletin* 31 (1983): 40–51, then published in *Notebooks* 437–38.

2. *HJL*, 4:801.

3. *HJL*, 4:590.

4. HJ2 to HJ3, November 26, 1911; HJ2 to HJ3, December 23–25, 1911; HJ2 to HJ3, June 11–16, 1911.

5. Robert Sayre, *The Examined Self: Benjamin Franklin, Henry Adams, Henry James* (Princeton: Princeton University Press, 1964), 145; *Master* 455–6; *Fictions* 124.

6. *Fictions* 71.

7. Goetz, *Henry James and the Darkest Abyss of Romance*, 37.

8. Lewis, *The Jameses*, 67.

9. *Woman Business* 141.

10. Thomas Cooley, *Educated Lives: The Rise of Modern Autobiography in America* (Columbus: Ohio State University Press, 1976), 112.

11. *Fictions* 77–8.

12. *Master* 445.

13. *Fictions* 81.

14. William Hoffa, "The Final Preface: Henry James's Autobiography," *Sewanee Review* 77 (1969): 284.

15. Quoted in *Untried Years* 43.

16. Quoted in *Untried Years* 151; *HJL*, 1:50.

17. *Untried Years* 64.

18. *The American Essays of Henry James*, ed. Leon Edel (New York: Vintage, 1956), 136.

19. Edel, *The American Essays*, 132; Leon Edel, "Autobiography in Fiction—An Unpublished Review by Henry James," *Harvard Library Bulletin* 11 (1957): 257, 256; my emphasis.

20. Goetz, *Darkest Abyss of Romance*, 17; "Is There a Life After Death?" Matthiessen, *The James Family*, 607; Goetz, *Darkest Abyss of Romance*, 17.

21. *Novel* 320–21.

22. *Henry James and H. G. Wells*, eds. Leon Edel and Gordon Ray (Urbana: University of Illinois Press, 1958), 128–29.

23. Edel and Ray, *James and Wells*, 173–74; "George Sand," *Notes on Novelists* (New York: Biblo and Tannen, 1969), 163.

24. *Novel* 221; *Treacherous Years* 15; *Novel* 246, 221; John Halverson, "Late Manner, Major Phase," *Sewanee Review* 79 (1971): 224; *HJL*, 3:300.

25. Matthiessen, *The James Family*, 610, 611, 607.

26. *Literary Criticism: French Writers*, ed. Leon Edel (New York: Literary Classics, 1984), 91; *Literary Criticism: English Writers*, ed. Leon Edel (New York: Literary Classics, 1984), 1205–1220.

27. *HJL*, 4:224, 302, 290; *William Wetmore Story and His Friends*, 2 vols. (Boston: Houghton, Mifflin, 1903), 2:30; 1:245, 5; *The Letters of Henry Adams*, ed. J. C. Levenson, et al. (Cambridge: Harvard University Press, 1988), 5:524.

28. Henry James, *The American Scene*, ed. W. H. Auden (New York: Scribner's, 1946), 25, 35, 13, 54; Gordon Taylor, "Chapters of Experience: *The American Scene*," *Genre* 12 (1979): 95.

29. Mutlu Blasing, *The Art of Life: Studies in American Autobiographical Literature* (Austin: University of Texas Press, 1977), 57.

30. *Novel* 4, 313.

31. *Novel* 47.

32. *Novel* 313.

33. *Notebooks* 437–38.

34. Edel and Ray, *James and Wells*, 128–29; my emphasis.

35. See *Fictions* (56–86) for a more detailed analysis of the relationship between James's autobiographical narrator and the small boy.

36. John Sturrock, "The New Model Autobiographer," *New Literary History*: 9 (1977): 58.

37. Veeder, "The Feminine Orphan and the Emergent Master," *Henry James Review* 12 (1991): 21.

38. *Fictions* 75.

39. Virginia Harlowe, *Thomas Sargeant Perry: And Letters to Perry from William, Henry, and Garth Wilkinson James* (Durham: Duke University Press, 1950), 344.

40. Lewis, *The Jameses*, 93.

41. *Untried Years* 137–38.

Chapter 4. Biographical Consequences of the Autobiographical Act

1. See *Untried Years* 75–76.

2. Veeder, "The Feminine Orphan and the Emergent Master," 49.

3. Edel and Ray, *Henry James and H. G. Wells*, 171.

4. HJ2 to AGJ, November 13, 1911; HJ2 to HJ3, November 26, 1911.

5. HJ2 to HJ3, June 5–11, 1911.

6. *HJL*, 1:115, 124; 2:60.

7. *Becoming* 196. The letter is taken from *HJL*, 1:125.

8. *Becoming* 194.

9. HJ2 to HJ3, June 11–16, 1912.

10. HJ2 to JBP, August 7, 1912. Over a year later, James's decision to write two books instead of one, and to devote a good deal of material to his own childhood, prompted Charles Scribner to write the following to James's agent:

Your letter concerning Mr. Henry James's new book "Notes of a Son and Brother" has just arrived and I am glad to hear that we may expect for our edition Macmillan's corrected proofs. Why is it that you give us no information concerning the two articles to be made from the selected Letters of William James? [Henry had originally intended to serialize his reflections on William's letters before publishing them in book form.] Your silence and the presumption that the book is to appear shortly lead me to think that the articles have been abandoned. I fear that Mr. James's Introduction to the Letters has grown into a second volume and that the Letters themselves (which were expected to make the bulk of the volume) will not appear in it at all. Please let me know about it. Of course this is for your eye and I do not wish to discourage Mr. James, but as you must realise, this enterprise is likely to prove diappointing [sic] if my fears are well founded. We started with the idea of a volume of William James's Letters and we shall have two volumes on Mr. Henry James's early life (October 27, 1913).

    11. HJ2 to AGJ, August 26, 1912.

    12. HJ2 to HJ3, September 23–24, 1912.

    13. HJ2 to JBP; September 9, 1912.

    14. HJ2 to HJ3, September 23–24, 1912.

    15. HJ2 to HJ3, September 23–24, 1912. Subsequent passages from this letter are taken from the manuscript copy and are quoted without additional citation in the text.

    16. Marginal notes on the manuscript of the September 23–24, 1912, letter. The sentence to which Harry responds reads as follows: ". . . I feel upset indeed at your allusion to poor Pinker's having perhaps *prevailed* upon me to 'give up' the Family Book!"

    17. HJ3 to HJ2, October 6, 1912.

    18. HJ2 to AGJ, October 29, 1912.

    19. *Master* 478.

    20. HJ2 to JBP, October 8, 1912; HJ2 to HJ3, October 22, 1912; HJ2 to AGJ, October 29, 1912.

    21. HJ2 to AGJ, January 5 and 17, 1913; HJ2 to HJ3, January 19, 1913.

    22. *Becoming* 225.

    23. *Becoming* 227.

    24. HJ2 to HJ3, October 22 and February 25, 1912.

    25. HJ2 to AGJ, October 29, 1912; HJ2 to HJ3, October 22, 1912.

    26. HJ2 to HJ3, November 25, 1912.

    27. HJ2 to JBP, October 8, 1912.

    28. HJ2 to AGJ, January 5, 1913; HJ2 to HJ3, February 25 and January 19, 1913.

    29. *Fictions* 71.

    30. *Fictions* 70–71.

    31. *Fictions* 86, 124.

    32. HJ2 to HJ3, November 25, 1912; HJ2 to AGJ, January 5 and 19, 1913.

    33. HJ2 to AGJ, October 29, 1912.

    34. HJ2 to AGJ, October 29, 1912; HJ2 to HJ3, February 25, 1913.

    35. HJ2 to JBP, November 26, 1912. Earlier in this letter, James says that "[m]y own history here remains dim, I'm sorry to say, to a degree that I'm getting to be ashamed of."

    36. Howard Brody, *Stories of Sickness* (New Haven: Yale University Press, 1987), x, 14, 30; Thomas Couser, "Introduction: The Embodied Self," *a/b: Auto/Biography Studies* 6 (1991): 4–5. For further discussion of illness narratives,

see the other essays in this special issue of *a/b* devoted to the subject of "Illness, Disability, and Lifewriting," and Arthur Kleinman, M. D., *The Illness Narratives: Suffering, Healing, and the Human Condition* (New York: Basic Books, 1988).

37. *Fictions* 124. In his recent biography, Fred Kaplan notes that the stories of illness Henry recited for his family in his letters from the 1860s fulfilled a similar purpose in the young writer's life. Quoting from a letter written to William in May 1869, Kaplan says, "He had 'told the long story because I felt a need of opening myself & taking hold of my situation.' He had told the story also because he had need to create a structure of words that would minister to 'the sacred influence of home,' bringing it 'into harmony with my idea' " (*Henry James: The Imagination of Genius*, 103).

38. Quoted in *Becoming* 298.

39. HJ2 to HJ3, November 25, 1912.

40. HJ2 to AGJ, January 5, 1913.

41. HJ2 to JBP, November 26, 1912.

42. HJ2 to HJ3, January 19, 1913.

43. *HJL*, 4:298.

44. HJ2 to HJ3, February 25, 1913. Of the militant language that in the 1860s James used to describe his European adventures to his family at home, Fred Kaplan says: "The coinage of illness was the most useful currency in the James family. So too was the rhetoric of self-exhortation, of romantic wilfullness, made even more powerful for Henry senior's sons because of his ostensible deprecation of it. For Henry, this, now, was histrionics on a grand scale, energizing military metaphors to heroicize, as well as to give force to, ordinary activities made difficult by emotional hesitation" (*Henry James* 111).

45. HJ2 to AGJ, January 17, 1913.

46. Ibid.

47. *Becoming* 193; *LWJ*, 1:80.

48. Henry James, Sr., "Woman and the 'Woman's Movement,' " 286.

49. *Becoming* 345; HJ2 to HJ3, January 19, 1913. As Feinstein says of Alice Gibbens' education in caretaking, "The eldest of three daughters born of a fragile, unhappy marriage, she became virtually the head of her family at the age of sixteen, when her long-separated physician father returned from the Civil War and a long battle with alcoholism, and committed suicide. Her mother had collapsed and Alice had taken over" (345). For more information on the father's suicide, see "The Strange Death of Daniel Gibbens," in Lewis, *The Jameses*, 589–93.

50. See, for example, Mary James's July 24, 1869, letter to Henry: "You know Father used to say to you, that if you would only fall in love it would be the making of you. Possibly Will's susceptible heart may be coming to the rescue of his back." In two separate letters in 1873, she likewise expresses concern over the extent to which Wilky's fiancée will support and encourage him. In the first letter, she feels "inclined to regret" his engagement, but with "his tendencies and temperment he needed some strong motive to stimulate him to work"; in the second, she concludes, "Poor Wilky! . . . I am afraid she is not a strong helpful woman, and does not help keep up his courage" (MJ to HJ2, March 21 and May 25, 1873). In chapter 2, I quoted a passage from an 1878 letter from Henry to

William in which, commenting on Wilky's "rude career," Henry adds, "but I hope his wife eases him down" (*LHJ*, 2:151). In *Henry James and the "Woman Business,"* Alfred Habegger quotes a number of letters which illustrate the fact that both Mary and Alice Gibbens James served as refuge and support for their husbands. Especially telling is Alice's remark that she had tried "to make my life serve his [William's], to stand between him and all harmful things" (244; see also 39).

Chapter 5. Divided Messages in *Notes of a Son and Brother*

1. Also quoted in chapter 4 of this study, James's September 23–24, 1912, letter to Harry claims that the completed material for *Notes* "begins with our time in Geneva from the end of 1859." "I am packing it in," he goes on to say, "all the vividness of reference & portraiture, all the *accompaniment*, that my strained estimate of my possible size of volume will allow, & in as much citation of other letters, your grandfather's . . . in particular, though as such too few & meagre (of the *useable*, I mean,) . . . My design is to follow more or less every hare I can start—& I have (as a slight illustration) a dozen pages of mere *introduction* of Minny Temple, 15 of evocation of our *1st* meeting with John LaFarge at Newport, about as many as to William Hunt &c, & about Miss Upham's old table at Cambridge (these being, as examples, but trifles, however.)"

2. HJ2 to HJ3, November 25, 1912, and January 19, 1913.

3. See Jane Tompkins, "The Redemption of Time in *Notes of a Son and Brother*," *Texas Studies in Language and Literature* 4 (1973): 681–90; HJ2 to HJ3, January 19, 1913.

4. *Fictions* 90.

5. *Becoming* 65.

6. Writing to a friend in 1868, William James made a similar statement about his need to make something of himself: "I confess that, in the lonesome gloom which beset me for a couple of months last summer, the only feeling that kept me from giving up was that by waiting and living, by hook or crook, long enough, I might make my *nick*, however small a one, in the raw stuff the race has got to shape, and so assert my reality" (*LWJ*, 1:132).

7. *Untried Years* 183.

8. Charles and Tess Hoffmann, "Henry James and the Civil War," *New England Quarterly* 72 (1989): 533.

9. Eakin, "Henry James's 'Obscure Hurt,' " 683.

10. See Fossum and Mason, *Facing Shame*, 6, and Helen Lynd, *On Shame and the Search for Identity* (New York: Science Editions, 1961), 27.

11. *Fictions* 91.

12. *Fictions* 94, 95.

13. Donna Przybylowicz, *Desire and Repression: The Dialectic of Self and Other in the Late Works of Henry James* (n.p.: University of Alabama Press, 1986), 218; Alfred Habegger, "Henry James's Rewriting of Minny Temple's Letters," *American Literature* 58 (1986): 166. It is also possible that, by deleting passages showing his father's attempts to combat despair, James was interested in

suppressing evidence not of the "strong resolution" in his father but of discouragement and depression (Przybylowicz, *Desire and Repression*, 218).

14. *Fictions* 95.
15. *Notebooks* 229; *Untried Years* 48.
16. *Notebooks* 229, 230.
17. "Woman and the 'Woman's Movement,' " 286.
18. Ibid, 281, 283.
19. *Woman Business* 222. See also my discussion of Mary James, chapter 1.
20. *Untried Years* 48, 49.
21. William Veeder, "The Portrait of a Lack," *New Essays on the Portrait of a Lady*, ed. Joel Porte (Cambridge: Cambridge University Press, 1990), 97.
22. Typescript copy of "The Portrait of a Lack." Veeder has published three versions of this essay which I read in early drafts: "The Portrait of a Lack" cited above; "Henry James and the Uses of the Feminine," *Out of Bounds: Male Writers and Gender(ed) Criticism*, eds. Laura Claridge and Elizabeth Langland (Amherst: University of Massachusetts Press, 1990): 219–51; and "The Feminine Orphan and the Emergent Master: Self-Realization in Henry James," *The Henry James Review* 12 (Winter, 1991): 20–54.
23. Veeder, "Portrait of a Lack," 97; Jean Strouse, "The Real Reasons," *Extraordinary Lives: The Art and Craft of American Biography*, ed. William Zinsser (New York: American Heritage, 1986), 175; Beth Ash, "Frail Vessels and Vast Designs: A Psychoanalytic Portrait of Isabel Archer," *New Essays on the Portrait of a Lady*, ed. Joel Porte (Cambridge: Cambridge University Press, 1990), 124.
24. I am grateful to Professor William Veeder for this reading of James's relationship to his parents in *Notes of a Son and Brother*.
25. Francis Hart, "Notes for an Anatomy of Modern Autobiography," *New Literary History* 1 (1970): 492.
26. *LHJ*, 2:346.
27. David Kirby, "Henry James: Art and Autobiography," *Dalhousie Review* 52 (1972–73): 637–44.
28. Jane Tompkins, "Redemption of Time," 684–85.
29. Ibid, 683.
30. Conversation with Professor Suzie Naiburg, Henry James Sesquicentennial Conference, June, 1993.
31. In a 1837 letter describing his plans, Henry, Sr., wrote somewhat grudgingly that "I should very much like to go on to Paris . . . but fancy I shall be obliged to go into Ireland, and spend a few weeks with an uncle's family there" (quoted in *Becoming* 63–64).
32. *Becoming* 64, 65.
33. John Byng-Hall, "Re-editing family mythology during family therapy," *Journal of Family Therapy* 1 (1979): 104–5; A. J. Ferreira, "Family Myths: The Covert Rules of the Relationship," *Confinia Psychiatrica* 8 (1965): 16.
34. Ferreira, "Family Myths," 16, 19.
35. Strouse, "The Real Reasons," 174.
36. Leon Edel, ed., *The Diary of Alice James* (New York: Dodd, Mead, 1964), 79; quoted in *Biography* 196.

37. Edel, *Diary*, 79.
38. Strouse, "Real Reasons," 180.
39. Edel, *Diary*, 149.
40. Quoted in *Biography* 168; my emphasis.
41. *Becoming* 251; quoted in Fred Kaplan, *Henry James: The Imagination of Genius* (New York: William Morrow, 1992), 267.
42. Quoted in *Biography* 195.
43. *Biography* 57. Maher's complete discussion of the fate of the letters is as follows: "It is possible that Bob's letters to his parents were included in the bundles of letters destroyed by Aunt Kate. It is also possible, however, that the letters were destroyed by Henry James, Sr., to protect Bob's privacy. Some of Henry James, Sr.'s, responses to Bob from this period [of military service] have survived, and they indicate that Bob's letters to his parents contained confessions that his conduct 'may not have been irreproachable.'"
44. Here the reader cannot help but question the "consistent tenderness" of parents who, having discouraged their two oldest sons from enlisting, were willing to surrender to the war a fourth son who was underage.
45. *Biography* 69. Maher claims that "Henry's crediting Bob with the deed," and with a deliberately heroic deed at that, "may simply have been an error; however, Henry frequently used his *Autobiography* to portray his family in the way *he* wanted them to be seen" (69).
46. Tompkins, "Redemption of Time," 686.
47. Compare, for example, Henry, Sr.'s, 1842 letter to Emerson as it appears in *Thought and Character* 42 with Henry, Jr.'s, version of the letter in chapter 6 of *Notes* (345).
48. HJ2 to HJ3, November 15–18, 1913.
49. *Fictions* 90.
50. See the Hoffmann's article, "Henry James and the Civil War," for evidence showing that James "had been exempted from military duty by reason of physical disability" (529).
51. See *Fictions* 109–16 for a comprehensive discussion of this passage.
52. For an extended discussion of this passage and its relevance to James's late fiction, see Charles Feidelson, "James and the 'Man of Imagination,'" *Literary Theory and Structure*, Frank Brody et al., eds. (New Haven: Yale University Press, 1973), 331–52.
53. Quoted in Edel, *Diary*, 8.
54. Strouse, *Alice James*, 49, 51.
55. HJ2 to HJ3, January 19, 1913.
56. HJ2 to AGJ, November 13, 1911; quoted in Edel, *Diary*, 19.
57. HJ2 to HJ3, January 19, 1913.
58. S. P. Rosenbaum, "Letters to the Pell-Clarkes from Their 'Old Cousin and Friend' Henry James," *American Literature* 31 (1959): 53.
59. Alfred Habegger, "Henry James's Rewriting of Minny Temple's Letters," *American Literature* 58 (1986): 161. The letter quoted by Habegger in this passage (HJ2 to Henrietta Temple Pell-Clarke, May 5, 1914) is published in Rosenbaum, "Letters to the Pell-Clarkes," 53.
60. Habegger, "Henry James's Rewriting," 163–65.

61. *Woman Busines* 129.
62. Habegger, "Henry James's Rewriting," 167.
63. *HJL*, 1:218, 221, 226.
64. *Woman Business* 143–45.
65. *HJL*, 1:219, 227, 223.
66. *HJL*, 1:219, 221, 224.
67. Tompkins, "Redemption of Time," 688.

Epilogue

1. *Master* 500.
2. *LHJ*, 2:240.
3. For interpretations of James's 1914 recovery and the means by which he effected it, see F. O. Matthiessen, *Henry James: The Major Phase* (New York: Oxford University Press, 1944), 118–19; F. W. Dupee, *Henry James* (New York: William Morrow, 1974), 245–48; Dorothea Krook, *The Ordeal of Consciousness* (Cambridge: Cambridge University Press, 1962), 353; Robert Sayre, *The Examined Self: Benjamin Franklin, Henry Adams, Henry James* (Princeton: Princeton University Press, 1964), 144–45; William Hoffa, "The Final Preface: Henry James's Autobiography," *Sewanee Review* 77 (1969): 283; *Master* 499–500; *Fictions* 56–125.
4. *HJL*, 4:706.
5. HJ2 to HJ3, November 15–18, 1913.
6. Henry's nephew, Harry, penned frustrated rejoinders to some of his Uncle's explanations in the margins of his copy of Percy Lubbock's 1920 edition, *LHJ*, 2:345–48. To his Uncle's claim (in the November 15–18, 1913, letter) that "I could *hear*" William "say Abraham and couldn't hear him say Abe," Harry exclaimed, "Yet he wrote it." To his Uncle's claim that he changed the wording of William's letters "to the end that he should be more easily and engagingly readable," Harry wrote, "But it ceased to be *he*. Poor Uncle H. could not make emandations that were *W. J.* They were *H. J.*"
7. *LHJ*, 2:309.
8. HJ2 to HJ3, April 24, 1913. An earlier version of the argument that follows appeared in my article, " 'Absolutely Acclaimed': The Cure for Depression in James's Final Phase," *The Henry James Review* 8 (1987): 126–38.
9. Virginia Harlowe, *Thomas Sargeant Perry: and Letters to Perry from William, Henry, and Garth Wilkinson James* (Durham: Duke University Press, 1950), 340.
10. Anonymous, "Mr. Henry James's Method," *Times Literary Supplement* (March 26, 1914): 147; Anonymous, "The Genius of Henry James," *Nation* (March 28, 1914): 1081. For a more detailed discussion of the British reviews, see Carol Holly, "The British Reception of Henry James's Autobiographies," *American Literature* 57 (1985): 570–87.
11. HJ2 to AGJ, March 18, 1914.
12. HJ2 to AGJ, March 29, 1914.
13. *Novel* 345.
14. James's claim was exaggerated, it seems, because nothing in his career,

not even the acclaim of 1914, could compare to the widespread reknown he enjoyed during his international phase in the late 1870s and early 1880s.

15. HJ2 to HJ3, April 7, 1914.

16. Harlowe, *Thomas Sargeant Perry*, 345–46.

17. *HJL*, 2:193.

18. HJ2 to HJ3, April 7, 1914.

19. Conversation with Tamara Follini, Henry James Sesquicentennial Conference, June 1993.

20. *HJL*, 4:521.

21. *Fictions* 124.

Index

Adams, Henry, 27, 94, 185, 194
Allen, Gay Wilson, 39
The Ambassadors, 61, 93
The American, theatrical production, 60
The American Scene, 94–95
Anderson, James, 30, 46
Anesko, Michael, 53, 63
Arnold, Matthew, 91
Ash, Beth, 156
Autobiographical act as biographical event, 5–6
Autobiography, See *A Small Boy and Others; Notes of a Son and Brother; The Middle Years*
Autobiography, history of criticism of, 5–6
Autobiography letters (1911–1914), 3–4, 6–7, 8, 11, 74–75, 94, 105–6, 109–20, 179–80; 185–94; on illness, interruption of work on autobiographies, 120–36, 145

"The Bench of Desolation," 70
Blasing, Mutlu, 95
Bledstein, Burton, 42
Bosanquet, Theodora, 71, 117
The Bostonians, 58
Bowlby, John, 18
Boyer, Paul, 205n7
Brody, Howard, 127

Confidence, 53
Cooley, Thomas, 86, 87
Couser, Thomas, 127

Eakin, Paul John, 5–6, 44, 75, 81, 87–89,

101, 123, 125, 127, 128, 138–39, 145, 148, 150, 151, 175, 194, 216n35, 221n51
Edel, Leon, 6–7, 8, 20, 31, 44, 52, 58, 61, 65, 70–71, 75, 87, 91, 93, 106, 121, 142, 154
Elsen, Miriam, 30, 33
Erikson, Erik, 33, 50

Family systems (therapy) theory, 8–10, 58; and family legends, myths, 11, 162–63; and family secrets, 28
Feidelson, Charles, Jr., 221n51
Feinstein, Howard, 9–10, 13, 20, 24, 26, 29, 34, 48, 50, 112, 114, 121, 134, 140, 162, 167, 204nn2,4,5, 206n30, 211nn15,20, 218n49
Ferguson, Francis, 53
Fletcher, Horace, 68, 70
Fletcherizing, 68–73, 83, 121
Follini, Tamara, 194
Fossum, Merle, and Marilyn Mason, 214n82

Gard, Roger, 60
Geertz, Clifford, 8
Goetz, William, 81, 91
Gosse, Edmund, 60
Gray, John Chipman, 138, 181
Green, Harvey, 68
Guy Domville, 60–61, 62, 66, 93, 192

Habegger, Alfred, 26, 27, 28, 31, 39, 40, 62, 85, 150–51, 153, 181, 182–83, 204nn2,6, 206n27, 207nn37,39,41, 210n75, 210n10, 218n50
Halvorson, John, 93

224

Hastings, Katherine, 17
Hoffa, William, 89
Hoffman, Charles and Tess, 221n50
Holly, Carol, 202n7, 214n90, 222n10
"Honoré de Balzac" (1902), 94
Horney, Karen, 40–41, 57
Howells, William Dean, 40, 47, 92, 96, 102

Illness narratives, theory of, 127, 217n36
"Introduction," The Tempest, 94
"Is There a Life After Death," 93–94

James, Alice (sister of Henry James), 29,
    30, 31, 32, 33, 34, 37, 48, 51, 73, 164–65,
    179. See also Notes of a Son and Brother
James, Alice Howe Gibbens (sister-in-law
    of Henry James), 40, 74, 105, 108,
    109–10, 115–16, 119, 132–35, 188–89,
    218n49
James, Augustus (Henry James's paternal
    uncle), 13–14, 19, 22, 51–52, 55, 66, 73,
    84
James, Garth Wilkinson, or Wilky
    (brother of Henry James), 10, 43, 45,
    51, 54, 55, 66, 90. See also A Small Boy
    and Others; Notes of a Son and Brother
James, Henry: aspirations to success and
    fears of failure, 40, 43, 49, 53–57,
    64–66; attempts to disassociate himself
    from family patterns, 48, 50, 52–57, 69,
    213n43; depression and recovery of,
    6–7, 43, 61, 70–73, 74, 165; dreams of,
    47–48, 57, 72–73, 86–90, 104; illnesses
    of, 11, 43, 48–50, 54–55, 67, 119–36,
    213n44; late autobiographical writings
    of, 5, 93–98; love of privacy and fear of
    exposure of, 90–91, 92–93, 210n7;
    negative or shame-based identity of, 10,
    43, 44, 46–48, 49, 51–52, 194, 211n20;
    and physicians, 67–68, 70, 71–72,
    128–31, 132; and problems with eating,
    50, 55, 69–73, 83, 214n82; professional
    disappointments of, 58–62, 65–71, 165;
    and relationship with father, 44–45,
    111–12, 208n53; and relationship with
    mother, 30, 45, 111–12, 156; and
    relationship with Wilky, 8, 167; and
    relationship with William, 8, 37, 38–41,
    44–45, 46, 68–69, 90–91, 106–9, 121,
    164, 211n15; on self-revelation in
    autobiographical writing, 91–93, 97–98;

sensitivity to, identification with, father's
    failure and shame, 37–41, 43, 44–45,
    58–63, 66–73, 210n75. See also A Small
    Boy and Others; Notes of a Son and
    Brother
James, Henry, Jr., or Harry (nephew of
    Henry James), 3, 40, 71–72, 74, 103–4,
    105–120, 122–23, 128, 132, 152,
    186–90, 217n16, 222n6
James, Henry, Sr., (father of Henry
    James): accident and disability of,
    18–21, 27; alcoholism of, 14; attitudes
    towards women, 31–32, 134, 153;
    autobiographical persona of, 26–27, 36;
    critical attitude towards Wilky, 51–52;
    and father, 10, 14–15, 16, 21–22, 27, 29;
    marital relationship of, 24, 30–31, 134,
    208nn53,55, 209n59; negative identity
    or self-loathing of, 22–25, 167; religious
    up-bringing of, 15–16, 20, 204n6; self-
    serving parenting practices of, 29–30,
    33–34, 221n44; secrecy of, 27, 28, 33,
    36, 164; and uses of autobiography, 25,
    27–28; vastation or emotional
    breakdown of, 22–24, 34, 48, 55, 73;
    vocational uncertainty of, 22, 25 32–33,
    206n27. See also A Small Boy and
    Others; Notes of a Son and Brother
—works: Lectures and Miscellanies, 25;
    Literary Remains of the Late Henry
    James (includes "Autobiographic
    Sketch") 26–27, 34–38, 58–59, 62,
    207n43; Substance and Shadow, 27;
    Society, the Redeemed Form of Man, 26,
    27, 34
James, John (paternal uncle of Henry
    James), 13, 14, 19
James, Mary (mother of Henry James),
    13–14, 24, 28; and husband, 30–31, 33;
    role in family of, 24, 30–33, 37, 45, 164,
    211n19, 218n50; and Wilky, 45, 51–52.
    See also Notes of a Son and Brother
James, Robertson, or Bob (brother of
    Henry James), 10, 51, 55, 133, 164,
    209n68. See also A Small Boy and
    Others; Notes of a Son and Brother
James, William (grandfather of Henry
    James), and the origins of shame-based
    psychology in the James family, 13, 23,
    37, 38, 41, 51, 66–67, 103, 206n16,17.
    See also Notes of a Son and Brother

James, William (brother of Henry James): death of, 74, 108; emotional breakdown and psychosomatic illness of, 26, 34, 48, 50, 51, 67, 73; negative or shame-based identity of, 42–43, 44–45, 46, 48, 219n6; and relationship with father, 10, 33–37, 45, 50; and relationship with mother, 30, 32, 37, 46; writings about, justifications of, father of, 25, 29, 34–37. See also *A Small Boy and Others; Notes of a Son and Brother*
—works: *Literary Remains of the Late Henry James* (ed.), 26, 34–38, 103, 174, 175; *Principles of Psychology*, 42–43, *Varieties of Religious Experience*, 34

Kaplan, Fred, 202n12, 218n37, 218n44
Kaufmann, Gershen, 23, 45, 209n68
Kett, Joseph, 15, 205n7, 207n41
King, John Owen, 23, 24, 26, 207n41
Kirby, David, 158

Laing, R. D., 4
Leverenz, David, 205n7
Lewis, R. W. B., 83, 103, 202n12, 218n49
Lubbock, Percy, 7
Lynd, Helen, 38

McIntyre, Archbald, 14–15, 23
Mackenzie, Manfred, 43–44
Maher, Jane, 170, 221n43
The Middle Years, 194
Miller, Alice, 156
Miller, Susan, 212n22
Morrell, Lady Ottoline, 47, 86, 87, 104
Mourning theory, 18–19

Naiburg, Suzi, 160
Narcissistic parenting, 29, 156, 203n22
Notebooks, 56–57, 62, 71, 152, 153, 208n58
Notes of a Son and Brother, 3, 5–6, 11–12, 25, 30–31, 66, 74, 77, 81, 96, 125, 135–36, 137–85; on Alice (sister), 136, 178–80; on Bob, 154, 166–67, 170–72, 176–78, 183, 207n43; on Civil War, 131–32, 141–42, 151, 166–72, 176–78; commemorative, protective purposes of, 138, 157–60, 165, 171–84; conflicting intentions of autobiographer in, 139–40, 156–57, 160–61, 172, 189; correspondence included in, 137–38, 150–51, 154, 165, 167–68, 172–73, 175, 179, 181, 186–90; critical reception of, 186, 190–95; on father, 139, 143–51, 154–55, 161–62, 163, 165, 172–74, 180, 208n51; fears, needs, anxieties of autobiographical narrator, 143, 157, 165, 166–67, 171–84, 187–88; on grandfather, 161–62, 163; on Nathaniel Hawthorne, 160; on William Morris Hunt, 141, 159–60, 183; and James family myth, 161–65; on James family women, 136, 151–56, 178–84; on John LaFarge, 141, 157, 158–59, 160–61, 175, 183; on mother, 134, 136, 139, 151–56, 160, 163, 173–74, 178, 180; on "obscure hurt," 127, 139, 142–45, 151, 168, 176; organization of, 138, 149–50, 151, 175; process of composition of, and family negotiations concerning, 105–6, 108, 109–110, 113–20, 122–23, 137, 138, 186–89, 219n1; on Cabot Russell, 168, 169; on William James Temple, 165–66; on Minny Temple, 136, 140, 145, 151, 179, 181–84; on therapeutic benefits of autobiographical act, 185–86, 194–95; on Catherine Walsh (Aunt Kate), 178, 180; on Wilky, 154, 166–70, 171–72, 176–78, 183; on William, 138, 141, 147–48, 150, 157–58, 159, 169, 174–76; on young Henry James's artistic development and professional commitment, 139, 140–51, 158–59, 171, 175; on young Henry James's negative or shame-based identity, 145–47

Nott, Eliphalet, 204n4

Palmer, R. L., 214n82
Perry, T. S., 90, 102–3, 190
Politics of illness (James family), 11, 48–49, 50, 114, 121; and women as caretakers, 134–35
The Portrait of a Lady, 182
Posnock, Ross, 202n7

Index

Prefaces to the New York Edition, 5,
63–65, 74, 91–92, 93, 95–96, 189, 192
The Princess Casamassima, 58
Przybylowicz, Donna, 150–51, 219*n13*

Review of *John Godfrey's Fortunes*, 91
Rosenzweig, Saul, 203*n13*

Sand, George, 91, 92
Saum, Lewis, 206*n14*
Sayre, Robert, 75
Scribner, Charles, 216*n10*
Shame psychology, 8–9, 19, 23, 24, 28, 38,
45, 58, 146
A Small Boy and Others, 3–4, 9, 10–11,
40, 43, 73, 74–104, 105, 158, 163,
176–77; alterations of historical record
of, 102–4; on Bob, 77; conflicting
intentions of autobiographer of, 76, 139;
critical reception of, 135, 190; dream of
Galerie d'Apollon in, 86–90, 104, 106,
139; evasions, qualifications,
justifications of autobiographical
narrator of, 101–4; on fostering of small
boy's identity, 75, 82–83, 98–99, 107; on
the James family fate, 79–81, 84–85, 87,
89, 104; narrative control in, 97–98,
104; problematic identity and behavior
of father in, 76, 77–79, 84–85, 99–101,
104; process of composition of, and
familial negotiations concerning,
109–120, 125, 188–89; relationship with
William in, 75–77, 85–86, 101, 106–9,
121; shameful identity of small boy in,
77–78, 80, 81, 106, 145; survival
strategies and enabling conditions of

small boy in, 81–87, 123–25, 127, 139,
140; therapeutic benefits of
autobiographical act of, 75, 127, 135–36
Strouse, Jean, 156, 164, 179
Strout, Cushing, 33
Sturrock, John, 98
Swedenborg, Emanuel, 22, 24

Taylor, Gordon, 94–95
Temple, Minny, 44, 45, 95, 182–83,
210*n10*. SEE ALSO *Notes of a Son and
Brother*
Temple, Robert, 51
Theatricals, introduction to, 60
Tompkins, Jane, 158, 160, 161, 172, 183
The Tragic Muse, 59, 93
"The Turning Point of My Life," 74,
96–97
Twain, Mark, 58

Veeder, William, 100, 155–56
"The Velvet Glove," 70

Walsh, Catherine, or Aunt Kate (Henry
James's maternal aunt), 28, 29. SEE ALSO
Notes of a Son and Brother
Weissbourd, Katherine, 17, 205*n13*
Wells, H. G., 92, 97, 109
Wharton, Edith, 62, 70, 92, 194
Whitman, Walt, 91
William Wetmore Story and His Friends,
94, 95
The Wings of the Dove, 61, 129, 130, 182
Wolseley, Viscount Garnet, 131
Wyllie, Irvin, 205*n7*, 205*n8*

Wisconsin Studies in American Autobiography
WILLIAM L. ANDREWS
General Editor

Robert F. Sayre
The Examined Self: Benjamin Franklin, Henry Adams, Henry James

Daniel B. Shea
Spiritual Autobiography in Early America

Lois Mark Stalvey
The Education of a WASP

Margaret Sams
Forbidden Family: A Wartime Memoir of the Philippines, 1941–1945
Edited, with an introduction, by Lynn Z. Bloom

Journeys in New Worlds: Early American Women's Narratives
Edited by William L. Andrews

Mark Twain
Mark Twain's Own Autobiography:
The Chapters from the "North American Review"
Edited, with an introduction, by Michael J. Kiskis

American Autobiography: Retrospect and Prospect
Edited by Paul John Eakin

Charlotte Perkins Gilman
The Living of Charlotte Perkins Gilman: An Autobiography
Introduction by Ann J. Lane

Caroline Seabury
The Diary of Caroline Seabury: 1854–1863
Edited, with an introduction, by Suzanne L. Bunkers

Cornelia Peake McDonald
A Woman's Civil War: A Diary with Reminiscenes of the War,
from March 1862
Edited, with an introduction, by Minrose G. Gwin

Marian Anderson
My Lord, What a Morning
Introduction by Nellie Y. McKay

American Women's Autobiography: Fea(s)ts of Memory
Edited, with an introduction, by Margo Culley

Frank Marshall Davis
Livin' the Blues: Memoirs of a Black Journalist and Poet
Edited, with an introduction, by John Edgar Tidwell

Joanne Jacobson
Authority and Alliance in the Letters of Henry Adams

Kamau Brathwaite
The Zea Mexican Diary
Foreword by Sandra Pouchet Paquet

Genaro M. Padilla
My History, Not Yours:
The Formation of Mexican American Autobiography

Frances Smith Foster
Witnessing Slavery: The Development
of Ante-bellum Slave Narratives

Native American Autobiography: An Anthology
Edited, with an introduction, by Arnold Krupat

American Lives: An Anthology of Autobiographical Writing
Edited, with an introduction, by Robert F. Sayre

Carol Holly
Intensely Family: The Inheritance of Family Shame and the
Autobiographies of Henry James